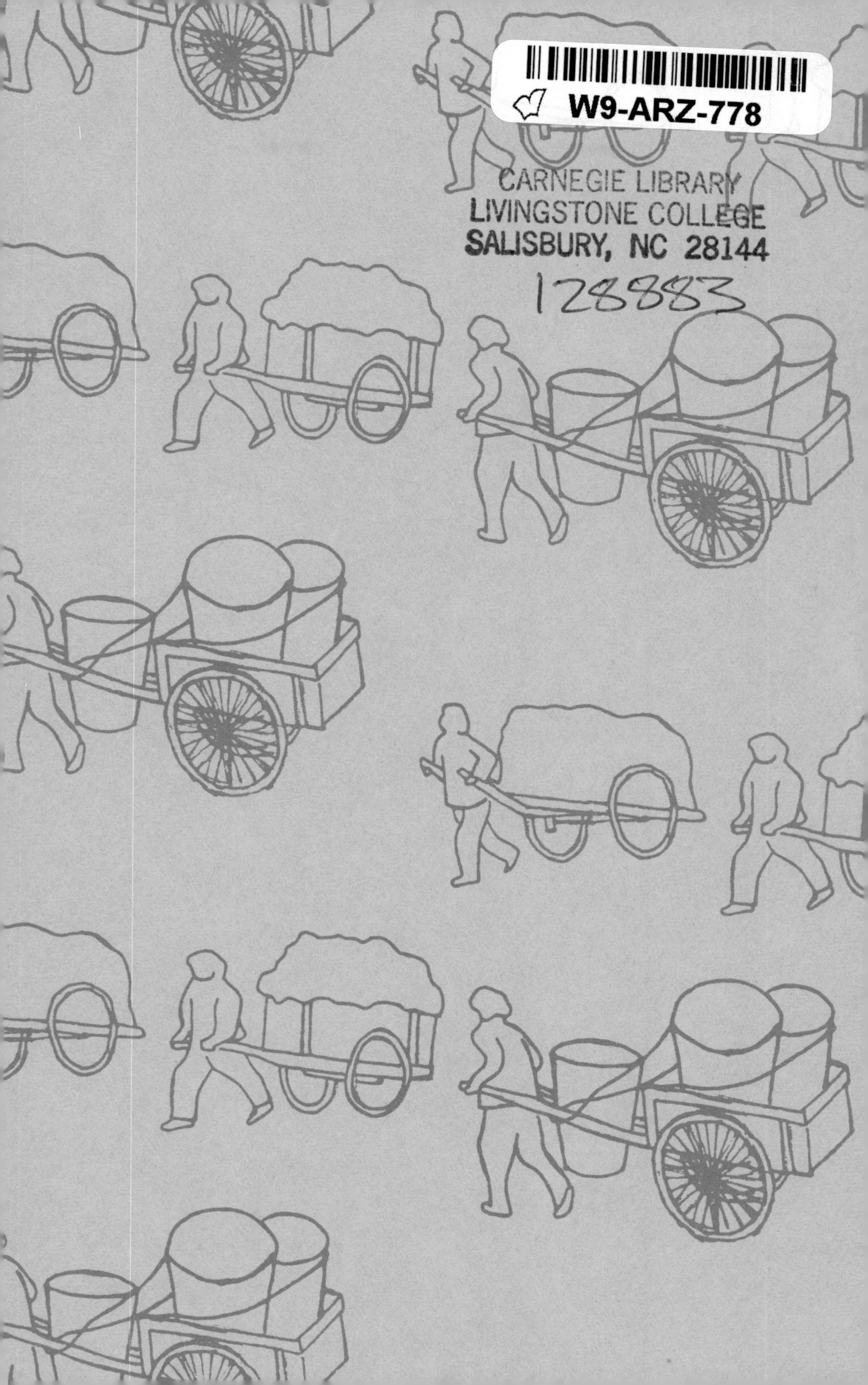

Revolution Postponed:
Women in Contemporary China

Revolution Postponed
Women in Contemporary China

MARGERY WOLF

STANFORD UNIVERSITY PRESS
Stanford, California   1985

Stanford University Press
Stanford, California

© 1985 by the Board of Trustees of the
Leland Stanford Junior University

Printed in the United States of America

CIP data appear at the end of the book

Endpaper drawings by Kazuko Smith

For Dorothy, Emily, Gail, Lisa, Margaret, Susan, Terry, and Yukiko,
who taught me much and made me laugh
when I badly needed to laugh

Acknowledgments

I knew when I went to China in 1980 that women's lives were not going to be a miracle of liberation, but I was not prepared for the frequency with which I would be told of this miracle in the very presence of women's continued oppression. As a result, I was often inclined to dismiss as propaganda what turned out to be real improvements in at least the material quality of women's lives. I have tried to rectify both the omissions and the tone in my final draft of the book. In this regard, the careful readings of the manuscript by William L. Parish, Burton Pasternak, and Marilyn Young have been particularly helpful; in their own ways, they all allowed me to listen with another ear. Martin King Whyte gave the manuscript the kind of close reading that every author dreams of and saved me from the many lapses in judgment and errors in fact that are slipped into manuscripts by subconscious demons (as well as ignorance). I am also indebted to Gail Hershatter, Robert J. Smith, and Arthur Wolf, all of whom took time out of busy schedules to read and comment on various drafts. Judith Stacey and Jess Bell were invaluable to me in that they both applied strong pressure to say more rather than less (although Jess wanted fewer words and more said). Judy's critical reading during precious vacation hours taught me more than she realized, and I only wish I could have written the book she had in mind.

I am grateful to the National Academy of Sciences and its Committee on Scholarly Communication with the People's Republic of China, who sponsored my research in China. Without the persistence of Robert Geyer and John Jamieson the work might never have been started, let alone finished. Arthur Wolf, who shared this difficult sojourn with me, remains, among many other things, my favorite traveling companion. I also would like to thank the staff at the Center for Advanced Study in the Behavioral Sciences for giving me the space and support that allowed me to complete most of the first draft of the book, and the Exxon Education Foundation and the National Science Foundation Grant BNS76-22943, which funded that support.

Finally, I would like to thank the many women in China who told me in a myriad of ways about their new lives. Nearly all of them expect a better future, and that in itself is an enormous step forward.

M.W.

Stanford, 1984

Contents

Revolution Postponed:
Women in Contemporary China

ONE

~

Eating Bitterness:
The Past and the Pattern

In 1980–81 I had the opportunity to talk to a good many women in the People's Republic of China (PRC). They told me about the things that occupy their daily lives, their hopes for the future, their perspective on the present. My younger informants were aware that their world was different from that of their mothers, but only the older women who had lived in both worlds could tell me just how different those worlds were. We cannot fully comprehend one world without a sense of the one that preceded it, so in this first chapter I will try to describe the old days as my oldest informants remembered them, as the handful of ethnographies and missionary accounts describe them, and as they have been described to me over the years by the Chinese of Taiwan. The second half of the chapter also provides background of a more recent sort and a few steps removed from the everyday existence of the average farmwife. The changes in women's lives that the rest of this book will document came about not through gradual evolution but through the political, social, and economic upheaval of a revolution. Since part of that revolution was ostensibly to liberate women from their past oppression, we must take a look also at some of the conditions that led up to the revolution and some of the policies that grew out of it. But first, the old days and "eating bitterness."

The birth of a daughter in traditional China was a disappointment; the birth of a second daughter brought grief and perhaps death to the infant; the birth of a third daughter was a tragedy for which the mother was most assuredly blamed. Daughters were goods on which one lost money. They could contribute little or nothing to their natal families in the way of enhancing their status, increasing their wealth, or providing for their care in their old age. They could not, except in very special circumstances, provide descendants who could worship the family's ancestors. And when the time came for a girl to be sent off to another family in marriage, most of the bride price had to be spent on her dowry if the family was not to lose its standing within the community. Unfortunately, the cultural stereotypes about the nature of women did nothing to make up for their structural handicaps. Women were narrow-hearted. They were incapable of understanding the finer points of human relations on which all civilized life depended. They gossiped and were jealous and quarrelsome, scolding other members of the family and even the neighbors when aroused. They were dependent, timid, and prone to weeping. They were ignorant and stupid and irresponsible. Worse yet, women were dangerous. Their menstrual secretions, if handled improperly, could cause men to sicken, gods to turn away in disgust, and families to decline into poverty. Their sexuality could drain men of their strength or drive them insane with lust. According to some they were sexually insatiable; according to others, they were frigid. In elite families they were expected to (and sometimes did) defend their chastity from even a suspicion of stain, with their lives if necessary, but they were considered morally and physically weak.

With a record of male chauvinism extending back at least twenty-two centuries, China has an inheritance of well-worked-out rules to control and confine the inferior sex. In traditional society, even illiterate farmers knew about the Three Obediences by which women were to be governed: as an unmarried girl a woman must obey her father and her brothers; as a married woman she must obey her husband; and as a widow she must obey her adult sons. During the three stages of a woman's life defined by male ideology, she was the property of different groups of men who were responsible for her care but who could, as with any property, dispose of her as they saw fit. An infant girl might be slipped into a bucket of water at birth; daughters could be sold into slavery at three or four years, or as prostitutes or concubines at twelve to fourteen years. Adele Fielde, a missionary-cum-entomologist, was told by a young woman living near Swatow (in Guangdong Province) in the 1880's:

Shortly after my birth a blind fortune-teller came along and told my mother that my brother, who was two years older than I, would die unless I was removed from the family. . . . It was in this way that my parents learned that they ought to part with me. They were very sorry to have me go, but as a boy is of so much greater value than a girl, they would not risk my brother's life by keeping me. They gave me to an acquaintance at White Pagoda, who had just lost a young child, and she brought me up as the future wife of her youngest son, then five years old. Little girls are worth nothing, but the bargain must be closed by money, so she paid my mother one penny for me, and I became hers.[1]

Even in the second stage of a woman's life, that of wife, she retained her position only at the convenience of her husband and his family. If she displeased her husband or her mother-in-law, she could be returned to her parents, and in times of economic stress, she might be rented, leased, or sold outright to a more prosperous man.[2] The marital history of another young woman who talked with Adele Fielde in Guangdong in the 1880's was probably not unique:

My parents were always kind to me, and would gladly have kept me at home till I was older, but my father died, and when I was fourteen my mother was forced to marry me. I went into a family in another village, and she got two pounds for me. I had never seen any of that family before I went to live in it. My husband, who was just my own age, hated me as soon as he saw me. There are a great many couples who hate at first sight. My mother-in-law was not unkind to me. I cooked the rice, fed the ducks and pigs, and helped her in the house all I could. But my husband was very cruel to me; he would not let me sleep beside him on the pine boards of the bedstead, but made me lie on the mud floor beside the bed; he had the coverlet, and I had nothing over me, and I used to lie and shiver all night. I did not tell any one how he treated me, lest that should make him more cruel. But he got to hating me so that every night he took a knife to bed with him, and told me that he would keep it there ready to kill me if he felt the desire to do it in the night. My mother-in-law saw how much he hated me, and fearing the consequences of keeping me with him, she engaged a matchmaker to marry me to someone else, and when I was sixteen I was again married, to a man at the village of Be Chia.

My mother-in-law received five pounds for me. This second husband was twenty-seven years old, and a gambler. His father was dead; the ancestral property had been divided among the sons, and the mother lived with her children, going daily to the house of each by turn. . . . My husband could not stop [gambling], and continually lost money. There was nothing for his mother to eat, and she ceased to come to our house for any meals, but lived with her sons. I had then three children—two boys and a girl. It seemed likely that we would starve. My husband had no money to gamble with either. He said to me: "You have a hard time with me; the children are thin, and you are miserable; it would be much better for you to be married to some kind man who would give you enough to eat. I will find such an one, and marry you to him. I myself am going away to foreign countries to seek my fortune, and I shall never come back." I assented to this, for I saw that the children would otherwise starve.

So my husband himself secretly took me and the children to Kam E, the village in which I was born, and to the house of the man to whom he had engaged me. He got five pounds for me and the children. He did not let anyone know about my going, because if people had known it, all the poor of the village would have come out and intercepted us on the road, and made him pay them a fine. . . . That is the way people do when a man marries off a wife that has borne him children. I did not cry at all when he left me, for I thought I could be no more wretched than I had been with him. He spent the money he got for me in gambling, and did not go to foreign parts, but died soon afterward. I was then twenty-four years old, my oldest son was five years old, and my daughter was ten months old.[3]

A woman who survived to the third stage of life was, theoretically at least, in a fairly secure position, for the balance of one set of obligations, that between young and old, had tipped in her favor. The Three Obediences might require her to obey her adult son, but rarely would a son risk the social opprobrium that would result from neglecting or mistreating his aged mother.

Thus far we have looked at male stereotypes of women's nature and male assumptions about women's obligations. I want to turn now to the day-to-day reality of women's lives in pre-Liberation China from the perspective of the women. No mother would wish on herself the grief of having her first-born child be a daughter, but in strictly practical terms, she would accept the birth of a daughter after the birth of her first son as a blessing. A little girl could be put in charge of later-born siblings, run errands, and help with household tasks. Unlike boys who ran freely about the village, a daughter was kept closer to home, hence socialized more thoroughly and at a younger age than her brothers. From her earliest years she knew that the biggest piece of sugar cane and the tenderest morsel of pork fat went to her brother, and if he also wanted her chair she must give it up without argument. Irma Highbaugh describes an incident among children at play in a village in Sichuan in the 1940's that I have seen repeated in many other villages in China.

Kuo-yung [a boy] came from his house. He saw the girls eating sweet potato and playing mother to their dolls. "I'll be the father," he said, snatching at the unfinished end of Mei-yu's sweet potato but Mei-yu held on to it. "Give it to me. I'm the father," he said angrily. Pulling at the sweet potato with one hand, he hit Mei-yu with his other fist. Mei-yu released the sweet potato and ran into Hsiao-hung's doorway. He followed and continued to hit her. "Fathers don't hit mothers," Mei-yu told him. "They do too," he said. "My father beats my mother. He's going to beat her to death," he stated in the same angry tones he had heard his father use. . . . Hsiao-hung had moved into her doorway as Kuo-yung continued to hit Mei-yu. She went inside and reappeared with another sweet potato which she gave to Kuo-yung saying, "You are the father, so I brought you the biggest sweet potato." Kuo-yung stopped hitting Mei-yu and started to eat his sweet potato.[4]

By the time a girl was five years old, she was the full-time caretaker of a two- or three-year-old sibling and might even have a smaller baby—cousin or sibling—tied to her back for part of the day. When her male relatives trudged off to school at the age of seven, she was likely to remain behind. In most areas of China before Liberation even boys had little opportunity for schooling. Education was lost on a girl. It might cause her to think beyond her station; it certainly would encourage her to talk too much; and it wasted time that she might devote to household tasks such as weaving. Since she would marry out anyway, a daughter's education was money lost to the family and might even make her a less desirable marriage prospect, for no man wanted to marry a woman who was better educated than himself. For many girls, this was also the age at which their feet were bound. (Parents

who hoped to marry their daughter further up the status hierarchy might take the physical risk of stopping the growth of the
child's feet at an even younger age.)

In fact, most of a girl's life was focused on the traumatic event
of marriage. If she was not sweet-tempered, her mother would
worry that the go-betweens might discover it. She was cautioned
and even punished for being too talkative. Anxious glances
passed between adults if she seemed sickly, since this made her a
less attractive marriage partner, but unless her family was rich,
medical care of any sort was reserved for her brothers. Her feet
were broken and crushed to make her gait halting, her appearance as weak and pliable as a willow. She was nonetheless expected to put in long, hard hours in the house, and in some areas
of China she might be required to work in the fields during planting and harvest. These contradictions may have been recognized, but they were rarely commented on. When I asked women
with bound feet how they managed to work in muddy fields or
flooded rice paddies (many of them did so for the first time at
Liberation), they told me of several methods that would keep
their tiny feet from sinking into the mud, such as sliding a tray
along or moving back and forth between two baskets. In dry
fields, they simply crawled on their hands and knees. Yet however much a reputation as a hard worker might become a young
wife, the most positive report neighbors of a potential bride
could make was that they knew nothing about the girl because
no one ever saw her. Chinese women were not in purdah, but
women, be they married or single, belonged at home. Those who
were seen too frequently in village paths were presumed to be up
to no good. The girl who was a stranger to her own neighbors was
assumed to be a paragon of virtue.

The cost of arranging a marriage for a son was likely to take
the equivalent of a year's income and could put a farm family in
debt for years after the event. Some of the cost was a cash payment to the bride's family, part of which returned with the bride
in the form of a dowry. Out of concern for her treatment in her
new home, most parents made their daughter's dowries as extravagant as they could afford. A woman in her late seventies whom I

spoke with in Fujian told me about her dowry. It consisted of twenty items of clothing, an apron, a carrying cloth for a baby, two hanging lanterns, a pair of brass candlesticks (for her husband's family altar), a pair of lead wine pitchers, a door hanging, bed pillows, linens and blankets, a large red basket, a small red basket, a red tea tray with matching cups and teapot, another tea tray with four covered cups, four small serving dishes, a hot water bottle, four covered glass jars, a gas lamp, two altar cloths, two chair covers, four hand towels, four foot towels, one wash pan, a looking glass, shoes and stockings for the groom and his parents, twelve pairs of chopsticks, and ceremonial hats for the groom and his father. All this was equivalent in value to about 300 bushels of rice, she said—an "average" dowry, according to her and some others who were present, neither particularly grand nor particularly small.

If the expense to the bride's family was heavy, the expense to the groom's family was worse. The girl who arrived as a bride into a family nearly impoverished by the gifts, bride price, and costly rounds of feasting was often resented by other daughters-in-law or siblings of her husband, no matter how elaborate her dowry. The expression on her mother-in-law's face changed gradually from the welcoming hopefulness of the day of the wedding, to irritation at the girl's clumsy inexperience in the months that followed, through anxious watchfulness when no signs of pregnancy turned up after the first year, and finally to open hostility if the son showed evidence of intimacy and affection for his wife. Ideally, a new bride was like a daughter to her husband's parents and like a polite stranger to her husband, threatening in no way the emotional bond between mother and son or the cool respect between father and son. In reality, few daughters-in-law managed their relations with their in-laws deftly, although their relationship with their husbands might stagnate at the ideal level for a good many years.

The months or years before the birth of her first child were hard and lonely for a young woman. Her husband, in most cases unknown to her until their wedding day, provided no companionship and might make her life even more difficult if he did express interest in her. Her sisters-in-law were often jealous of any act that might indicate favoritism on the part of the mother-in-law. And the mother-in-law was herself watching for signs that the young woman had designs on her son, whose primary emotional ties were and should remain with his mother. Amidst all this tension the model wife was expected to remain calm, compliant, and ready to serve her husband, his parents, and his siblings. She was not supposed to gossip or complain to the neighbors or to her husband. If she was the youngest daughter-in-law, she had to be the first one up in the morning and the last to go to bed at night. And she must get pregnant and bear a son preferably within a year after she married.

These were things that a model wife was expected to do. There was another agenda, however, in the mind of the young woman who would eventually become a successful wife and mother. Her first task was to form good relations with the women in her new village so that in time of need—financial or political—she would have a community to turn to for support. If her mother-in-law beat her excessively, it would be ignored as none of their business by the other women, unless she had established herself early on as part of their community. The older woman soon learned whether or not her daughter-in-law had access to this all-important court of appeal and would not risk her own relations with that community of women by letting herself get a reputation for cruelty. Although one finds evidence in early accounts from all over China for the existence of what I have called elsewhere the women's community, few of the writers are aware of its significance for women and of the role it often played in forming community opinion.[5] Martin Yang, for example, describes the gatherings of women in the village he studied in Shandong as opportunities to "gossip":

After supper, men go to the hard and clean threshing grounds at the outskirts of the village. Large groups gather and community life is at its height. At home the women rush through the washing as quickly as possible because they also want to have a neighborhood gathering. Since they are women, they do not meet on the threshing grounds, but in the little open spaces in the lanes between their homes. . . . In the women's groups freedom of speech and freedom from convention are also enjoyed, but to a lesser degree. Older women lie down on a mattress and swing their fans without embarrassment. Younger married women can joke at the expense of each others' husbands, or tease the grown-up girls by saying they are dreaming of handsome young men. The daughters can laugh and talk much more freely than in any other circumstances. The women return to their homes before the men come back, so that the latter cannot see their gathering nor hear what they say.[6]

If the men *had* overheard them, I daresay they would have been taken aback at how keenly some of the women understood what they as women were not expected to understand, and how politically astute they were in manipulating each other and through each other the men of the community.

But for the quality of her life, a young woman could not depend on the women's community. She had to create her own base of security by creating a family from her own body. That family would be the scale by which her life was measured and the staff that eased its burdens. She was a stranger and an outsider in her husband's family, but her own uterine family was composed of children who valued her praise, her affection, and her support of them over that of all others, including that of their father. Once she had established her uterine family, a woman was well on her way to subverting the men's family. In future discussions of family strategy, she might speak up for the interests of her sons if her husband would not speak for her, and as soon as her sons were able, she could speak through them. If she did her job well, by the time she was a grandmother the men's family—that bastion of male power in rural China—might in fact be dominated by her wishes, though expressed by her adult sons. As Martin Yang described the situation, perhaps a bit romanticized, in Shandong:

Middle-aged sons have almost invariably developed strong attachment to their mother but not to their father. . . . When the son and his wife are middle-aged parents, the mother-son relationship comes to include the son's family. In the winter, when the men are not busy in the fields and supper is usually finished earlier, sons, wives, and grandchildren will gather in the old mother's room and the grandmother will play with her youngest grandchildren, while the wives and older grandchildren and the sons talk about what they have seen and heard outside. The father may take part in this gathering if he likes, but he usually keeps himself aloof in order to maintain his patriarchal status. If he attempts to disrupt the free atmosphere, he will be chased out by his old wife.[7]

Because proper behavior in China demanded that men maintain a dignified reserve with their children, women had little competition for the affection of their sons. Society dictated that sons be loyal to their fathers and their father's relatives, but emotionally they belonged to their mothers. When boys came into conflict with their father and his family, the mother was careful to hear out the boys' side of the story, to support their interests in family disputes. And when they reached marriageable age, she did her best to find them good wives, but of necessity she chose daughters-in-law first and wives second. A model mother treated her daughter-in-law like a daughter, but in fact the younger woman was a source of continuous anxiety to her. If not handled properly, the young woman could endanger the uterine family the older woman had sacrificed so much to build. She might, for instance, cause quarrels between brothers, forcing family division. To guard against this, the model mother had to treat her sons and their wives with an even hand, and any daughter-in-law who threatened family harmony might well find herself subject to constant criticism, extra chores, and hushed conversations between mother and son about how to handle her.

In Taiwan, the greatest fear of an aging mother was that her daughter-in-law would seduce her son totally and talk him into leaving the family and abandoning his mother to a cold and hungry old age. This was not a very common occurrence but it was a common anxiety, and many households were full of strife as the two women battled for control of the man who was crucial to both their uterine families. In some households, the older woman accepted the inevitable and kept her hand in by spoiling her grandchildren outrageously, which of course had the effect of weakening the uterine family of her daughter-in-law. Nonetheless, she slowly relinquished control of the family to her daughter-in-law, settling into second place and gradually into honored onlooker, an invaluable source of advice but no longer responsible for other than minor tasks. Some women found the transition more difficult to make, often because they had daughters-in-law who were too eager or sons who were not loyal. Suicide rates, which were extremely high among young Chinese women, dropped dramatically when they entered their thirties, and began to climb again as women in their fifties recognized that though they could compete with the men's family, they could not compete with the woman in their son's bed.[8]

This bare-bones synopsis of a story with many subplots runs the risk of misrepresenting the importance of one gender in a society infamous for preferring the other. Sexism has plagued social science, history, and literature from their beginnings, and it is with conscious irony that I admit my bias here. Lest this analysis of the lives of Chinese women get too far away from the context in which those lives are lived, I hasten to point out that China was—and still is—a patriarchy. Women, in their struggle for some security in their day-to-day existence with the all-powerful male-oriented family and its larger organization, the lineage, worked like termites hollowing out from within places for themselves and their descendants. These small units, which I call uterine families, overlapped with and weakened the male family, but they could not overcome it. Uterine families were in fact only a way of accommodating to the patriarchal family. Property, hence power, was (and remains) in the hands of men, and even though mothers could often wield strong influence over their sons, they did so as individuals. When sons acted "for the good of the family," it was for the family of their male ancestors, not for the family their mothers so painfully created, maintained, and watched dissolve with the natural progression of the family cycle. Nonetheless, in most rural farm families, by the time a woman had grandchildren, demographic factors had made the living personnel of the men's family and the members of her uterine family nearly one and the same. Against the *ideology* of the men's family, however, she had no protection beyond the emotional bonds she had created between her sons and herself. Sometimes that was not enough.

To make intellectual amends to the reader for presenting the above female-biased view of what is in fact a male-oriented system, I must now sketch briefly some of the limits to that stereotype. Again and again in the pages that follow, statements will have to be qualified because of differences between life in the rural and urban sectors of Chinese society. Although those differences are now much greater than they were in pre-Liberation days, the rural-urban discrepancies in times past were nonetheless large. For a man, the difference between being a member of the urban elite or the rural poor was the difference between ease and misery. For a woman, a similar generalization could not always be justified. Even among the elite, women were property, and they might be physically mistreated, isolated, or ignored with impunity, as long as the abuse was not so extreme that it came to the attention of a powerful father whose face might be at risk. Elite women, unlike village women, had little support from other women. They were more confined than their poor or rural sisters and might not see anyone other than their servants or the other women of the family (often hostile second or senior wives of their husband) for weeks on end. Thus they had no women's community to mobilize if their situation became unbearable. Moreover, in elite families the sons were often removed from the women's quarters at an early age, thus rending before it was properly formed the web of love and obligation country women used to bind their sons to them.

Urban women of a more middling sort suffered from some of the same physical privations of country women, that is, hunger, lack of medical care, and all the other ills of poverty, and they also bore some of the disabilities of their wealthy urban sisters. Country women, particularly the young ones, would be soundly criticized if they wandered too much in village paths, but at least they could meet other women when they went to draw water from the well or wash clothes at the side of a nearby stream. The urban poor had no such freedom. Only women who had gone out of the family and were therefore outside the rules of respectability appeared openly in the streets. These were the beggar women, the slave girls, the prostitutes, the vendors, the servants. Few women, no matter how close to starvation, made the decision to go out easily, for there was no going back.[9]

Around the turn of the century for a small minority of women, mainly those who lived in or around cities or on the Pearl River Delta, the opening of textile factories produced unprecedented new opportunities for independence. In fact very few of these women actually used their new earning power to acquire autonomy. Most young women turned their wages over to their parents until they married and over to their in-laws after they married. Even in the 1930's when Olga Lang did her interviews in Jiangsu, the women valued their work only as a way to earn money; they were not in favor of "new style" marriages, and they believed in the traditional distinction between women's rule inside the home and men's rule outside. They had maintained these values despite their exposure to the unrest and dissatisfaction of the urban intelligentsia. Some of them worked in factories that had been closed down the decade before when women went out on strike for short er hours (ten) and more pay (five cents a day). When the Guomindang suppressed the unions, a few women continued to organize surreptitiously, even joining the outlawed Communist organizations, but most women remained aloof.[10]

This is not the place and I do not have the competence to describe the movements and campaigns for reform and eventual revolution that swept the cities of China in the first three decades of this century.[11] For my purposes here the interesting question is why these pressures for change had so little influence on the lives of ordinary women. The answer is, I fear, all too simple: the demands being made by students and urban intellectuals of the May 4th era were realistic for students and urban intellectuals, but they were hopelessly irrelevant to the lives of rural or working class women. One goal, for example, was an end to all-male schools and the opening of all schools to women students. When I asked village women who had grown up during this period about their schooling, they laughed at my foolishness. "I didn't even know where the gate to the school was," they said, and often added that in their village there was no school at all. Essays appeared attacking the "big family system" and the economic and marital oppression it inflicted on women and men alike. Many women, both urban and rural, must have considered this almost frivolous as they struggled to get food and shelter for their children, tolerating beatings and other abuses to remain in a family, since this was the only source of support available to them. City women pushed for birth control and the vote. Farm women probably had no notion of what the vote was, for their menfolk had little acquaintance with it. Contraception would have been a blessing to some, but they were shocked to hear it spoken of in public, and for many it was beside the point—even bearing a child every two years could not guarantee that enough would live to support one in old age.

Many farm women and even many urban working class women felt threatened by what they did hear about the reforms demanded by elite women. Eager but naïve women students demonstrated their own liberation by confronting older women on the streets and forcibly bobbing their hair and unbinding their feet. In their fervor, these committed young people took from country women the symbols of respectability essential to their lives. Men students demanded that they be allowed to divorce their old-style wives in order to make "love marriages," further threatening the only security rural women knew or could hope for. However obvious the need for these reforms seemed to urban elites, they had little support among the women in the towns and villages. Rural women had worked out their own ways of coping with the oppression of the "big family system," and the new freedom espoused by the students threatened not only their sense of propriety but their very survival.

As the women's movement matured in the 1920's, greater efforts were made to appeal to women in the villages and the factories, mainly by focusing on issues relevant to their needs, such as wife beating, divorce for cause, footbinding, and literacy.[12] Attempts to organize women's unions in the villages often provoked conflict with the men, including the leaders of the peasants' unions. In many villages attempts at organizing women were hopeless, for the mere arrival of the big-footed, bobbed-haired, uniformed women walking openly without chaperones was enough to outrage the local people. It was at this point in 1927 that Chiang Kai-shek, secure in his military triumphs, decided to eliminate his Communist competition and suppress all unions—worker, peasant, and women. The story of this period is gruesome; thousands of young women lost their lives in a bloodbath of revenge. When the Guomindang (GMD) finished cleaning out its women's quarters, it unveiled the "new" women's movement, which was little more than an alms-giving club run by upper class women. The philosophy supporting it is illustrated by Zeng Bao-sun: "For the modern Chinese woman, let her freedom be restrained by self-control, her self-realization be coupled with self-sacrifice, and her individualism be circumscribed by family duty. Such is our new ideal of womanhood and to realize this is our supreme problem." [13]

From this period of suppression onward, the Communist Party followed a separate path, by necessity turning its "woman-work" toward peasant women. The techniques that would later be used to bring women out of the household and into production and to "free" them from "feudal" ideas were developed during the hard years in Jiangxi and the war years in Yenan. Mao's oft-quoted statement—that women, like men, were subject to the three oppressive systems of political authority, clan authority, and religious authority, but also had one more, the domination by men —was *not* to be the keynote of the Chinese Communist Party's (CCP) approach to peasant women. In fact, after some initial male hostility not unlike the early days when the GMD and the CCP were tenuously united, the orthodox Marxist solution was adopted and women were to liberate themselves through full participation in production. In the 1940's the Party and the nation were in desperate straits. Cut off from supplies in the south, the CCP could not carry on a war of resistance in the north unless it got cloth and other manufactures from the north. Although the vocabulary was different, women were mobilized as the reserve labor force that has been the lot of women everywhere and continues to hamper the struggle of Chinese women for equality even today.

During the Rectification Movement of 1942–44, Ding Ling, a radical woman writer who came to Yenan in 1937, called on the party in a Women's Day speech to include an attack on sexist attitudes in their new campaign to educate lower level cadres and

village leaders in matters of theory. Although the CCP claimed
the emancipation of women, even within the party hierarchy
women were not comrades of equal rank. They were expected to
be activists and to fulfill their traditional roles as well. Falling
short in either brought expressions of contempt. Ding Ling's position is summarized by Kay Ann Johnson in her fine study of
women and revolution in China: "The party had proclaimed
lofty theories of gender equality, but failed to deal with the actual
conditions and attitudes which held women in an inferior position. Ting Ling claimed that male leaders 'should talk less of
meaningless theories and talk more of actual problems. Theory
and practice should not be separated.'" [14] But the Party refused to
consider risking the loyalty of male peasants over an issue that
they considered secondary themselves. And Ding Ling, for her
frankness, was withdrawn from both political and literary activities for the next two years. [15]

In February 1943, the Party's decision to avoid discussions of
women's social and political inequality was made explicit at the
meeting of the Central Committee in a directive on women's
work in the Anti-Japanese Base Areas. I quote again from Johnson's account:

> According to the directive, women were not to be called to mass politi-
> cal meetings. The village women's associations were to be de-emphasized
> and supplanted by small production groups as the basic unit for women's
> organization. Political, cultural and educational work was to be carried
> out among women only to the extent that it directly contributed to im-
> proving their production skills. There was no mention of the 1934 Mar-
> riage Law, no work to educate against child betrothal, no mention of
> oppressive traditional practices except those practices, such as foot-
> binding, which it said directly hindered production. Instead, women
> leaders were instructed to "lessen the unnecessary mobilization of rural
> women" so they could devote more energy to production.
>   To justify this policy and defend its narrow focus against its feminist
> critics, the directive fully developed the notion that this singular em-
> phasis on production was not only necessary to the war and the peas-
> ants' livelihood, but was the best, indeed the only, way to further
> women's own liberation. [16]

As Johnson goes on to point out, this directive became the
standard for all subsequent policy decisions on the woman ques-

tion. Where once the CCP had said that women's lot would be equalized through class struggle and revolution, it now seemed that the women must make their own way by proving that they could contribute to production equally with men; only by doing that could they change men's attitudes. At the same time, of course, as Ding Ling had pointed out, women were expected to bear the truly heavy burden of their traditional roles, economic and social, within the household. Throughout the Sino-Japanese War and the civil war that followed, the primary function of the women's organizations remained that of mobilizing women for production. Party leaders spoke from time to time of the need for village women to take part in political action, and they talked of the problems of mistreatment of women by husbands and mothers-in-law and the selling of women and children into (and out of) marriage. But any woman who seemed to be suggesting revolution rather than reform as a solution to the burdens of women was quickly accused of error, of neglecting the class struggle in favor of a narrow feminist one. This was an early manifestation of a pattern that would become all too familiar: the set of reform goals and social education projects that could and would most easily and most often be set aside until the current economic or social crises were solved were those pertaining to women.

Shortly after Liberation, however, such did not appear to be the case. One of the first major directives from the new government was the promulgation of the Marriage Law in May 1950. The features of the new law that received the greatest attention, both favorable and unfavorable, were the rights of women to demand divorces and the rights of young people to choose their own marriage partners without parental interference. Marriage by parental arrangement was forbidden, as were child betrothals and the selling of women or children into marriage. Initially, the right to divorce caused the greatest havoc as hundreds of thousands of unhappy women sought to assert their newly discovered rights. That this threatened many men and their mothers, also seeking to enjoy *their* newly discovered rights in the new society, goes without saying. And the local level cadre who might have wished to help women acquire a legal and morally justifiable divorce was caught in between. If the cadre (usually a man) carried out his duties under the marriage law, he might find himself faced with an angry village and a serious handicap in the "important" work to come. If he did not, he was returning women, illegally, to families who would undoubtedly make them feel their anger for the loss of face they had suffered. The cadre was in fact caught between two Maoist dicta: he (rarely she) must be sensitive to the will of the masses, and he must use the Maoist method of confrontation, struggle, and education, risking polarization to achieve eventual consensus.

For many cadres, the dilemma was resolved by the implementation of the Agrarian Reform Law, which was announced the following month. Why these two major campaigns were introduced in such quick succession remains a source of speculation among China scholars. As Kay Ann Johnson points out, one might think that they were intended to be mutually supporting: "Land reform redistributed property and power in the villages, marriage reform redistributed property and power in the family. The marriage reform law gave women and children equal property rights, the land reform law gave them real property." [17] But this (as Johnson recognizes) seems not to be what they had in mind. Reform cadres were urged to bring women into the struggle against the landlords and to encourage them to speak out in public meetings on the land reform issues, but they were also warned explicitly not to let women's "special problems" interfere with the important land reform work. Land reform cadres were given special training and spent many hours of study before they went into the villages to mobilize the peasants for this very basic transformation of their society. [18] Even local level cadre knew the law inside and out before they began to work with their fellow citizens. Their knowledge of the marriage law and its implications was quite another thing. Often as not they were ignorant of its basic content and, equally often, they were hostile to the ideas they understood it to be espousing. They had interpreted, probably correctly, the barrage of material on land reform coming to them as meaning that marriage reform was to be mentioned and forgotten while the land work proceeded.

Land reform apparently was to benefit women as much or more than men in that for the first time they too would receive a share of land equal to that of each man. The hidden benefit to women was the experience they would gain in speaking out as political beings in a public setting. For some this did occur, but I suspect most let their menfolk do the talking. Reports from some areas of China indicate that the women who did speak out were looked at askance or were reprimanded. Though land deeds were made out in women's names, they were handed over to the male heads of household just as women's wages were. The presumption that land ownership would increase women's power within the family is arguable under some circumstances, but since the land of all family members was soon turned into collective land, there was insufficient time for such changes to occur, let alone be documented. The failure of land ownership to automatically produce gender equalization is readily apparent in the debates that took place in the rural areas over who should be given the shares of land for unmarried women. This land became a new item in marriage negotiations.[19]

If the kind of publicity and education given to the principles of land reform had been applied to the Marriage Law at the same time, the developing contradictions might eventually have been resolved. But at that point the government needed to convince the rural male community that the benefits associated with support for the CCP were immediate and personal. To give land was an enormous gift, but to take away male authority over the other half of society was a threat more basic than a new revolution could tolerate. So, the fact that women "owned" land was rendered impotent by the fact that women themselves remained the property of men who still could transfer them and their property with a fair amount of ease. Whatever women's legal rights, their actual control over the means of production or even over their own bodies did not change much as the result of land reform.

By 1953 reports of the failures in the implementation of the Marriage Law were made public both as a nudge to factions within the government who preferred not to move at all on family reform issues and as a beginning campaign to spread knowledge about the law's intent. Statistics were published describing the tens of thousands of murders and suicides that had resulted from the lack of support for women who wished to annul betrothals or free themselves from unhappy marriages. The figures tell us little since we have no population baseline from which to judge them, but the fact that they were being collected and publicized indicates the determination of at least some section in the government to confront the issue.[20] Even as cadres were being trained and pilot campaigns launched in rural areas, the Central Committee was still debating the wisdom of such a disruptive program and attempting to devise (or force through) moderating tactics.

The conservatives were successful. Mao's response in 1927 to criticism of "going too far" had been, "Proper limits have to be exceeded in order to right a wrong, or else the wrong cannot be righted"; here the marriage reform cadres were cautioned to tread carefully.[21] Mass struggle meetings, which had been so successful in the land reform campaign, were not to be used. Individuals were not to be targeted for mass criticism unless they had caused a death or serious injury. Past failings were not to be investigated; instead, the good models were to be held up for emulation. And finally, to gain the cooperation of local cadres who were known to be a major stumbling block in the movement, cadres were to be investigated only by other cadres and not held up for public criticism and confession. The local cadres were also given broad discretionary powers to suspend or limit the campaign in case it produced major social conflicts, disrupted production, or the like. According to Elisabeth Croll, "The Women's Federation noted in a report on the state of affairs in southern China that to get a divorce, there were three obstacles to overcome: the obstacle of the husband, of the mother-in-law and of the cadres. Apparently it was the latter which was often the hardest to overcome."[22] Once again, it seems, the continued cooperation of local cadres took precedence over marriage reform.

In other words, the goals of the much-touted campaign were long term and primarily "informational." If the provisions of the law were known widely but did not spread anxiety widely, the campaign would be considered a success. By those criteria, Johnson feels that it was:

Even though the publicity month did not get off on schedule in many areas, more people learned about, studied and discussed the Marriage Law than at any time since the law was passed. . . . Not only does it seem that millions became more clearly aware of the major issues of marriage reform and women's rights, but people also became more aware of some degree of government determination in supporting such changes—something which, given the past behavior of local officials, may not have been clearly understood in many areas prior to the 1953 campaign."[23]

It is worth noting, however, that when I asked a number of women in Jiangsu and Shaanxi to tell me about the marriage re-form campaigns in their area, only one of them could remember such a campaign occurring and she was not at all sure of its con-tent. "My children were small at that time, and I had no time to go to meetings," she said.

By 1956 the rhetoric and, one assumes, the emphasis on the new law had changed. Editorials supporting young people against the restrictions of the patriarchal family stopped appearing. Pub-lications that dealt with the family spoke instead of the need to prevent sexual laxity and licentiousness and to guard against the bourgeois attitudes toward marriage that were creeping into the country. These latter included such failings as contracting mar-riages for monetary gain or security and the whimsical changing of marital partners. It seems rather unlikely that many such breaches of China's stern moral standards occurred during that early period, but the message being conveyed was unmistakable. The nation had important business ahead and was not to be dis-tracted by the selfish individualistic needs of unhappy women. The first Five Year Program was under way, and while men were urged to push ahead, women were urged to "link up closely the household work with the work of constructing a socialist society" by way of the Five Goods Movement.[24] Since the economy was not yet ready to provide full-time employment for women, they should (1) unite with the neighborhood families for mutual aid, (2) do housework well, (3) educate children well, (4) encourage family production, study, and work, and (5) study well them-selves.[25] Women's magazines concentrated on domestic topics, including fashion tips and self-beautification, leading presumably to a happier and more productive husband, not to bourgeois partner-switching.

In the countryside, collectivization was stepped up, and women were being liberated by labor—that is, if labor needs allowed. Where single-cropping created labor surpluses, women remained in reserve. And, as part of the developing Chinese pattern, efforts were made not to let women's issues interfere. As Judith Stacey describes it:

Where the demand for labor allowed the mobilization of women to proceed, the regime exercised concern to avoid undue threats to patriarchal sensibilities. Activists stressed the benefits to family prosperity peasants would derive if they allowed their women to work in the fields. Peasants with traditional beliefs about pollution—that menstruating women would harm the crops—were reassured by measures barring women from agricultural labor during their menses, this on the "scientific" ground of protection of health. Official investigation teams even published reports appreciative of local communities that excluded pregnant, lactating, and menstruating women from agricultural work. Likewise, peasant concern that women who labored in public were subject to immoral temptations was allayed when cadres organized separate female work teams for work conducted away from direct familial supervision. Even when the government conducted ideological campaigns to combat peasant resistance to female agricultural labor, it attempted to reassure the public that families had little to fear. . . . The collectivization of agriculture succeeded in expanding the contribution of female labor and in modifying the specific contents of the traditional sexual division of labor, but it leveled no fundamental challenge to the traditional view that female labor was naturally different from and subordinate to that of men.[26]

The Great Leap was Mao's attempt to achieve dramatically higher levels of production within the limits of China's still backward technology. For the Great Leap to succeed, some 300 million women had to be mobilized, and that mobilization obviously required some new institutional arrangements. For the first time and only a few short years after the Five Goods had relegated women to the sidelines, the patriarchal citadels were to be challenged. This was apparent in the rural areas, less so in the cities. If women were to work long hours in the fields every day, they could not also take care of children and prepare and preserve food in the old time-consuming ways. The newly formed communes were instructed to set up child care facilities, communal kitchens, even service centers for mending. Since such needs were identified as women's needs, they did not receive the planning and funding associated with other aspects of production. The cafeterias were the cause of the most grumbling, producing poorly cooked food at the wrong times. More importantly for a staggering economy, they were wasteful not only of food but of fuel, since it was the firing of the stove for cooking that also provided necessary heat to the *kang* (sleeping platform) during the icy winter months. But many analysts suggest that in fact it was the pressure to change women's role and status that caused the most distress in the rural areas. Workpoints were not raised to the level of men's, but they were raised. Women were assigned tasks formerly done only by men; they were trained in male skills and performed them with ease. This did not make the Great Leap policies popular among rural males. As Phyllis Andors says, "Of all the policies adopted in the Great Leap the attempt to change the role and status of Chinese women probably resulted in the most widespread, consistent, and far-reaching opposition. It was both qualitatively and quantitatively different from other problems for it involved questioning basic traditional cultural values and institutions, and half the population was involved in its scope."[27] Andors's conclusion fits the pattern that is the theme of this chapter. The policies underlying the Great Leap assumed that women's progress would come only as a result of their own labor: "But it is clear that at this stage the Chinese had decided that the advancement of women must not be at the expense of economic growth and technical change; i.e., the opportunity for female employment and participation must be within the context of increasing production and expansion of social services."[28]

In the cities, the recruitment of women did not produce as much anxiety about patriarchal institutions as it did in the countryside. Partly this was because women were often brought in to take over simple basic tasks that would free men to do more technically advanced processes and were thus not a threat to the familiar sexual division of labor. And the neighborhood collectives wherein most women worked in the early days were by definition totally outside the male sector. Many of these small factories are still in operation today, and they are a tribute to the women who organized them and continue to keep them going. Some of them are a kind of collective jobber, doing piecework for a nearby factory. Others produce a complete product, such as binding sheets of paper into accounting books. Still others have isolated and taken over a basic process through which raw materials must go before a factory can assimilate them.

The restrictions placed on these neighborhood organizations, which developed in response to the government's call for women to join the labor force, are indicative of how much sacrifice the policy makers were willing to make toward women's efforts. The women were told they could not ask the government for funds, raw materials, machines, premises, or workers from state-run factories.[29] If with none of these things they could create a factory, they would be fulfilling their patriotic duty. But their achievements brought them no nearer to equality with male workers since the wages were very low, there were no benefits, and advancement was out of the question. If the entry of women into labor was the path to equality, it would appear that the government was unwilling to provide more than an ill-drawn map.

In the late 1950's a three-year drought combined with generally inadequate central planning turned the Great Leap Forward into an economic disaster from which the country was unable to recover for more than a decade. Retrenchment on all fronts again forced women out of the labor force. In the mid-1960's Mao launched the Great Proletarian Cultural Revolution in an attempt to regain among other things ideological control of his revolution and rid the nation of its crippling bureaucracy. Mao turned to the young people for support, but some effort was made to involve women. As Johnson puts it:

Thus the Cultural Revolution, more than previous periods, placed emphasis on the need to mobilize women to participation in politics as well as production. Not only were barriers to women's rights of participation attacked, but intense normative pressure was also generated to impress upon women that they had an obligation to devote themselves more fully to social and political responsibilities outside the home. Red Guards and the mass media widely propagated norms of behavior which stressed that the individual's role and responsibilities to the collective should take precedence over more narrow and individualistic family roles and responsibilities.[30]

The Cultural Revolution was the first major campaign that focused with any depth on women's needs since the ill-fated Marriage Law Campaign of the 1950's. It was followed in the early 1970's by the Anti–Lin Biao, Anti-Confucius Campaign, which ostensibly attacked traditional family structure and explored the causes of women's subordination. The effect of the campaign seems to have been negligible for women. Although in 1980 women occasionally repeated slogans from the Anti-Confucius Campaign in answer to my questions, they also told me that it was "natural" for men to rule outside the home and women to rule within. Indeed, many seemed to think their newfound voice within the house, limited though it might be, was the victory they had been preparing for.

Judith Stacey maintains that this in fact was what the revolution *had* promised them—a stable family life in the traditional patriarchal style.[31] At the risk of oversimplifying an elegant synthesis, let me try to pinpoint where I differ from Stacey. She perceives the events leading up to the Chinese revolution and much that has happened since as predetermined by the intention of policy makers as well as citizens to preserve—indeed strengthen —the patriarchal basis of Chinese society through whatever social or economic transformations it might pass. She argues her case eloquently and I have no trouble accepting that this has been the effect of the policies and actions she cites. I am less convinced that the conscious intent of China's revolutionaries has been the resuscitation of patriarchy. I am more inclined to believe that a revolution dominated by men and a postrevolutionary government organized by men accepts a different set of priorities than would a government or a revolution shared by both sexes or, for that matter, led by women. Although sexual equality as a principle has not been vacated, it has been set aside at each economic downturn or show of rural resistance without recognition that such casual treatment will in time devalue a principle until it is but a hollow slogan. I do not think this was a conscious effort on the part of the CCP to keep women subordinated but rather a consistent failing on the part of an all-male leadership to perceive and be aware of their own sexist assumptions. As a consequence their ignorance of the costly effects of gender inequality in their society continues.

Only the most ardent anti-Communists would deny that life for the average person in Communist China has been raised to standards beyond the hope of the previous generation. People live better and longer lives, and they have that most valuable of emotions, hope—hope for an even better future. The criticisms I have made in the last few pages and will be making in the next few hundred are not intended to deny that accomplishment or even to diminish it. What concerns me is the frequency with which a revolutionary government has stepped aside from one of its most earnestly stated goals, gender equality. Though the revolution for women has never been repudiated, it has been postponed all too many times. Once again, under the radical new policies of the Four Modernizations, women are being told to step aside in the interests of the nation. As Phyllis Andors explains:

Articles which appeared in the press on [International Women's Day, 1978] clarified the extent to which women's roles were being reevaluated in light of the new strategy for Chinese development. The theses were clear. Even though women were held up as "the other half of the sky," with important contributions to socialist construction, their release from "backbreaking manual labor and tedious housework" was to be *gradual*. In the meantime, a double burden was clearly stated. "Women workers, commune members and women scientists and technicians need to work hard and study, but they have to spend a considerable portion of their time tending to housework and children." The clear identification of women with familial responsibilities and the lack of discussion concerning male participation in these matters and a redefinition of the sexual division of labor contrasted sharply with publicity given to precisely these kinds of innovations a scant two years ago. Images of the 1960s continued to appear. By the time the Women's Congress opened in September 1978, any lingering doubts about the shift in policy toward women were dispelled.[32]

Women are again being encouraged to give up their jobs in favor of their children and to value their roles as socialist mothers and wives. As Andors puts it in her stimulating new book, "Thus in political-ideological terms, the resolution of the women question in China is to be dependent upon the future success of economic modernization."[33] I will return to this latest turn in China's cycles at the end of this book, but now it is time to look at some of the problems and pleasures of doing research in the new China.

TWO

Speaking Bitterness: Doing Research in the People's Republic of China

All too often, a researcher studying the sex-gender system of her own society finds that she has become a part of her own research problem. A foreign researcher attempting a study of the sex-gender system of China can easily, if she is a woman, find her work enmeshed in a web of conflicting observations and ideological statements, and her person subjected to a confusing alternation of gender discrimination and equally unwelcome deference. Since this makes data collection in China difficult and its analysis complex, a somewhat fuller description than usual of the process of doing research in China seems called for. I, as the researcher, still find myself puzzling over whether a particular statement I am about to make is a fair and necessary description of sexual discrimination or a fair but not at all necessary description of behavior toward women or toward me as a woman that roused my pique. Explaining in some detail the unusual research process that put me in such a mental state does not absolve me of the responsibility for making or not making the judgmental statements in question, but it does provide my reader with another context from which to evaluate the analysis that will follow.

The process of doing anthropological research in China begins with getting permission from the People's Republic. Having survived an American peer review committee and been designated a Research Scholar by the Committee for Scholarly Communication with the People's Republic of China (CSCPRC), a committee of the National Academy of Sciences, I had next to gain acceptance by a sponsoring agency in the PRC. Everyone, foreigner and citizen alike, must have a unit. Because of the nature of my research, my first choice as a unit was the All China Women's Federation. This group declined, on the grounds that they did not have the facilities, that there was no precedent. Reasonably enough, the American academic adviser in Beijing for CSCPRC, John Jamieson, who carried on these negotiations on my behalf, turned next to the Chinese Academy of Social Sciences (CASS), through which Arthur Wolf, with whom I am associated in marriage but not in research, was also seeking sponsorship. That was the beginning of my fall from Research Scholar to Wife of Research Scholar. Unlike many of the Chinese leaders who fell, I never managed to achieve reinstatement; but then, as any PRC specialist will attest, a year is hardly long enough for rehabilitation.

However, the Research Scholar to whom I was now categorically appended was having his own problems getting sponsorship with CASS. The details of how this was eventually accomplished, so far as they are known to us, might interest a political scientist or a sociologist concerned with bureaucratic function, but they may be omitted here. At the time, when we had taken leave for a year, had rented our house, and were financially dependent on grants that were dependent on our being in China, I found these details both fascinating and enraging. It is sufficient to say that I was made to feel unwelcome and to believe that I was somehow taking advantage of a society for which I have great respect, simply by participating in a freely and openly negotiated scholarly exchange program between our two countries. Nor would it be the last time these unpleasant thoughts were pressed upon me.

For the field researcher who has worked in other countries, the most frustrating aspect of doing research in the PRC is the loss of autonomy. When we arrived in Beijing, we found that although no preparation had been made for our work, we were not going to be allowed to do any of the necessary groundwork ourselves. Normally, we would have got in touch with friends and relatives of friends, looked over potential research sites, talked to local leaders, made contacts with scholars, or consulted relevant archives. Instead, we had to sit in our hotel for six weeks while some unidentified officials and committees "made arrangements." Other scholars, foreign and Chinese, report the same lengthy process. Decisions vital to the quality of your research are made on your behalf by committees or individuals who know nothing about social science or the needs of your project. Often as not these decisions are unworkable, and the committee must be recalled any number of times before a satisfactory plan is achieved. The problem may be as simple as the number and age of the people with whom you wish to speak, and the problem on their side—rarely revealed to you—might be something you the researcher could easily work around. No matter how you plead, however, you will not be allowed to attend these planning sessions.

In a pattern that was to become all too familiar (and uncomfortable for us both), Arthur's research needs were attended to first. When the people from CASS finally turned to my project, they expressed amazement and disapproval. Other wives of visiting scholars had been satisfied with interviewing one or two women, but my minimum sample for Beijing alone was fifty. Worse yet, I wished to study one neighborhood and to interview women in their homes. Impossible.

I will never know how many meetings, phone calls, softening-up dinners, and so forth were needed before CASS got permission for me to interview fifty women in one neighborhood (I gave up early on the notion of doing a real neighborhood study), but I was led to believe they were numerous. CASS could not simply call around to a number of neighborhood committees to see who would accept me in their midst. There is little or no lateral interaction between Chinese bureaucracies, so that often as not a simple request must move all the way to the top of the bureaucracy in which your unit is located, cross to the top of the bureaucracy within which is located the unit you want to contact, and then, with painful slowness, move down through that hierarchy. At each stop along the way, the request is examined to see what ill-effects might accrue to that office if the next level is allowed to accept or pass it on down. Even a safe "no" can backfire if the source of the request wants to use the rejection to your disadvantage, and there are all sorts of elaborate calculations of relative power, accumulated debts, and future usefulness to the other units involved. The Chinese distrust of the social sciences did not improve CASS's bargaining power, and I daresay more than once even this national-level academy had to go back up its own hierarchy and across to that headed by the Minister of Education to get one American researcher permission to interview the women a national exchange committee had committed them to. All told, hundreds of hours must have been spent on this; for me, at any rate, three full months in Beijing were devoted to obtaining approximately 125 hours of interviews.

Many restrictions were placed on the way in which I was to conduct my research. After a good many years of fieldwork in Taiwan, I know that my best insights come from the casual conversations I have in kitchens, fetching water from wells, or hanging around the flat rocks where women gather to do their washing. My first bit of bad news in Beijing was that I would not be permitted to go to people's homes, even if invited by my informants. I was to be allowed only formal interviews in an office, attended by representatives of the street committee, the neighborhood committee, the Women's Federation, and various branches of CASS. With some firmness but as gracefully as possible, I resisted suggestions that I interview several women at once, and I also managed to secure a certain amount of privacy. After my first day of work, in which the women being interviewed were faced not only with their first foreigner, mangling their language with a heavy Taiwanese accent, but also with a room full of male officials, all smoking, I again raised objections. It seemed to me outrageous that these women should be asked to discuss questions about their personal lives and opinions in the presence of strange men. My objections were, I now see, based on a quaint old code from pre-Liberation days, but they worked: from then on, in all my subsequent research sites, men were never present at my interviews. Since there are very few women officials in China, the unexpected side effect of this display of righteous indignation was that, unlike Arthur who was burdened with as many as six observers from every level of government, I rarely had more than two women in addition to my informant's family members.

If the loss of autonomy is the most frustrating aspect of doing research in China, the pervasive influence of politics is the most awesome. Every few months educational campaigns sweep the country, covering billboards and newspapers with exhortations to clean up the backstreets or show respect for mothers-in-law, and filling the airwaves and rural public address systems with explanations of the Five Goods or the Three Bads. If you are not aware of what has passed through your research area in the few months before your arrival, you will be puzzled to find even the most senile old lady parroting a slogan in response to any question you ask that has key words in it, rather like the advertising jingle you cannot get out of your head. In asking questions, you can with patience get from some people how they feel about an issue of public concern, not just what the CCP's view is. Many other people can tell you nothing but the Party line. At first I assumed such people simply were not willing to tell a foreigner their personal views on any subject, and in many cases I was correct. However, quite a few women who answered my questions with the Party line seemed neither reticent nor ignorant. They, like the average American worker, had absorbed, uncritically, what they heard on the radio or through other communications media. They were no more aware of the degree to which their opinions were shaped by the Party than American workers are aware that theirs are shaped by the corporations that own the broadcasting systems.

Nonetheless, questions that might elicit answers contrary to Party policy seemed to produce uneasiness in many of my informants if I was too curious about their personal opinions. The most threatening questions seemed to be those that required comparisons of men's and women's access to some limited resource. I was surprised by how many of the women I talked with would trot out a slogan, such as, Men and women in the new China are equal, in direct response to the question, but later in the interview casually provide me with exactly the comparison I was seeking. The kind of interview situation in which I was required to work is by its nature alien to the usual setting of women's interactions with one another. I suspect their insistence on giving answers in at least the verbal context they found appropriate was another example of the subtle flouting of authority I have long admired in Chinese women everywhere.

Before I move on to describe the research project that finally evolved out of these compromises on both sides, I should make one final set of observations about Chinese attitudes toward Americans. Americans are charmed by Chinese. An even slightly outgoing tour guide in China is surrounded at all times by an admiring gaggle of American tourists asking her about the details of her personal life, pressing little gifts and large compliments on her, and generally being ingratiating. This friendliness may be well intended, but the patronizing tone is often unmistakable. The Americans look on with sophisticated amusement as Chinese fumble with advanced Western technology, and comment wittily on their childlike fascination with science. And yet we are hurt and offended when *our* childlike offers of friendship are not accepted in good faith.

As a nation, our record in China is not good—not as bad as some other countries, but not good. We recall our slightly more acceptable policies during the colonial period and our generosity during the Second World War. China recalls the Second World War as a time when they fought both with and against American arms. And they remember all too vividly the ultimate betrayal and the years of isolation and conflict that followed. Their textbooks are full of anti-American sentiments, and until recently Americans were the unifying devil figures nursery school children bravely attacked in song and dance. Although government policy has changed dramatically, a basic attitude of distrust must remain in most Chinese minds. For example, one day when I was walking with an assistant to an interview, some very small children began pelting us with pebbles from a cliff above the road. My companion yelled at them and told them that the foreigner would come and get them if they didn't stop. They looked stunned and scurried off, obviously not realizing until then that their targets included a foreigner. I was amused but told my companion, a college graduate and urban sophisticate, that I would rather she not use me as a threat. I then laughingly recounted some of the rumors missionaries used to have to contend with—such as that their orphanages adopted Chinese children to grind up for medicine. "But that is true!" my companion said, looking surprised. "Everyone knows the big American hospitals in Beijing experimented on Chinese and took their babies to make medicine for foreigners." She had read it in a textbook, and nothing I could say would ever convince her that it was untrue. I learned two things from this incident, both unsettling. The first was that this woman and many like her who received the same political education manage to work amicably with Americans. The second was a better understanding of the sudden withdrawal of a number of women who had seemed to be interacting with me on a human-to-human basis. Xenophobia is deep and widespread in China, and for anthropologists it must remain a profound influence on their research.

My original research proposal outlined a project that would allow me to examine in socialist China some observations about the behavior of women based on my study of traditional Chinese society in Taiwan. Specifically, I wanted to spend six months living and working in a Beijing neighborhood and then a month in one other smaller city and a month in four or five rural collectives. I was interested in the change socialism had brought to the lives of women and whether these changes differed in different parts of the country and between city and countryside. I hoped to find evidence for the continued existence of a particular family dynamic that was a source of domestic strength for women in old China, and of a women's community, a source of political strength for women in old China. These last two goals would have been better served if I had settled in one village and spent the year there, but the prospect of discovering, of "surveying" China, and the very real possibility that a shift in the political winds might make a return trip impossible led me to prefer this more peripatetic approach. This also meant that at least half if not more of my field time could be spent with my usual traveling companion, Arthur Wolf, whose research design required a number of different sites.

All the collectives I lived in or studied in were "model" collectives, that is, they have been designated by a regional authority as worthy of their neighbors' emulation, either through some miracle of labor such as redirecting a frequently overflowing river or by organizing prosperous sideline enterprises that compensated for poor agricultural conditions.[1] For a long time to come, if ever, foreigners in China are not going to be allowed to live in whichever village or city they choose; Chinese can't either.* Nor are the officials in charge of foreign research projects going to allow them to be carried out in villages that might embarrass China by their poverty or disorganization. Studying model collectives does not necessarily mean studying atypical communities, though some are. Shijiazhuang, the brigade I worked on in Shandong, was one of the exceptions. There is reason to believe that a great deal of outside money was poured into it to provide a showcase for visitors. If one's research concerns the economic operations of a typical collective, a model unit like this with an indirect or unacknowledged state subsidy is not the place to be. If one is interested in the success of the current birth limitation program, a model collective will have an optimistic bias. However, if demographic history or gender relations or a host of other less potent (from the state's view) topics are one's major concern, a model collective will do nicely—so long as one always bears in mind the fact that it is a model collective. Research that focuses on women, of course, is even less adversely affected than most in that married women grow up in and retain ties to other villages that are unlikely to be model units.

My negotiations with CASS in Beijing eventually resulted in a quota of fifty interviews at each field site. Any variation from this quota, such as when I heard of a former woman shaman and wanted to talk with her, produced expressions of grave concern on the part of the cadre accompanying me, and in this particular case meant giving up an interview with another woman in my sample.

---

*Not all foreigners are assigned to work in model villages, however. Victor Nee, Helen Siu, and others who are "overseas Chinese" or have Chinese relatives have been allowed to do research in non-model settings.

My tardy request to add five male informants at each field site was taken as a show of bad faith on my part since my quota had already been agreed to. I now realize that in the new China, new organizations are having to learn new ways of interacting with one another, but until they do the old ways continue. When CASS had to ask for yet another favor from a rural collective or urban organization with whom they had no accumulated history of debts and credits, my request to interview five more people seemed an outrage to them; their reaction (phone calls to Beijing, etc.) seemed to me absurd. My finickiness about whom I would like to interview—no schoolteachers, no wives of team and brigade leaders, no women cadre—struck my handlers as perverse; from their perspective, these were the women who could most articulately explain to me the way things were for women now. I, of course, wanted to know how things were for women who were not articulate and educated.

Because the scholarly exchange program was new and the presence of foreign field researchers in rural areas was a particularly sensitive issue—many countries now resent the presence of anthropologists or putative anthropologists in their hinterlands—I was extremely cautious about pursuing lines of questioning that our hosts found distasteful. Not all my research sites were in Mandarin-speaking areas, but I did talk whenever possible with people off the collectives and often found these contrasts informative. In each field site, either jointly or separately, Arthur Wolf and I interviewed a set list of collective officials, including accountants, birth limitation cadres, Women's Federation representatives, and production team or brigade leaders. In many cases these officials were very helpful in providing statistics that put "my" brigade or team in the context of the larger collective, the commune. We learned, as I will explain below, to treat these statistics with a degree of suspicion after we were presented with two sets that were clearly fabricated. In other cases there was simply a relaxed attitude toward statistics that probably was not related to a desire to mislead. Lucien Bianco, who struggled with local level statistics during his survey in 1979, made the same observation.[2] One must simply take this into consideration when one tries to work with them.

Like most foreigners, we were required to live in a hotel during our Beijing stay, but fortunately it was a hotel that had not been used for foreign tourists until that year. More importantly, it was on the edge of Dazhalan, one of the neighborhoods I had requested as a research site. In 1980 the area was a mixture of major shopping streets, small factories, a few larger factories, schools, and middle class housing. The city museum has a splendid early Qing scroll portraying its small shopping district character. Prior to Liberation some part of Dazhalan was Beijing's red light district. The present residents giggle about its lusty recent history, but claimed to know nothing about it when I asked for details. They were all, they told me, post-Liberation newcomers.

The first half of my Beijing interviews were carried out in the tiny office of the Baixu Residents' Committee. Once I had barred male observers and the chairperson had the coal-dust stove installed (a month early in my honor), the place was quite cozy. The Women's Federation Representative from the Neighborhood Committee sat through each of my interviews; CASS sent one and sometimes two women to observe my "methods"; and one or two women from the Residents' Committee were always present. When the women discovered that my tastes ran to those of the "masses," an endless stream of snacks from street vendors and native places added to the growing informality of our sessions. I recognized that it would be impossible for me to achieve anything like a random sample, so I settled for occupational diversity and a strict spread of ages (ten in each ten-year cohort). Most but not all of the women turned out to be either members of the Residents' Committee or their relatives. All lived in Baixu.

But then one day my CASS representative told me that I would be given a house and factory tour the next day and my interviews would begin on Monday in a key school in the district, but not in Baixu. This removed the last vestige of the "neighborhood study" I had hoped for. When I arrived at the school, I found that they had arranged for me to take most of the second half of my sample from the school's teachers. I had discovered early on that schoolteachers provided very uniform answers to even the most individualized questions. I reminded CASS of my research proposal and my concern to interview workers, not intellectuals. Their impatience with this "new" problem was not quite visible. Then I discovered that the school had many workers, so I requested permission to interview the cook, her assistant, the sweeper, the janitress, the gatekeeper's wife, the nurse's aide, and so forth. When I ran through this category, I again referred to my research proposal and asked to interview some shopkeepers and store clerks. Enough were found to fill out my remaining Beijing quota. So far as I could tell no more state secrets were revealed by the shopgirls than by the schoolteachers.

We left Beijing in mid-December, climbing on the train out of an icy wind appropriate to the city's psychological climate. The long slow train ride to south China was an ever-unfolding panorama of China's amazing climatic variety. My spirits made a decided jump as soon as we dropped off the edge of the dismal, lifeless North China Plain. Arriving in Fujian was, for two old Taiwan hands, like coming home. We spent a few days in Fuzhou and then traveled by bread truck (vans are shaped like loaves of bread) down the coast to Quanzhou and Zhangzhou, ancestral homes of the Taiwanese. It was unmitigated pleasure to see again colorful clothing and fresh fruit and vegetables, to smell incense, and to hear loud voices and laughter. People responded to our greeting "Have you eaten?" with a hearty "Come on in and have a cup of tea." Our Beijing handlers couldn't understand a word of it, and we revelled naughtily in our newfound independence. We peered into houses to see if they had ancestral altars (many do), counted new Tu Di Gong temples freshly rebuilt after the destruction of the Cultural Revolution, and stared in amazement at the highly unconventional houses designed by returned Chinese workers in the plantations and shops of Southeast Asia. Even our Beijing handlers were visibly impressed by the amount of housing space a farm family had when compared with urban dwellers of north China. They also went slightly mad over the fresh fruit, consuming literally dozens of oranges each day.

But all vacations must come to an end, and we headed south one fine morning for Jiaomei Commune, the site of our next five-week stint of interviewing. Jiaomei is only a few miles southwest of Xiamen (Amoy) as the crow flies, but the crow flies across the long, wide estuary of the Jiulong River, so if one needs a city from Jiaomei one either goes west to Zhangzhou or travels three hours around the sea's inlet to Xiamen. We lived in the guesthouse of Jiaomei Commune, and our interviews were carried out primarily in the production brigade of Shicu. We were their first foreign visitors, and the two rooms they had prepared especially for us were in the style of most "new rooms," that is, bridal. Our gaudy quarters were resplendent with frilly pink mosquito nets, red satin comforters, and pink pillows. Two young women were assigned to attend to our needs, and throughout our stay one or the other was always present, refilling thermoses, plumping pillows, serving meals, and doing laundry—if I didn't hide it in a suitcase.

To get to the brigade in which I was interviewing, my associates and I walked down the main street of Jiaomei, a street lined with what had formerly been shopfronts but were now housing a mix of shops and families. Most mornings there was a vigorous "free market" in the street itself where the real buying and selling took place. One could have shirts hemmed and buttonholes made while another family member bought fruit, meat, cheap ready-made clothing, altar pictures of the gods (sold by the same vendor who carried pictures of Deng Shao-ping, Hua Guofeng, and Mao Zedong), incense both for mosquitoes and spirits, fresh fish, and a variety of cooked foods. One of the regulars was the comic-book vendor who didn't sell her wares but rented them for a few pennies to adults and children who squatted on one of the bamboo stools and read, with whatever light the sky provided, one of the smudged and tattered pamphlets of few words and many drawings. A habitué of the main street was an enormous sow who cleaned up the orange peels and then settled down near food stalls, waiting for a child to have a tragedy. Main Street ended abruptly at a large drying ground. On some days a third of the drying ground was a brilliant purple, covered with sticks of freshly dipped incense. On other days the more subdued hues of yellow, tan, or gray prevailed, depending on what vegetable was being dried. On the north side logs from the lumber mill often encroached. During our stay a gas-engined carriage was installed in the mill, but the logs, large and small, were still transported to the carriage by straining teams of men.

Once past the noisy mill, we encountered the low-slung building from which issued the shrill voices of children chanting their lessons, then the dark, unwelcoming storefront that served as a day care center, and finally the walled garden and surprisingly urban-looking apartment house that was home for many retired People's Liberation Army families (and before Liberation was the district execution grounds). One then crosses a canal and is suddenly in the villages or what is now known as the brigade. Here old and new confront and refuse to confront one another in intriguing confusion. Splendid old wooden farm houses with finely carved lintels and inner columns lean slightly to one side as if in disdain of the sturdy concrete utilitarian structures that have grown up around them to house the sons and daughters-in-laws of the older houses. The new houses are without character, often following their predecessors in design but with the ostentatious lack of attention to artistic detail that is appropriate to a socialist society. Still, they defiantly flaunt bits of red at the crucial openings and lines that once required the attention of geomancers. Inside, the houses reverse themselves in appeal. The old buildings reveal (with the help of a flashlight and a good bit of imagination) carved and painted beams, and a few splendid panels, but they are stained dark from the smoke of several generations' charcoal fires. The new houses, though furnished in a decidedly tacky style with plastic and shoddily constructed furniture, are lighter and brighter and easier to live in.

Most country houses around Jiaomei, old and new, have an ancestral altar facing the door. In some homes when I came to visit there was a vase of plastic flowers or an odd blank space in the center of the altar, but in others the center of the altar boldly displayed a photograph of a god from the main temple in Jiangzhou and a tin can with a few burned-out sticks of incense in it. On either side of the altar are pictures of recent ancestors which people fairly openly admit are focal points for offerings, substitutes for ancestral tablets burned by Red Guards during the Cultural Revolution. The altar also holds other important family possessions: a radio, new thermos bottles, a clock, fancy glass or plastic objects, and other bits of decoration. On the walls hang the family's awards: children's certificates of school achievements, mothers' awards for clean and peaceful homes, sons' or husbands' awards for being model workers. A table and some benches are the basic furnishings, but chairs and farm tools, plus a much-prized bicycle, might also be found. In some of the older houses, the tables and altars show signs of former elegance, but in general fine furniture was either destroyed during the Cultural Revolution because of its decadence or was sold long ago.

The central room of the old-style houses was too public and, in winter, too drafty for interviews with foreigners, so I was usually ushered into one of the sleeping-rooms of the house. Even though a sleeping-room is considered the private domain of the conjugal unit, I was nearly always received in the room of the most recently married son—no matter whom I was interviewing—for this was the room into which the family had poured its recent savings. Even in the oldest, most dilapidated house, every square inch of what is known as the "new bride's room" is pasted over with fresh paper. Comforters with new red or pink satin covers are stacked on the *kang*, and the new mosquito net (often pink) is held back with red plastic ornaments. The new furniture is spotted with doilies (trimmed in red or pink), and the wedding gifts—thermoses, mirrors, clocks, a radio, and a collection of glass and plastic thingamajigs—are on careful display. The cheerful "new bride's room" stands in sharp contrast to the stark and dingy rooms of the long-married or as yet unmarried children of the household.

Every morning and afternoon my assistants and I trooped down to the brigade, interviewed the women selected for the day, took

Polaroid pictures of each woman as a gift, and trooped back. We were discouraged from making informal visits (our Beijing cadres wanted everything cleared with our hosts first), but no restrictions were placed on chats with passersby. When I objected to having too many wives and relatives of team leaders or other officials in my sample, the local handler cheerfully made the changes I requested. In general the local people found the whole affair amusing and even entertaining. But once again I was appalled at the number of people who were pulled away from their normal activities to "handle" the foreigners. One male and one female cadre from Beijing traveled with us to "make arrangements" throughout the year. Because I was not confident of my fluency in a language I had not used for ten years, I agreed to hire an assistant, who, it turned out, spoke more English than she understood, which fitted nicely with my ability to understand more *putong hua* (the national language) than I can speak. Each province we worked in felt obliged to send with us a member of their own academy of the social sciences; each county made sure that one of their foreign affairs officers was within hailing distance; and each brigade provided (at our expense) at least one and usually two local assistants. It was with this cumbersome entourage in tow that I set out each day to try to talk casually with women about their lives—all the while feeling guilty about the hours my companions were wasting on my behalf and a touch irritated at having them imposed between me and the people I was trying to get to know. Attempting to alter our working conditions was impossible; I was told time and again that each of these people was essential, or that that was the way it was done in China. (I am sure that my frustration was no greater than that of the people responsible for this huge outlay of time and to some extent money—for which they could see no conceivable benefit to China. Lower level officials had little understanding of scholarly exchange programs or were unaware that there are far more Chinese scholars in the United States than there are American scholars in China.)

The five weeks in Fujian talking to feisty, tough-minded farm women were a psychological restorative, after the bleak months

in Beijing. They were followed by two weeks of physical restora-
tion in Hong Kong, where a persistent Cantonese doctor finally
cleared my lungs and supplied me with the drugs and confidence
to face subsequent attacks of Chinese bacteria on my breathing
apparatus. Just after Chinese New Year Arthur and I arrived in
Zhejiang; we spent a few days in Hangzhou, and then went our
separate ways, with Arthur and my former Beijing handler going
up to a mountain tea commune where they endured snow and
frostbite for five weeks, while my assistant and I settled down in
Shaoxing in an old teahouse now used to house visiting dignitaries (foreign and Chinese). Anyone who has read Lu Xun can
imagine the excitement of wandering the alleys and peering
down the canals from the very bridges mentioned in his stories.
Because of my experience in Beijing, I did not look forward to
interviewing in another, albeit smaller, city, but the Foreign Affairs Officer assigned to handle me seemed motherly and interested, an appearance that turned out not to be misleading. She
took care of our housekeeping arrangements without a hitch and
plodded along to each and every interview, fading into the wood-
work when the work began—a rare and valuable quality. I went
with considerable anxiety to the first meeting with the Residents'
Committee that was hosting me, for I had discovered in Beijing
that these were the women who would make or break my project.
It didn't look too promising. They were an unsmiling group, and
the two Women's Representatives assigned to be my local watch-
ers and handlers appeared to be the worst of the lot—one a
tough-looking lady who could have been a prison warden and the
other a slightly skittish young woman who seemed easily dis-
tracted. The head of the Committee, a short, sturdy woman in
her mid-fifties, toured me around her neighborhood at a breath-
less pace, ticking off the items of interest, and then rushed off to
attend to other affairs of, I was sure, greater import. I was thoroughly intimidated.

First impressions are often wrong. Both my local handlers
eventually won my heart for their separate virtues. The older of
the two, who seemed so forbidding, on many occasions "saved"
an interview with a word of reassurance either to me or to the

informant, and on the day I departed waved farewell with tears in her eyes. The younger woman, who had to contend with a new baby, a series of bad colds, and a long commute by bicycle through the nonstop winter rains, was an inspiration of good humor. But the Residents' Committee as a group and in the person of its director, Comrade Chen Su-zhen, was my greatest source of good fortune. These women were extraordinarily busy, running several neighborhood enterprises as well as administrating a sizable district of the city. They took me and my unusual needs on in the same way they had taken on the other enterprises: they found out from my Beijing assistant what I needed, *checked it with me*, set about lining up informants, made someone responsible for the day-to-day organization, and then settled back to watch the fun. Although I added enormously to their workloads, I truly think they enjoyed it. It is still hard for me to make a "professional" evaluation of my research setting in Shaoxing without remembering the day they discovered that my hand was often numb in those icy houses as I took notes on interviews. A hot water bottle appeared and followed me from house to house. Or the wet gray afternoon that mysterious noises in the kitchen of a house I was working in climaxed (timed to my last question, which everyone recognized by then) with the appearance of the head of the Residents' Committee and her sister carrying platters heaped with spring rolls for which all the rest of the family and some of the neighbors had been waiting. This was only one of several impromptu parties that did much to make my Shaoxing research a pleasure.

Shaoxing in February is miserable. We interviewed for thirty-two days, and the one day that it didn't rain it snowed. Some days it did both. On several days the temperature in the dining hall of my guest house never rose above 2°c. My room was provided with a sturdy old wire-coil electric heater, *circa* 1930, but Shaoxing homes have no space heaters, and many buildings are in such poor repair that the drafts ruffled the pages of my notebook. Aesthetically some of the big old two-story townhouses are elegant, displaying carved posts and panels, inner courtyards with delicate balustrades on the upper galleries, and sliding painted interior screens, and containing a surprising quantity of handsome old furniture that somehow survived the barbarism of the Cultural Revolution. One young man showed me his lovely old-style bed with inlaid and painted scenes from the classics. He sheepishly pointed out where he himself had slopped paint over these scenes, probably as much to prevent outrages by Red Guard inspectors as to indicate his patriotic disgust with feudal values. Because of my interest in this bed I was taken to another house to see an even more elaborate old bed, which was almost a room in itself, with built-in chests, cabinets, and benches. Often as not these old houses were festooned with laundry and had several families living in what once must have been quarters for one, but some were privately owned and were not at all crowded. About half the houses I interviewed in were so old that I was more than a little nervous about sitting in an upstairs room in which the furniture—including the stool I was sitting on—bobbed up and down when anyone walked across the floor. Nonetheless, the newer housing was far, far less pleasant—concrete boxes with small rooms and a chill that seemed to emanate from some dark, dank underground place.

Perhaps it was this chill and the hot cups of tea that made the small groups of women I spent my days with in Shaoxing huddle closer together and at least seem to include me in their lives for a brief hour or two. I am not sure whether this influenced my impressions, but I left Shaoxing convinced that these women more than any others I had met in China were proud of their sex, not always content with their achievements, but not without hope. They were energetic and as devoted to socialism as any women I met in Beijing, but they also liked to wear colorful blouses under their somber jackets, curl their hair, and even wear a bit of makeup. The monotonous uniformity both in thought and appearance that made Beijing such an unpleasant place to live and work was absent in Shaoxing, and the revolution did not seem to be any less well served.

It is well that the Shaoxing experience was so happy, for from the minute we set foot in Jiangsu, we were again deeply mired in bureaucratic paralysis. We spent a week in Nanjing, awaiting permission to continue to our next field site. When we finally got to Yangzhou, we discovered I could not interview in the city "because it was not yet open to foreigners," a curious statement in view of the tour buses that came and went with great regularity. I suspect the real reason was simple enough. There were no women cadres, hence no one to "handle" me. We could not live on the commune we were finally assigned to work on, nor would we be allowed to interview in homes there. Instead we were housed in Yangzhou's tourist hotel and went by cab each day to the commune. I continued to request house visits, and on my last day was finally taken to three carefully selected (and carefully cleaned) homes. On the way, I saw many houses made of mud and wattle with thatch roofs, but my hostesses all lived in newish, concrete, single-family dwellings. Many of my informants had told me that they lived in the economical concrete two-story row houses now popular in China's collectives. There is probably a reason why my home visits were all to families in old-style scattered housing, but I will never know it. None of the houses I visited had cheerful gaudy bride's rooms (which may have been due to the family's stage in the domestic cycle), nor did any of them have the endearingly frivolous touches of decoration I saw in Shaoxing. I saw no direct evidence of ancestor worship, but all three houses had curiously bare altar tables. Several women had remarked in interviews that they or other members of their family made regular offerings to ancestral spirits.

For four weeks, six days a week, I interviewed in a concrete cell in Wantou Commune headquarters with my Beijing assistant, the commune Women's Affairs Officer, and a Women's Representative from each of the two brigades that provided my sample. After the warm and friendly relations I had with Shaoxing officials, the bored but watchful attitude of the Wantou women depressed me. Even more disheartening were their attitudes toward the women who had been selected for my interviews. My assistant and I were by now accustomed to problems of language and problems of incomprehension unrelated to language, but the Wantou officials were impatient and cross with my struggling informants. When all went smoothly, the Women's Affairs Officer in charge smoked and sighed, sighed and smoked. She often slept, no doubt because she was up until all hours fulfilling her domestic responsibilities after she put in her eight to ten hours with me. The two Women's Representatives from the brigades hadn't worked with foreigners before and found it all more of an adventure. They also were not infected with the established bureaucrat's ennui. Unfortunately, one was too young to be trusted by the anxious country women she ushered in, and was not even known to many of them. The other was a cheerful woman in her early thirties who knew personally the women from her brigade and was good at reassuring them. Most of the women had never before been to commune headquarters and found that experience in itself upsetting. They worried about where they would get their lunch, whether they would get home in time to start supper, where they should be, how they should sit, when they could spit, whether they could smoke, or in a couple of cases whether they could *not* smoke. We would all have been more comfortable in their homes.

With all this going against the project, it is as surprising to me now as it was then what good interviews these women gave me. So often in the years I have worked with Chinese women I have been struck by their capacity to force aside the multiple obstacles of language, illiteracy, fear, cultural misunderstandings, and political difference to tell me something about themselves and their lives. Once again, almost against my will, in this cheerless room the Jiangsu women told me haltingly about their new lives. It was not the happy story that I had heard in Shaoxing or even the story of struggle continuing I had found in Fujian, but it was their own story. Most but not all of the women had worked in the fields before they married, but in recent years as the state factories began to ring their commune, drawing off the young and middle-aged men to wage labor, more and more of the agricultural tasks had fallen to women of all ages. As one woman put it, "Now women do all the farm work. Men just supervise." Since a family's grain ration depends on the workpoints they earn as part of the collective, a major part of the family's livelihood comes from the sweat of the women's brows. And yet when I asked women what their jobs were, they nearly always said, "I have no job; I am at home." The collective's fields are now like the kitchen garden, and working in them is simply part of the domestic toil for which women never are rewarded with dignity, let alone cash. I was not sorry to leave Jiangsu. But I left with a renewed appreciation of Chinese women's capacity to endure.

Long before we left Beijing, CASS officials told us, with a certain air of disbelief, that the Shandong Academy of Social Sciences "welcomes your visit, really welcomes your visit." We were greeted in Weifang by the Academy's Foreign Affairs Officer who exuded goodwill, energy, and enthusiasm. With a now more practiced eye I could see that Shandong was not a rich province; the wheat was sparse in many places; the housing looked grim. When we turned off the unpaved road we had been bumping along for some miles onto a paved avenue lined with trees whose trunks had been painted white, the fields of wheat were suddenly a foot taller and a brilliant shade of green that can only be produced by chemical fertilizer. In the distance loomed an imposing three-story building that we found was to be our home for the next four weeks. Alas, a very model collective. This time the model was the brigade, and the commune was barely mentioned. We had driven through its headquarters without even slowing down, or having it pointed out.

Certainly our accommodations were palatial: two large, airy rooms, the usual separate dining room (foreigners are allowed to dine with Chinese only at banquets), and a spacious bathroom (albeit without hot water). We were given a whirlwind tour of Shijiazhuang's many enterprises and were properly impressed with its orchards, rabbit farm, and so on. When I hesitantly asked if I would be allowed to interview in homes, I was assured that I would. My assistants seemed friendly and a part of the community. But what was wrong? First of all, the enormous building we were in had been built to house a United Nations demonstration unit that had decided not to locate here. Why? No one knew. Then when we walked down to the brigade store, which was the size of most commune stores, we found a main street of new buildings, also commune size. The majority of the inhabitants, we were told, were either in or about to move into new housing. The new buildings were the usual row-house style, but with interesting gates, front courtyards, and auxiliary sheds that had been adapted from the local style. We both recognized what was missing on our first stroll through town: the people didn't stare. They glanced at us when we appeared and then went on with what they were doing. Even the children hurried off. Only once, at the brigade store, were we surrounded by the curious, and this was a group of rather dirty, rather ragged kids who were quickly shooed away and who, I later learned, were children from another brigade come to look at the sights of Shijiazhuang. Unpleasant as I find the nonstop staring that is the lot of every foreigner in China, its absence in a field site suggested that the people were either very sophisticated farmers, had seen so many foreigners that they were no longer interested, or were under strict orders. I asked about the number of tour groups that came through and was told they came every week or two (only one came during our month-long stay). When I asked about previous researchers, I discovered there were a number of them, including an American anthropologist who had visited several times. Not exactly fresh territory, but still not so saturated with foreigners as to account for such complete disinterest in their peculiar ways.

By the end of my fourth day of interviews, it was abundantly clear that my informants were anticipating my questions. For another few days I asked a new set of questions, and it become obvious that not only had answers to the questions I no longer asked been memorized but themes had been rehearsed as well. If my questions did not give my informants the opportunity to say their piece, the less sophisticated women simply blurted it out, all using much the same language. Finally, as much out of curiosity as anything else, I removed from my questions *all* items asking for gender comparisons. I continued to get little speeches about sexual equality in the new China. When I raised the problem formally with my local handlers, they denied that anyone had coached the women, suggesting only that the women might have gossiped with those who had already been interviewed. Since I was not working with a formal interview schedule but with a list of questions, it was easy enough for me to switch to another set of topics every few days that would still elicit the information I was interested in, but I became a more wary interviewer as a result. Also, Arthur and I both began to look more carefully at the other kinds of information the brigade leaders were giving us. We discovered that some of it did not agree with data we were collecting on our own. Two batches of statistics in particular were so at odds with what we had obtained from individual interviews that they could only have been fabricated.

One set concerned the success of the birth limitation program and will be discussed in Chapter 10. The other discrepancy is more amusing than troubling, although it will plague anthropologists and historians of the future. Part of the family background information I asked for from each of my informants was whether or not their fathers and fathers-in-law had owned any land at the time of their marriages. After sitting through nearly fifty of these interviews, my local handlers told me one day in casual conversation that before Liberation 70 percent of the land in the area was in the hands of two or three very large landlords and that all the people in Shijiazhuang were either poor tenants or farm laborers. When I pointed out the discrepancy between their remarks and those of my informants, they said, "Oh, they are just ignorant women and don't really know." (One of these women was herself illiterate and the other could not write.) Since they were so confident of their facts, I pursued the matter further than I might have ordinarily, and the two women told me quite firmly that this information had been obtained from an exhibit set up by the Party. It showed, with maps, that before Liberation most land was in the hands of a few landlords. Unlike their fellow brigade members, neither of these women believed that their own fathers and fathers-in-law had owned land. The "reality" presented to them by the Party was so much more meaningful that they had forgotten their own childhood experience.

Shijiazhuang was by far the most comfortable place I lived in, but with each passing day the realization that I was living in a stage-set became stronger. Finally, on the last day of my interviews, the older of the two local assistants invited me to dinner with her family. She suggested that I come over immediately after my last interview and "help" her cook. I was delighted, and it proved to be an interesting and pleasant evening. She and a neighbor made *jian bing* (a corn pancake), squatting over a smoking fire of cornstalks. Her husband came home from work and pitched in to scrape vegetables, and when the children came home from school they too had tasks, one of which was to keep the foreign lady from doing anything that might injure her (such as pumping water or peeling hard-boiled eggs). After dinner we were sitting around finishing the beer and picking our teeth when the Foreign Affairs Officer came strolling in. He proceeded to give me a ridiculous lecture on what a treat I had just had, dining in a typical peasant home on typical peasant fare. The Wu family were hardly typical peasants, and after interviewing in fifty-five homes, I was well aware that few families ate like this except on holidays, even in this very affluent brigade. I could not decide whether to laugh or weep. Mrs. Wu knew what she was doing and she knew I knew, but we both, I think, had enjoyed the process whatever the purpose.

By the end of May we were settled in our next field site, Fenghuo, way on the other side of China in Shaanxi, some forty miles north of Xian. When we arrived it was at last pleasantly warm, but by the time we left, it was unpleasantly hot. Fenghuo was also a model brigade. It had been honored with a visit by Jimmy Carter, and it had even had a foreign researcher (a Yale economist) for a few days, but our living quarters were primitive compared with our Shandong palace. Rooms were bare, dirty-walled, and without running water. The outhouses were across the courtyard, shared with many, and unpleasant as the days got hotter and the insects larger. On the brighter side, there was an openness about things that was a genuine relief after the heavy cosmetics of Shandong. My Fenghuo assistant was very helpful to me while at the same time being supportive to the women she represented. People we met were curious but friendly, and although we were often warned about the dangers of the countryside, we managed to walk off the model brigade and talk to people in the less fortunate brigades round about. For the inhabitants of these poorer brigades, the living conditions were grim, but the old-style architecture was aesthetically far more appealing. The new houses into which all of Fenghuo had been moved were the usual two-story brick rowhouses with some local touches on courtyards and outbuildings, but the housing in the non-model villages was built to resemble the cliff dwellings in which many still lived, with arched doors and windows that gave them a Moorish look. Obviously in winter these villages would be in a sea of mud and the houses damp and dark, but in late spring they were cool and attractive compared with the tightly packed rows of the model brigade.

The local school served a couple of other brigades as well as Fenghuo, and was itself very picturesque, each room being hollowed out of the high cliff behind the village. The model classroom that had been set up for visitors was comfortable enough, but when I did a survey of the other classrooms, I got some sense of how committed children had to be to get an education. They must contend with all the natural miseries of rural China (poor lighting, poor ventilation, uncomfortable makeshift furniture, insects) as well as the unnatural miseries of Chinese schooling (overcrowding, long hours, dull textbooks, and boredom). Moreover, most of them must have realized that their education was not going to take them anywhere.

Like many model brigades, Fenghuo has its miracle and its hero. The hero is a model worker, whose picture receiving congratulations from Mao Zedong and Zhou Enlai is conspicuously displayed at various places in the brigade. He seemed rarely to be in residence during our tenure, but one hot sleepy afternoon he granted us an interview. He has put on a bit of flesh since his days of labor miracles, and the presence of one long fingernail asserts that he no longer engages in physical labor.* Fenghuo's miracle, under the leadership of its model worker, was to change the

---

*In pre-Liberation China, men who did not have to do physical labor allowed one fingernail, usually on the little finger, to reach an inch or more in length. It was, they said, a handy tool, but its more obvious function was that of a status-marker.

course of the river, build new fields in the old riverbed, dig deep ditches to get water to other fields, and install an elaborate pumping station. Although local leaders would like us to believe that it was entirely a self-help project, clearly a good deal more money than a rural collective could manage was poured into the initial project. Moreover, this is the same collective visited in 1973 by an American delegation studying early childhood development. At that time the Americans interviewed some of the hundreds of students and workers who came out from Xian each year to spend a month "learning from the peasants" and working on their earth-moving project.[3]

Our stay in Fenghuo covered the busiest season of the year, when the wheat is harvested and the land is prepared for the next planting. The paths were lined with young women pushing and pulling carts laden with wheat stalks on the way to an enormous communal drying ground where the men did the processing. But even during this busiest season, there were still many women to be found at home during work hours. Like much of China, Fenghuo has an oversupply of labor. When asked, women said they worked every day, but when you look at individual income records in a family, it is clear that they worked considerably less than their menfolk. They explained this in terms of having to stay home to do chores; older women simply retired when they had a daughter or daughter-in-law to take their place in the production team labor force. The teams were disproportionately female, nonetheless. Most of the men were in special groups such as irrigation, agricultural research, or machinery, wherein they usually earned more workpoints, which were worth more in cash at the end of the year. Those men who were left in the teams were leaders, according to the women.

When we were given the usual "brief introduction" at Fenghuo, Arthur and I exchanged knowing smiles when we were told that nearly every family in the brigade had a television. We assumed that this was the usual patter given to people who would never go into every house in the brigade and so would never know. To our surprise, nearly every family in the brigade *did* have a television. When I asked how they could afford this luxury item, I discovered that the brigade subsidized them, paying for as much as half the cost. Why? The answer given was one of the frankest I received from a brigade official: "Life is very dull in the countryside. There are no movies here and no big shops and no books. People need some amusement, so we decided to buy everyone televisions." And they did. Houses that did not own enough cups or bowls to give tea to guests had a television in a prominent position, carefully covered with a lovingly crocheted or embroidered "cozy." One wonders whether the world seen on television makes people more or less satisfied with rural living. Certainly life in the communes without the annual cycle of religious festivals is colorless. Efforts to keep weddings and funerals simple have further diminished the once frequent breaks in village monotony. However, most of the things shown on Chinese television are urban in origin, with urban values and styles, a fact that must make rural young people even more restless to become a part of the glamorous life that they mistake to be the lot of all city dwellers.

For me, the high point of my research in China was to be the last of our field sites, Sichuan. Set deep in China's interior in a rich basin that is the source of the mighty Yangtze River, bordered by forbiddingly high mountains, Sichuan had always seemed to me the heart of China. It was with great disappointment that I finally admitted that the intensifying heat and humidity were taking a toll on my lungs that I could no longer afford to ignore. The male half of our entourage continued on to Sichuan and I and my (delighted) female companions returned to Beijing.

Nothing seems to come easily in doing research in the People's Republic, even to the final analysis of the data collected. Although I have been referring to my sessions with informants as interviews, the pages and pages of notes that came from each interview are not the sort of data that can be tabulated neatly on graph paper. Rural women often answer questions obliquely after thinking on the topic for a bit. They may be unwilling to give a direct answer to a direct question, but not necessarily unwilling to provide the information later on, at a time of their own choosing. As a result, I have had to analyze much of my field data like a text, extracting the answers whenever they occur. Not surprisingly, the reader will find more quotes than tables in these pages. Whenever possible I have tried to give some sense of the number of women who gave similar answers to a particular question, but even then I must caution the reader against generalizing too far. China is vast, and my travels there have if nothing else convinced me that a handful of women in Beijing are no more typically Chinese than are fifty women in Xian, or for that matter in Taipei.

THREE

Women Workers
in the Cities

What is the best time of life for a woman? I don't know about other women, but for me the best time was my first job. The best day of my life was my first payday. A woman who has no work cannot control her own life. Later, when my husband died, I put all my energy into my work. If I had not had a job life would have been intolerable and I could not have borne the grief. My son is very good to me now, but I would not be happy depending on him entirely. I have my pension and my independence.
—*Retired dining room cashier from a wheel factory in Beijing, age 58*

I was assigned to this job [as a nurse] in 1972 and at that time I felt lucky to get it. Most of my classmates got sent to the countryside. I would like to have been an architect, but that wasn't suitable for women. I feel cheated. I wanted more education—I would like to have learned about literature and history, but now I will never have that chance. Nurses get low pay and they are not respected by either the patients or by society. But this is my lot. —*Nurse in Beijing, age 28*

In both cities in which I did research, Beijing and Shaoxing, the women who served as my guides and cultural interpreters were members of Residents' Committees. These women, ranging in age from mid-forties to seventy, were the "officials" in charge of the neighborhood's day-to-day affairs. Their duties were many: inspecting courtyards and houses for cleanliness, organizing study groups, settling domestic quarrels, overseeing the local clinic, running several small and not-so-small enterprises, coordinating and finding jobs for the "waiting-for-work" youths, and organizing the neighborhood security patrols. Their level of education was generally low: some of them were illiterate, others were painfully self-taught, long after learning comes easy. They were political in that they were appointed by the local party apparatus and motherly in that they had all grown up in a society that valued them primarily as mothers. Some of them were overworked—in particular, the women I met in Shaoxing—and all of them took their jobs seriously. They, more than the younger women I interviewed, had a sense of history, for their lives had spanned an enormous social revolution that their daughters experienced only by hearsay. When young women glibly answered my questions with political slogans and spoke scornfully of their parents' feudal ideas, I had to fight back my impatience with their shallow understanding; when the older women told me laughingly of their dowries, their arranged marriages, and the new society where none of these things occurred any more, I found it easier—sometimes too easy—to believe. From an outsider's perspective, the women who composed the Residents' Committees and the women who worked in the small enterprises they managed were being exploited; from their perspective, they had been liberated from a life of isolated household drudgery.

I interviewed 100 women (and ten men) in Beijing and Shaoxing about their and their families' jobs and lives. The women's occupations were varied. Although, as I mentioned before, the authorities preferred that I speak only with teachers and administrators, they eventually allowed me to talk with factory workers, shop employees, and service workers in restaurants, hotels, and business establishments. Each informant took a half-day off work (for which I compensated their units) in order to be interviewed. Some clearly enjoyed the experience and others would have preferred a full day at hard labor. Of all the urban workers I spoke with, only five (one of whom was a man) said that if they had all the money they needed to live on they would happily stay at home. And yet throughout the interviews there was a theme of constant weariness. As one woman put it, "Rush in the morning, stand in line at noon, headache in the afternoon, angry in the evening." None of the men I talked with (admittedly a much smaller sample) alluded to this, but when I asked them if they would rather have the life of a man or a woman, they nearly all said they wouldn't want to be women because women had so many "other" duties. They were referring, of course, to the women's "second shift," familiar to working women the world over: the shopping, cooking, cleaning, laundry, and child care that must be squeezed into the hours before and after work.

Most, but by no means all, of the women I interviewed under the age of forty had what we would call real jobs. They worked in factories, clinics, schools, stores, restaurants, and hospitals. Their units provided them with medical care and some had canteens where they (and sometimes their families) could eat lunch and dinner. The larger institutions had nurseries for their children (although there were never enough spaces) and gave them fifty-six days' paid maternity leave and pensions at retirement that amounted to 80 percent (70 percent prior to 1978) of their last salary. They were paid on pay scales graduated within different kinds of work that ostensibly guaranteed pay raises with seniority. And, of course, they received equal pay for equal work regardless of gender. The catch here, as we shall see shortly, is getting equal work and defining equal pay.

The work day is eight hours, the work week is six days, but the time women (and men) put in at the workplace is usually much longer. The workplace, one's unit, has far, far greater significance in the life of the urban worker than it does in that of the average Western worker. Following the four-hour morning shift, some women rush home during their lunch break to prepare a midday meal for other family members, or they may join queues for scarce or poorly distributed commodities or attend committee meetings. After another four-hour shift, workers attend political study groups one day a week or oftener if there is something special to be discussed in the ever-shifting sands of Chinese policy. There may also be meetings to discuss work skills, production lags, and so forth. And for those who wish to get ahead, there are "volunteer" jobs, committees to discuss reorganization of shops, or implementation in their shop of a new policy directive concerning some new campaign.

It is not just sheer hours spent that makes the unit central to the urban worker's life, however. It is through your unit that you get ration cards for meat, grain, cloth, appliances, and scarce items of furniture. Your unit must approve your marriage plans, your fertility plans, your housing; if brought to their attention, even your marital problems may be subject to group discussion. During certain swings of the political pendulum, you and your spouse's political attitudes may be examined and reformed. There is literally nothing in your private life that is considered unsuitable for your unit to be concerned about. Women are often told (and tell the foreign interviewer) that the unit "shows concern" (*zhao gu*) for their welfare. This is the same term that is used to refer to men's obligations to protect and nurture their wives and children. In the West, in the context of labor relations, we might call it paternalism. For the woman worker in China, it includes such things as arranging light or sitting-down work for women who are pregnant, nursing, or menstruating, as well as the exclusion of all women from jobs in heavy industry that may or may not require heavy lifting but are nearly always better paying.

Working conditions in factories are certainly far superior to those described in the factories of pre-Liberation China, but by Western standards the amount of "concern" shown for the workers' welfare is debatable.[1] Foreigners are only allowed to see the very best factories, and one wonders what conditions are like in average factories. Even factories that are standard tourist stops show a stunning lack of safeguards. Tour groups routinely comment on the need for ear plugs in textile mills and are told by their guides that they are available but the workers are unwilling to use them. In one factory I visited where items were being glued together, the fumes were so strong that members of my group felt faint. Yet two women workers were obviously pregnant, and given the ages of the other women it is likely that there were others who were in earlier (and more damageable) stages of pregnancy. One of my handlers asked, not quite out of my hearing, if these workers were given "hazardous working conditions allowances" and was told that they were. Such things as gloves, protective goggles, hard hats, and safety screens are seldom seen in Chinese factories, but every inquiry about their absence is met with the response that they are available but not used.

Some of the franker Women's Representatives I spoke with in various parts of China were aware that many of the policies designed to protect women from poor working conditions also kept them out of many industries. In fact, they told me that some factories, when approached by people from the Women's Federation who wanted to place more women workers, simply refused out-right to consider any of their arguments. Now that factories are again expected to show a profit, managers are even less willing to take on women workers. They are afraid of having to add special facilities, such as nurseries, and they assume that the factory would be less efficient because of women's "special problems." One Women's Federation Representative said she had simply given up with the established factories and concentrated her efforts on improving conditions in the traditional workplaces for women and in making sure that new factories included provision for at least some women employees.

Given that the working conditions are not the best, why then *do* women work? The simplest answer is that they have no choice: men's wages are not enough to support families. However, that answer does not begin to describe the complex motives involved in women's work lives. Older women, no matter how dreary the work, truly do seem to see their jobs as a symbol of their personal liberation from the tyranny of domestic labor. They may com-plain about the double shift and about being tired, but few of them willingly give up their status as workers. Younger women, particularly those who have entered the labor market in the last twenty years, take it as a natural part of their lives. When they finish school they are assigned a job, in due time. They may have to wait as much as two years for permanent work, and when it comes it may be totally unsuited to their particular talents, but until they have a job, they cannot get on with their lives; they are not truly adults. Neither men nor women would consider (or could consider) marrying until they have been given a job and worked at it for a period of time. Without a unit of their own, they remain children of their parents, receiving from them their rations, their pocket money, their identity. When their names finally turn up on a job list, most young people are delighted to be freed from the boredom of hanging around home or the mo-notony of futureless part-time jobs in Residents' Committee enterprises.

By far the most common reason women give for wanting to

work is that it is not interesting to stay at home. At home, there is nothing to do, no one to talk to, no way of finding out what is going on. When I asked women if they would continue to work if they didn't need the money to live, 30 (41 percent) of the 74 positive responses (some gave more than one reason) indicated that boredom at home was the main reason. The fact that this attitude was somewhat more common in Beijing (46 percent of the responses for that city against 34 percent of the responses in Shaoxing) would not come as a surprise to anyone who has seen workers' housing in the two cities. In winter, Shaoxing's un-heated houses are spartan to be sure, but they are light and spa-cious compared with the cramped, dank, drafty homes of Bei-jing's families. I suspect that what was meant by a good many of the Beijing respondents was that staying home was not only un-interesting, it was uncomfortable. Spending most of your waking hours in an unpleasant room without the collection of material goods with which Americans amuse themselves would make em-ployment look attractive to the most determined sluggard.

The remaining responses to this question (excluding those who rejected it outright by saying one worked because one needed the money and the thought that one might not was silly) were more or less political. Ten (14 percent) said they wished to work in order to contribute to socialism or the Four Modernizations, and another seven (10 percent) spoke of the symbolism of work: it was both sign and source of the improved status of women in the new China. There is a certain irony in these responses when one turns to look, as we soon will, at the wages women earn in the cities. They are indeed the symbol of the extent to which women's status has improved. Nonetheless, a good many of the older women, those who were the most poorly paid, did seem very pleased with their jobs, and that pleasure was associated with being something more than a housewife and working on something that did not have to be done over again the next day and the next and the one after that. They liked having a prod-uct; they liked seeing a stack of account books they had sewn together piled by the workshop door at the end of the day, in-stead of a clean floor casually dirtied by an unnoticing family.

However, if working conditions in real jobs were less than ideal, the conditions which these older women (and some of the waiting-for-work youths) found at the neighborhood workshops were much worse. The two most common miseries were overcrowding and poor lighting. Safety precautions were one's own lookout. In effect, every shop I looked into (and some of my visits would have been frowned upon by the authorities) was what we would call a sweatshop. In one shop I visited, as many as thirty women were crowded together cutting, sewing, and gluing a product in a room no more than twelve by fourteen feet. The only light came from windows on the front side of the room so that those working in the back were always crouched over their work. Another shop, not much bigger but much better lighted, was half filled with feathers that were being sorted for size and for down. The women were not wearing masks and there was no ventilation system. A woman who had left the shop reluctantly after many years told me that it was only because of her lungs that she had returned to tailoring; she still had a deep dry cough some two years later.

The miserable working conditions of the shops set up and run by the Residents' Committees in no way reflect their concern (or lack of it) for the welfare of their employees. Many of the Residents' Committee members work or have worked in these shops, or shops of the same sort, ever since they were set up during the Great Leap Forward. They are well aware of their discomforts, but they are equally aware of the constraints under which they operate. The Party offers them high praise and very little else. When these shops were established, the women were warned that they were bootstrap operations, and, except for a few very successful such enterprises that were subsequently taken over by the state, they have remained so. Wages are very low, usually between twenty and thirty-five yuan per month, and they are often on a piecework basis that is geared to the low profit the collective makes. Unlike the state enterprises, few of these shops provide benefits. The women who work in them take the neighborhood as their unit, as do housewives and some of the retired people whose workplaces have disappeared in reorganization schemes.

Their medical care comes through the neighborhood clinic, if there is one. They do not have pensions and they do not build seniority toward higher pay. They do not have paid holidays, sick leave, maternity leave, or death benefits.* In some shops the women who have been there a long time and/or are involved in management may be on a salary so that they can count on a certain amount each month. In other shops, or if one is a new worker, wages are paid for the days worked, which often may be determined by the availability of supplies or the demand for the product (in China, the former is usually more unstable than the latter).

Insofar as possible, the Residents' Committees try to find at least part-time work in one of their enterprises for the many unemployed youths in the neighborhood, and it is for them that the dead-end quality of work in a neighborhood enterprise is most frustrating. For the older women it has many advantages. Their homes are often right around the corner from the shop, so they can dash home at midday to make lunch for members of the family who return. They can bring a sick child or grandchild to sleep in the corner, and they can take off at unusual hours that would not be tolerated in a more formal work atmosphere. They are not under pressure by younger, more experienced workers but are instead surrounded by friends of their own age and interests. None of these advantages make for an efficiently profitable organization, but because wages are low, many of the enterprises carry on for a good many years. Nor are they all so badly managed: the women on Shaoxing's Fu Shan Residents' Committee seemed to be running a profitable wine house and a couple of other enterprises, owing probably to a good supply situation and competent administrators. If one thinks of the neighborhood enterprises as sheltered workshops, they are very successful in that they provide some income and productive work for individuals who might not otherwise be able to earn anything. If one thinks of them as stepping-stones to the incorporation of categories of people into the mainstream of China's economy, they are less successful. Few

---

*Truly successful urban collectives that have not been absorbed by the state can now offer their employees some benefits, but nothing like those available to state workers.

skills are learned, and the attitudes toward the work world remain amateur.

The involvement of women in production was at some points in the last thirty years essential for the economy as well as essential for the good of the women involved. As we have seen in Chapter 1 the former unfortunately took priority over the latter. Nonetheless, in the cities of China most adult women between the ages of twenty and fifty are now employed.[2] According to Mao's interpretation of Marxist theory, when women become full partners in the economic life of the family instead of being unpaid household workers or unpaid laborers in their husbands' or fathers' shops, they will receive equal recognition in their families and in society. The degree to which that goal has been reached in China will be discussed in later chapters, but first we must look more closely at the first half of the proposition. How fully have women been taken into economic partnership? Although equal pay for equal work is a rule frequently cited, it is readily apparent that equal work is a myth among the older women in my sample. Their husbands are employed in industry and other state enterprises, whereas they are, by and large, in neighborhood workshops. Income figures I obtained for 236 women and men in Beijing and Shaoxing show that, on the average, the women are paid 71.7 percent of what men are paid—¥545.84 per year for women and ¥761.01 per year for men. This ratio may seem good when compared with the American figures usually cited for women—that is, 58.6 percent of men's wages—or even those of Canada and the United Kingdom at 66 percent and 65 percent, respectively; but I must remind the reader that my sample was carefully selected for me by government officials who were unlikely to introduce me to poorly paid sectors of society. Also, China is ideologically committed to sexual equality, and the United States is not. Sweden, an industrialized country that shares China's commitment to sexual equality, has achieved a wage ratio for women of 88.7 percent.*

---

*These figures come from a talk on labor market policy given by Marianne Janjic of the Women's Department of the International Labor Organization at a conference held in honor of Alice Cook in October 1983 at Cornell University.

When I discussed these sex differences with Chinese officials, I was told about the pre-Liberation conditions that accounted for present practices: women had not been educated and therefore were not able to handle jobs requiring skills or special training. Still, when I arrange my data by level of education, the gender asymmetry remains: in Beijing the men with middle school educations earn 22 percent more than women with middle school educations, and in Shaoxing they get 18 percent more. The differences are even more dramatic among the less well educated, with Beijing men earning 39 percent more than similarly educated women and Shaoxing men earning 37 percent more. Obviously, education does improve a woman's salary, but not relative to men.

Since it is possible that my two gross categories, primary school or less and middle school or more, concealed within them a major discrepancy in years of education, I calculated the average number of years in school for each group and discovered that primary school women had an average of 2.8 years of schooling as against 3.3 years for primary school men, but their wage discrepancy was still 36 percent, with the women averaging ¥44.20 per month and the men ¥69 per month. Women with educations of middle school and better averaged eleven years of school; their male counterparts averaged 11.4 years, but the men earned an average of ¥62.10 to the women's ¥52.90 per month. In other words, though the discrepancy decreases with education, it certainly does not disappear—even in this selected sample.

These data reveal something else that is interesting: whereas the expected positive relationship between income and education exists for women, it reverses for men. Why is this? The differences are not large, but in both cities they are in the wrong direction, that is, the more highly educated men actually make less than their less educated comrades. The data presented in Table 1 shed some light on this peculiar finding. For men, there is a steady rise in income with age, and the fact that the younger men are better educated and undoubtedly have better-developed technical skills is less important than the traditional values on age and seniority. Another factor affecting the relationship be-

Table 1. Average Yearly Income by Age and Sex: Urban

Age	Women Number	Women Income	Men Number	Men Income
Beijing				
20–29	20	¥460.20	16	¥462.00
30–39	11	600.00	9	632.04
40–49	13	697.80	12	924.00
50–59	7	646.32	6	999.96
60+	8	531.00	3	1,128.00
All ages	59	587.06	46	829.20
Shaoxing				
20–29	24	¥506.96	19	¥526.68
30–39	19	537.48	21	689.76
40–49	8	604.56	14	858.84
50–59	6	482.04	8	871.56
60+	3	392.04	9	517.20
All ages	60	504.62	71	692.81
Combined urban				
20–29		¥483.58		¥494.34
30–39		568.74		660.90
40–49		651.18		891.42
50–59		564.18		935.76
60+		461.52		822.60
All ages		545.84		761.01

tween age and wage level is that for nearly ten years during the Cultural Revolution wages were frozen, catching the more highly educated younger men at low beginning wages. A Cultural Revolution policy that eliminated the wage scale differences between skilled and/or professional workers and unskilled workers further handicapped the younger better-trained workers. The sharp drop-off in wage level at age sixty and over among the Shaoxing men is due to the fact that many of them were retired at 80 percent of their last wage. The Beijing sample in this age group is quite small, and only one of the three men in it had retired, with a pension of 79 yuan a month. Although these are far too few cases from which to generalize, such a finding would not be surprising. Beijing is a city top-heavy with officials, and officials are long-lived and unlikely to retire at an early age like sixty-five, although the current campaign to force earlier retirements may eventually have some effect. The wage structure for Shaoxing males probably is a more common urban pattern, with average wage rates dropping substantially as older men retire. Until that drop, however, the correlation for men between wages and age is positive, and that between education and wage is not.

For women, however, we find quite a different pattern. As we saw, education is a decided advantage in the earning potential of women. In both Beijing and Shaoxing, there is a nearly ten-yuan-per-month difference between the salaries of women with a middle school education and those without. Education does not make a bit of difference when women are competing with men. Men with a primary school education or less still make 26 percent more than better-educated women in Beijing, and Shaoxing men maintain a 21 percent salary superiority over their educational superiors. For women, as for men, age is a strong determinant in wage levels; but the drop-off comes a decade earlier for women, reflecting their earlier age at retirement.

I do not have data on seniority so I cannot examine the effect this might have on gender differences, nor is my sample size sufficiently large to subject it to the statistical manipulations that allay uneasiness among sociologists and economists. Fortunately, the work of Martin King Whyte and William L. Parish suffers from neither of these flaws.[3] Although the conclusions we draw from our data differ somewhat, our basic findings are satisfyingly similar. Working with emigrés from cities in China, Whyte and Parish were able to generate income data for 666 individuals. The mean income levels they computed are very close to my smaller sample from two cities. The women in my sample earned four more yuan per month than did theirs, and the men earned two more yuan per month.* Using a linear regression analysis, Whyte and Parish conclude that kind of job and seniority have a greater influence on pay levels than does education, a conclusion with which my data concur, insofar as they can speak to their

---

*The generally higher pay probably reflects across-the-board wage increases that have been granted since the Whyte and Parish study in 1978.

point. More surprisingly, at least at first glance, they find that when the other three variables (occupational classification, seniority, and education) are controlled, "the independent influence of gender is considerably reduced. . . . This means that when Chinese authorities say they are providing women with equal pay for equal work, they are not distorting reality too much. The main sources of the lower incomes women receive are attributable to their being placed in lower wage jobs where they benefit less from seniority. . . . As long as tendencies exist for women to be channeled into jobs with lower pay and fewer chances for advancement, some wage gap that widens as people advance in age will persist."[4] Whyte and Parish develop a table displaying the average wage levels and percentage of women in occupational groups from the information given them by emigrés for about 1,232 people. In the highest-paid half of the thirty-two occupational groups, only four occupations show women as half or more of their employees. Among the lowest-paid half of these groups, *all* but four have 50 percent or more women employees.

In a socialist society that takes as one of its explicit goals the equalization of male and female status, the channeling of women into inferior jobs should not be a problem once the women have had the benefit of an equal education, equal work experience, and so on. I will speak to the reality of equal education in a later chapter, but if one can use wage levels as one indicator of equal job placement, it would appear that the young people in Beijing, and generally speaking, Shaoxing, are starting out fairly evenly. Table 1 shows very little difference in wages in the first cohort of workers. The differences appear in the older cohorts, which have been less affected by the educational advantages provided since Liberation. On the other hand, acquiring the skills to do the work does not necessarily mean being assigned to the work. Thus far, decisions about which industries are suitable for women have not paid much attention to women's actual physical and intellectual capacities, and the assignment of tasks within an industry may be even more capricious or, indeed, biased.

It is here that we run into that knot of prejudice—labeled feudal ideas by the young and biological differences by their elders—that confine many in the barely concealed traditions of the past. For women, physiology, or rather beliefs about women's physiology, has been the most constraining. After one has observed Chinese women every day for a month pulling cartloads of bricks along a five-mile stretch of road, their clothes dripping with sweat, one begins to doubt the sincerity of the cadre who explains that women are too weak to drive the tractors or manage the horses men use to pull *their* cartloads of building material. Confronted with these pretty obvious discrepancies, cadres remind foreign questioners—and I suspect Chinese women as well—that there are other physiological differences that must be taken into consideration. For example, they say, an entire workshop could be brought to a halt if a woman in a key position has to take a half-hour off morning and afternoon to nurse her baby. Since urban women now have at most two children (and usually only one) and wean them at six months, the applicability of this example is limited, as is the pregnant woman example and for that matter the menstruating woman example, for women in leadership positions are in fact likely to be beyond the age of childbearing. What is being expressed by reticent officials and employers is not simply a blanket attempt to keep women out of their factories, but an old and deeply rooted conviction that women are not and never will be the equal of men. For example, I was told of a factory that until recently had an all-female work force. In 1980, for the first time, they mechanized one of the processes. Men were hired to run the machines. According to my informant, the women were never considered as possible candidates for the new jobs. The most widely accepted explanation for excluding women from such jobs is that their bodies are weaker, their energy level lower. They cannot take the strain.

For many occupations and factories, this argument is clearly irrelevant, and in them one finds young men and young women working at the same tasks in the same pay grade. Even then, however, the take-home pay may still be unequal, because men, who do not need to concern themselves about family duties at home, can work overtime. Bonuses for exceeding quotas go to those who have time to work late or to devise new methods for increasing production. Women who know a family is waiting for them to pick up the groceries and cook the evening meal or have only one hour to get from work to the baby's nursery before it closes are not going to put in much overtime. And these constraints are not reflected in their paychecks alone. They feed into the stereotype of the woman worker on one level and they reduce the upward mobility of the woman worker on another. If she foregoes bonuses in favor of fulfilling her domestic obligations, the woman worker must also forego advancement at the same rate as her husband or brother. The myth of her incompetence and the reality of her burdens serve to hold her longer in each grade level. Seniority is not simply putting in time. To make the big jumps one must earn merits. A good example of a typical outcome is that of a young woman in her early thirties whom I talked with in Beijing. She and her husband had been classmates in the same technical school and both had had the good fortune to be assigned to a factory in Beijing. They began work the same month. The only leave time she took was six weeks for the birth of their one child. Now, about eight years after they began their work careers, her husband is an administrator in the factory, she is a worker; he earns 64 yuan a month, she earns 52.

In an attempt to discover why women neither expected nor received occupational advancement as rapid as men's, I interviewed women and some of their male counterparts about women in leadership roles, asking them to compare women with male leaders, describe the strengths and weaknesses of both, and tell me how they thought managers, foremen, or whatever reached that position. I also asked them which sex made better workers, and I tried to find out how many women were actually in leadership positions in their factories. Their answers ranged from the blunt and informative to the evasive political slogan, but after a hundred interviews a fairly clear picture emerged of the attitudes and actualities of work in China's cities.*

---

*One of the challenges of interviewing in such a self-conscious society is in listening for answers to questions not asked and coping with questions that are rejected when first asked but are answered later in another, often less threatening, context. Just how to report data gathered in this way can be a problem if one is tied to an interview format. I was

Reliable data on just how many women occupy managerial or leadership positions in China's industries and businesses are not available to my knowledge anywhere other than in the Whyte and Parish survey of urban emigrés.[5] In their sample, 23 percent of the managers and shop heads were women, no foremen were women, and 33 percent of the sales supervisors were women.[6] This is fairly consistent with my smaller sample. Most of the women I talked with said that their immediate supervisor was a man. In a few cases in which the leader was a woman, the workplace was a Residents' Committee workshop. A retired textile worker summed up her observations about her factory when she grew impatient with my tedious line of questioning and said, "It is simple. The managers are all men; half the foremen are men, half are women; the workers are all women. It's always that way."

How come "it's always that way"? Two men, administrators in a Beijing factory, told me quite frankly that women didn't become foremen or managers because they weren't good workers. One said, "Men are better workers because they have more energy." His superior elaborated, "Men don't need other people's help to do their jobs, but women do, and that isn't just on the job, either. They need it at home, too, with the heavy chores, because their strength is limited. Besides that, it is more convenient for men to study and improve themselves. Women have children and housework, so they can't." To my surprise, many women shared this attitude. I was told by a woman in her forties who worked in a factory, "Women can't do heavy work or technical things like repairing machines." I asked why technical work was difficult for women; the only reason she could offer was that men had more experience with it. I asked if she thought women could do heavy work if they had to and she said they could, but it wouldn't be good for them. When I suggested learning to do "technical work," she seemed uninterested in the prospect for herself and the question in general. Like many women her age and older, she gave the impression that she regarded herself and

---

not, either in the interview session itself or in the analysis of the results. What follows, then, comes from the responses to a variety of questions concerning work and work attitudes.

her fellow female workers as amateurs who were playing one of the parts in some revolutionary drama. She was committed to the revolution, heart and soul, but was still slightly embarrassed to find herself holding a wrench.

Inadequate commitment to the job was hinted at by more than one worker and a number of management level cadres. The single-minded devotion with which men supposedly approach their work is not to be found, they imply, among women after they marry. On close questioning, a hospital administrator finally admitted that she feared there was a decided difference in the topics women workers—nurses, doctors, and technicians—discussed after they married. Instead of talking about new developments in medicine, they compared notes on child care, husband management, and the wearying load of domestic burdens. A woman who was very highly placed in a factory complained that women workers lost their enthusiasm after they married and the loss was reflected in both the quality and the quantity of their work.

The explanation for this loss of commitment or enthusiasm is not openly revealed—indeed, the full partnership of men in child care tasks and household chores is a set piece lit for every inquiring foreigner with any sort of feminist credentials. But so far, at least, little evidence (beyond observing men carrying babies about in the park on Sundays—as they did before Liberation and do in Taiwan today) has been gathered that will support these assertions. Whyte and Parish find their sample no more impressive at housework than other socialist and capitalist countries; and they point out that because China has not made much progress toward providing consumer products that would ease that workload, the double burden for women in China is probably more onerous than in many other parts of the world.[7] When I asked direct questions about men's participation in household chores, I got the usual political slogans, but women let me know in response to other questions that the domestic burdens were their responsibility. After a group of nurses told me their husbands and fathers shared equally in the housework and child care, I told them about the Swedish policy of allowing either mother or father to take six months' leave after the birth of their child. This was greeted with peals of laughter and many jokes about the uselessness of men with infants, their unwillingness to get near soiled diapers, and so forth.

The toll this burden of full-time work and full-time housework takes on women physically is serious, yet accepted by the Party with little more than a concerned shake of the head. The toll the double burden takes on women psychologically may well be more far-reaching. Though the foreign researcher is the last to hear explicit criticism of Party policy, she may be privy to a lot of carping that government policy makers take too much for granted. Women are told that labor is their liberation, but their bodies are telling them something else. They and their work supervisors know that many women are beginning to believe their weary bodies over the propaganda. Since women comprise nearly half the urban work force, the problem becomes not one of theory but of production, a difference the current Party leadership must eventually take seriously. The acceptance of the double burden as woman's lot by both Party and populace is the virtual acceptance of women's second-class status. A young woman worker told me that a good wife (as opposed to a lazy or bad one) did more household chores than her husband so that he could devote himself fully to his work. She was a full-time worker in a department store. Another woman who held a political post at her place of employment was a very articulate spokesperson for the new equality of the sexes. But when I asked her to describe a good wife for me, she said, "A good wife takes full responsibility for the house and the children so that her husband is free to work." When I asked, "What about the wife's job?" she answered offhandedly, "Oh, his work will be more important than hers." And, as we have seen, that is true. Women remain in the lower-paid positions and men move up into the better-paying jobs.

When we look in a later chapter at women's education, it becomes clear that the reasons involved are not the double burden alone but also include some more depressing beliefs about innate differences in the capacity of men and women. Most informants, however, spoke of the double burden as the primary handicap for working women's advancement. A young married woman in her late twenties told me that men, of course, made better leaders. "They are stronger and they can work longer hours. To be a foreman you must be able to do every job in the shop yourself. Women can't do that. They can't stay after work to learn these things; they have work waiting for them at home. Well, maybe some can . . ." Another young woman who had told me proudly that all women in China wanted to work added, "If we had to live off a man's money the way you Western women do, we would have to obey our husbands' every command." But when I asked her later on why there were so few women in management positions in her factory, she said, "Men don't have as much to do as women. There are more male managers because they don't need to worry about the family. They all have wives to take care of those things." An older woman said succinctly, "Women bear children; men become leaders."

If the goal of the Party leadership is to make productive labor as important to women as it is to men (and in 1980 that was still the avowed goal), the lack of pressure exerted on men to take up their share of the domestic burden is ensuring failure. Many of the comments quoted above attest to the priority women give their domestic duties. This should come as no surprise to the policy makers. If you get to work late, the effect is slight, but if you don't get breakfast for your family, everyone's day is messed up, and you are responsible. If you don't get your quota done at the factory, someone will finish it up. If you don't get the laundry done, your son will have to wear a dirty shirt to school, and he and everyone else will recognize it as a sign of a badly run household, and you are responsible for the running of the household. No matter what Mao may have expected from the social transformation, the arenas in which women and men are judged remain separate. Men are judged in the workplace and women are judged in the home. For the average woman worker, the "model worker" serves less the function of a role model and more the function of the Hollywood starlet. You might wish you had her attributes and rewards, but she is too far removed from the realities of your world to emulate.

One might expect a more work-oriented view to be common among the younger women workers since they have been bombarded with propaganda all their lives, but instead they seem to be modeling their lives after their mothers', and their mothers still give family first priority. Some of the more touching, but often unproductive, instances of this sense of priorities are apparent in the degree to which mothers give up their jobs in favor of their children. I have many examples in my notes of women retiring early (hence at lower pensions) so that they could give their jobs to their children who were languishing in the countryside or waiting for work assignments.[8] Certainly fathers also do this on occasion, but in every case I have come across, the men are retained by their workplace in some capacity (usually the same job with another name) and take no more than a nominal drop in pay. For women, the retirement is actual. The state exchanges an experienced worker for one who is younger and stronger. From the state's perspective the exchange may be equal, but from the woman's perspective the exchange is traditional and unequal. She is taken out of the labor force and returned to the domestic scene to provide free services for her husband and adult children. It may be a welcome relief from the double burden, but there was something in the voices of the women who told me of "their" decisions to retire that I found disturbing. As I mentioned earlier, many older women were more enthusiastic about their status as workers than were the younger workers. I suspect that they were bullied by children or state or both into retiring for the good of their family. I never could get a woman to admit this to me, but several came close. In the end, they always said it was their decision. I suppose in some sense it was.

Finally, in probing about women's advancement in work, I was surprised to hear some of my informants say quite openly that women made poor leaders. "There is always more trouble when the leader is a woman. More gossip, more fuss." "Women leaders aren't fair. They have favorites." "Women foremen are harder to work with. Their hearts are narrower and there is a lot of *shi* (fuss, trouble)." All these comments were made by women who

had had women leaders at one time or another. Other informants were gentler on their sex, only criticizing them by saying
why men were better in management positions. "Men are better
leaders; they are bolder." "Men arrange work better; they are better organized." A woman who worked in a clock factory told me,
"I'd rather have a man leader. They are more generous in their
thoughts and in what they do. Men just have a broader perspective on things." A young worker said, "No, I would rather work
with men. They are franker. If you do it wrong, they tell you
right now." And a sweet old dear in her late sixties who had
never worked outside her home in her life said, "Oh, I'm sure
men are better leaders. They think bigger than women." Some
women preferred women leaders but nearly all of them praised
them for their feminine virtues. "I prefer a woman leader. It is
easier to talk to her about things." "Women leaders are more understanding." Only one woman said she thought the woman
manager in her factory was better than the man who had been
there before because she was better organized. "And I'm not the
only one who thinks that. She wasn't appointed, she was elec-
ted—by us."

Predictions about China have not been very successful, but I
think it is fairly safe to say that urban women in China are unlikely to find much improvement in their work status in the near
future. The equalization of education, if it does indeed come
about, will not have a major effect on the average woman
worker's advancement. As long as women are considered divided
in their commitments between home and job, they are not likely
to be assigned to the higher-paid occupations. They are not
likely to move up the pay scale as quickly as men, because they
do not have the time and energy to learn new skills, do "volunteer" tasks, and so on. Because of their physical weakness and so-
called recurrent physiological handicaps (childbearing, nine
months per lifetime; nursing, six months per lifetime), they are
not going to be enrolled in heavy industry or high technology.
And because they are considered temperamentally handicapped,
they are probably not going to move into the management positions in the industries for which they *are* considered suited. For
all these reasons, it seems likely to me that the asymmetrical

wage pattern for men and women will remain for years to come. In their first years of work they will have similar wages, but men will pull rapidly ahead as women marry and have children. The women's wages will level, as they do now, in their forties and then drop sharply as they retire at fifty. Men's pay will continue to increase as they rise in rank and seniority until retirement when they will drop, but to a level considerably higher than their female counterparts.

Pensions are another area of gender inequities in the urban workplace. The most glaring inequalities arise from the simple source of employment: men, of all ages and occupational levels, are much more likely to be working in the state sector, where they are assured of pensions. Women are more likely to be working for neighborhood enterprises that offer no pensions of any kind. If the data reported in Table 1 included workers who were no longer working and had no pensions whatsoever, the gender differences would be much, much greater. The inequality that results from women being "allowed" to retire a decade earlier than men is large and permanent. I mentioned earlier the fact that women were more likely than men to retire so that their children could have their jobs, and that when men did retire under these circumstances they often continued to work with a "bonus" that supplemented their pensions to the original salary amount. Another apparent gender difference that affects women near retirement age is that of ill health. I ran across several men among the relatives of my informants who were totally and irreversibly incapacitated yet who were nonetheless on full salary. I encountered considerably more women with minor physical ailments who had been told to retire even before they reached the age of fifty. I suspect the reasoning (insofar as it is ever conscious) is the same that afflicts our own society: men need the income to support their families; women don't. The fact that women will live a decade or two after their husbands (and their husbands' pensions) cease to exist seems not to be considered.

Another fundamental determinant of gender asymmetry is even less likely to change in the near future. The saddling of women with the responsibility for everything outside of work is too readily accepted and too easily attributed to the nature of their physical selves. The state made attempts to provide some of the services once only found in the home, but for economic reasons they have been severely reduced over the years. Canteens are found only in large factories; nursery schools are even more rare; laundries are more trouble than they are worth; mending and sewing stations faded out of existence soon after they were set up; food distribution centers are arranged for the convenience of the supplier. The fact that women's energies are not focused solely on their extradomestic work should be a surprise to no one. Unfortunately, the conclusion apparently reached by policy makers is that women are simply different from (read inferior to) men, and the logic circles back on itself: there they are, fully incorporated into productive labor, and they are not performing as well as men—you cannot change biology.

It is here, where traditional prejudice overwhelms socialist theory, that the promises made to China's women are being broken. The following innocent comments made by women about management practices in their workplaces are damning. I asked a young woman why there were so few women foremen. She said, "All the foremen in my division used to be women, but the Party sent a new Party secretary and he is a man."* A woman in her early forties who had persisted in asserting women's equality told me, with obvious irritation, "Of course women are capable of managing the shops [factory units]." I asked her why then there were so few, and she said, "The higher authorities decide these things." "What if the workers decided?" I asked. "Well, then we would have a lot more women foremen." Yet another woman told me that one had to be a Party member to be in a management position and that since few women were Party members, there were few women in management. And finally, a woman section leader told me that there were several women in her position in the factory. "Positions above this, however, are only for men." "Why is that?" I asked. "These positions are appointed by higher authorities outside the plant."

---

*The party secretary holds a very powerful position in any organization, representing the Party and reporting directly to the Party, but also taking an active role in factory organization.

FOUR

Women Workers in the Countryside

It used to be that the men did the heavy work and the women did the
light work, but now there are more women workers than men workers, so
the women do it all and the men just supervise them.
                                                    —*Female farm worker, age 46*

To judge China by her cities is to judge her in her most self-
conscious state. It is in the rural areas, where 80 percent of the
population lives, that the weight of the past drags most heavily
on plans for social change. The team of urbanites who traveled
with me through Fujian, Jiangsu, Shandong, and Shaanxi showed
genuine apprehension about some aspects of the life I had got
them into, even though it was by any anthropologist's measure
quite comfortable. (On one commune we even had a flush—
sometimes—toilet.) But if the visitors' uneasiness was noticeable, the local suspicion was equally evident, albeit more polite.
Trouble comes from the top down, from the urban centers to the
countryside. Certainly on both sides there is a sense of difference.
When I asked rural women if they thought men would want to
marry women who had more education than they, the answers
often assumed that I was asking about marrying city women.
(The question was designed to elicit attitudes toward marital relationships in which women might dominate.) One woman said,
"Farmers wouldn't dare think of marrying city women. Even if
they did, the women wouldn't be interested. Farmers have less
education and they work in the fields. They are just too different.
It would be no use even if a man wanted to."

Two of the Three Great Inequalities that were emphasized in
the rhetoric of the Cultural Revolution were those between industry and agriculture and those between rural places and urban
places. By and large, the attentions of the Cultural Revolution

activists were not particularly welcomed in rural places and indeed seem to have had little influence in the hinterlands. Their main contribution to rural life was the devaluation of the things that once provided the farm cycle with relief from monotony. In the colorless world created by the excesses of the Cultural Revolution—sans local opera (feudal), sans religious festivals (superstitious), sans bright-colored clothes, jewelry, or paintings (decadent), all that was left was television, and a good many of the rural districts do not have access even to that. For them, radio is still the source of their information and amusement. Movies are a rarity that usually come with a political message. Books are alien to most farmers.*

More importantly, from the perspective of women, a woman's access to paid employment differs greatly depending on where she lives. Estimates of the proportion of urban women between the ages of twenty and forty-nine who are in the labor force run as high as 93 percent.[1] Marina Thorborg concludes, after a painstaking analysis of the very uneven rural employment data available from China, that only about one-third of the rural women work full time in agriculture and two-thirds work part time.[2] Other estimates coming from unpublished census material are even lower.[3] These admittedly rough estimates are not strikingly different from those we have for the period preceding Liberation. In his agricultural surveys of the 1920's and 1930's, John Lossing Buck estimated that women did somewhere between 9 and 16 percent of the farm work, depending upon whether they lived in the north or the south: in the winter-wheat- and millet-growing areas of the far north, their share of the farm work was a mere 5 percent.[4] Regional differences were large and apparently varied even between small districts, so the safest generalization that can be made about pre-Liberation China is that women worked in the fields more in the south than in the north, and they usually worked only during the busy seasons of harvest and planting. Few women were full-time regular laborers in the fields.

* I am told by recent travelers that colorful clothing, curled hair, and even a flash of jewelry are now to be seen regularly in China's cities, but how far this extends into the countryside I cannot say.

The objections to women working outside the home were far easier to overcome in the cities than in the rural areas. Some women in urban areas, particularly among the educated but also among the small-shopkeeper and working classes, had entered the work force before Liberation, but in the countryside, decent women from decent families stayed indoors and tended to domestic tasks. *Nei ren*, "inside person," was and still is a common term of reference for wives in China. Education and the exposure to new ideas brought by the revolution made the idea of women working more tolerable to rural men, but the sheer necessity of their mobilization in response to the labor demands of government programs was the most effective means of getting them into productive labor. Nonetheless, many objections and criticisms remain, coming both from men and from women. Since these attitudes color so much of what I will be discussing in this chapter, I will raise them briefly at the outset.

Nowadays, few people in China would publicly acknowledge harboring any beliefs about women's pollution, but the lingering effect of such beliefs can be seen in some of the so-called protective regulations concerning women's participation in field work. In the old days, if women were allowed anywhere near a well that was being dug, no water would be produced, or only sour water would fill the hole. If women came into the area of a brick kiln when it was being fired, the bricks would all crumble. Pregnant or recently delivered women could kill growing silkworms, and menstruating women who stepped into a rice paddy would cause the shoots to shrivel. These are all referred to as "superstitions" today, but after childbirth, country women are still expected to stay at home, indoors, for thirty days after delivery, and menstruating women are "allowed" to take three or four days off work each month during their menses. I found these restrictions in every collective I visited, and they were always explained as ways in which the leaders protect women or show concern for women. Sometimes when I followed up with questions about pollution beliefs, they were denied; sometimes the relevancy of those beliefs was admitted with a rueful smile or an offhanded comment. Very few women recognized the pollution belief system as discriminatory, or at least very few were willing to discuss it with me; and women were as likely as men to explain to me that women couldn't be tractor drivers for "physical reasons," their reproductive organs being more vulnerable than men's to being jostled about on tractor seats. However, men were far more likely than women to complain about the special arrangements that had to be made for women who were pregnant (light work), nursing (work near home), or menstruating (dry work if any work at all).

Even where pollution is not a problem, older farmers still object to training young women to do any of the technical jobs involved in farming. A woman cadre in Fujian told me a story that has a variant in every region of China, for it has become part of the mythology of the revolution. When women's enthusiasm was high, Comrade Li and some of her young friends begged to be taught to plow. They were told that the work was too heavy for girls, that the water buffalo would just run off with them, that the men were too busy to waste time on this. Finally, the women began to mess around with the plow and water buffalo during lunch hours and rest breaks and after work until finally they taught themselves how to plow. Then one glorious day during the Great Leap Forward when the fields were flooded and ready to plow, the men were all ordered away by the county government to work on a massive water project. Disaster threatened until Comrade Li and her young friends came forward and saved the year's crop by plowing all the brigade's land in the men's absence. Like most of these stories in China, it ended there. Women still do not plow in this brigade in Fujian.

The reticence to teach technical skills to women may be due in part to male need for superiority, but frank informants give a considerably simpler explanation. It is a waste of time and effort. No matter how long they delay marriage, young women will eventually marry out, taking their talents to benefit other families and other brigades. In Shandong, two of my informants were former barefoot doctors. One had received a year's training in a county hospital and worked for eight years as a barefoot doctor before she married. The other had had only six months' training but had worked in the brigade clinic as a midwife for six years. Both women had married into their present homes about three years before and had been working in the fields as common laborers ever since. Their skills were lost to their natal teams, but their new homes were not about to hand over prized jobs to newcomers. My interviews turned up all too many women who had worked in small local enterprises in their natal villages and were common laborers in their new homes, women who were Women's Representatives or Youth League officers in their natal villages and were demoted or ignored completely in their new brigades. More commonly, however, the skill of pruning trees, driving tractors, germinating tricky seeds, or treating sick livestock is kept from young women completely so it won't be wasted and, as I was told in one place, "so the secrets of our success won't go to others."

Not a few of the older cadres say bluntly that it is a waste of time to try to teach women special skills because they can't learn them. Aside from basic stupidity, women reputedly cannot concentrate on the task before them; they are forever running off to see if the children are being cared for properly, or they quit early in order to prepare a meal for the family. Women simply cannot think beyond the petty affairs of the stove, and if they do manage to learn, they are irresponsible about carrying out their duties. Women are also too timid to acquire such skills as plowing or cart driving ("they are afraid of draft animals") or pruning ("they don't dare climb trees").

After an otherwise helpful brigade cadre expounded the failings of women to me for half an hour, my Beijing assistant told me of an interview she had carried out on her own the evening before. While strolling after dinner, she encountered three people working in the fields. One was a man who was squatting next to the pump house. He told her he was waiting for the women in the field to tell him to turn off the pump that was feeding water into the wheat. To do this he had to pull a switch. As a technician, he earned 10.5 workpoints a day. Walking on, she interviewed the two women, both in their thirties, who were rushing back and forth ditching and damming to keep the water moving evenly through the fields. Although the evening was cool, they were sweating with the effort it took to move the heavy waterlogged earth onto the banks of the ditches. They were unskilled workers and earned 6.5 workpoints for their day's labor. If they came out and put in an hour before breakfast, however, they would get seven workpoints. But who would cook the family's breakfast?

If women are ill-equipped to do technical jobs, they are, according to male cadres, even more poorly equipped for what is known as "heavy work." In each of our field sites there were one or two jobs that were listed for me as just too heavy for women to manage. In Fujian it was managing the water buffalo pulling the plows in the wet paddy, so instead the women carried fifty-pound sacks of chemical fertilizer to the fields while the men trailed along after the water buffalo. In Jiangsu women couldn't carry things on a carrying pole or pull carts. I observed a good many of these carts on the heavily trafficked road I traveled morning and evening between Yangzhou and the commune where I was interviewing. On the way into the city the carts were heaped with produce, bricks, and other building materials; on the way out they carried a more miscellaneous cargo, including barrels of nightsoil. The strain on the faces and in the bodies of the cart-pullers made it clear that it was a hard, heavy job. Over one three-day period I did a count of the kinds of cargo-vehicles I passed and the sex of their drivers. I listed 553 carts, trucks, and other wheeled conveyances. Of the 450 hand-drawn carts counted, 206 (46.2 percent) were drawn by women. Of the 103 motorized vehicles (many of them tractors pulling the same carts), only four were driven by women. Women may be poorly suited to cart-pulling in Jiangsu, but on the road to Yangzhou they did nearly as much of it as men did. In the physically less demanding job, guiding a tractor, they were oddly underrepresented.

In Shandong I had another fine display of the division of labor just outside the window of my room. A small garden workshop was being built of brick and mortar. Each morning the crew would show up and the men would kick open a sack of cement and wait for the women to bring buckets of water and baskets of sand on carrying poles. Then the men would stir them together. When a proper mix was achieved, they went over to stand by the house and have a smoke, while the women began the parade that would occupy the rest of their day, carrying first the bricks and then the mortar to the men who set the bricks one by one on the growing wall with a slap of mortar. As the wall got higher and the men farther off the ground, a pulley arrangement was set up to get the mortar and brick up to them. I waited with bated breath to see who would work the pulley. Sure enough, it turned out to be technical work, so the women were only allowed to bring the heavy loads to the lift where a man attached them to the hook and hoisted them up. Women in Shandong were also too weak to manage the incredibly clumsy and heavy wooden barrows that date from at least the second century. When I sighted one of these monsters in the yard of my local assistant's house, I asked if she could handle it. "Of course. With my husband away in the army I would be in a bad spot if I couldn't, wouldn't I?" However, women cannot use barrows in collective work, and those who do (men) are more highly paid. And finally, in Shaanxi where pulling carts (a more modern two-wheeled affair) was also listed as work done only by men, I watched nearly the entire wheat harvest pulled into the brigade drying ground on two-wheeled carts by sweating young women between the ages of eighteen and thirty. The men were cutting the wheat.

Before we turn to work incentives, we must look briefly at the way in which rural life in China is organized. The old system of towns, villages, and hamlets has been overlaid by a new system of communes, brigades, and teams. The communes are based more or less on the old rural marketing area and can vary considerably in population. The one I worked in in Fujian had a population of 80,000; the one in Jiangsu was about 28,000. Production brigades are usually centered on largish villages or a cluster of hamlets composed of two to three hundred families. It is at this level of organization that one finds clinics, primary schools, and small factories. The production brigade may also be responsible for collective orchards, fish ponds, and large livestock farms. The production team, composed of former hamlets or neighborhoods of larger villages, has in it twenty to forty households and was at the time of my visit (1980–81), in most areas of China, the basic accounting unit. The team level is where land-use rights are held, job assignments are made, and the profit and loss (which sets the income of individual households) is determined. Unfortunately for women, far more of the old structure of village organization remains than the names imply. In much of China in the old days, villages and hamlets were composed of lineage members and their wives and children. Sometimes two or more surnames might be represented in a village, but the men within each surname group were, or considered themselves to be, relatives. At some point in the long line of ancestors each man worshipped, there was a common ancestor who linked them all to one another. Not so women. When they reached marriageable age, all that was proper said they must marry outside their home village into a village of strangers, totally unrelated. Even a man from the other end of China who bore the same surname was, for marriage purposes, a relative. In parts of south China, the animosity that existed between surname groups was often bloody. The cohesion within a surname group might not be obvious until danger threatened, divided as the villages were by economic and class differences. But when outsiders, such as the relatives of a woman who married in from another surname village, made a complaint about her treatment, they were united in opposition.

In modern China, as I will explain in detail in a later chapter, women still marry outside their own village or brigade into a world of strangers. The implications of this are most poignant when one considers the plight of a young woman who finds her marriage intolerable. She must take her case first to the leader of her team, one of her husband's relatives, and from there, if it is allowed to go any further, to the appropriate officer of the brigade, who is likely to be one of her husband's people also. Obviously this has a major influence on the extremely low divorce rate in rural China.

This community of male relatives also has considerable influence on the allocation of resources. Men are inclined to see their own and their relatives' daughters as temporary residents for whom job training, let alone leadership experience, would be a gift to another community. The young women they receive in marriage are equally untrained and, for the first years of their residence, "outsiders." Moreover, they are likely to be absorbed in accommodating themselves to their new familial relationships and to having a child or children, still their first obligation in the countryside. Marriage in the rural areas almost automatically turns a woman into a part-time worker with a list of "special considerations" that disqualify her for many jobs. Gender is certainly her biggest handicap, but as Norma Diamond points out and my own interviews corroborate, the few women who do remain in their natal communities by making uxorilocal marriages are much more likely than the newcomers to occupy what few leadership positions or skilled jobs are allotted to women.[5]

In many areas of rural China, the economic organization is being radically transformed yet again. The basic accounting unit is being changed to "small groups" or even single household units within the team, making collective labor the source of a much smaller proportion of the farmer's income. None of the communes I worked on had yet had much experience with such radical departures from the principle of communal organization. In Fujian and Jiangsu the basic accounting unit remained the team, although two of the brigades in Jiangsu were experimenting with a four-unit work group division rather than the usual residential groups, and in Fujian they were "discussing" smaller units. In Shandong the brigade I lived in had returned to the team level of accounting from the brigade level only the previous year. In Shaanxi, the brigade in which I worked was divided into twenty-eight work groups, some of which were residential and the rest of which drew members from the entire brigade. Accounting was done in the work group, but a large proportion of the land had recently been reallocated to families to farm more or less as tenants of the collective. In all the communes I studied, sideline endeavors such as raising pigs or rabbits or salable crops in private plots accounted for a large share of a household's income (see

Table 5 below). Most of the work in the private plots and virtually all the care of the domestic livestock was in the hands of the women of the household.

Payment for labor in new China has been and continues to be a topic of much debate. In 1980–81 there seemed to be no uniform system. In some areas the old standard set number of workpoints per day's labor continued, usually 6.5 or 7 per day for women and 10 per day for men. In most areas this simple method usually was applied only to the kinds of work that could not conveniently (or fairly) be compensated in terms of hours or effort expended. Some jobs were paid on a simple piecework basis—for example, the number of baskets of tea or cotton picked. Women much prefer this method, for, they say, they can easily make ten or twelve workpoints in a day. Brigades find it expensive in that there is an unspoken commitment to provide a higher wage for men who are much slower at tea or cotton picking. The compromise is usually to devalue the work traditionally assigned to women and upgrade the work assigned to men. Another method of payment, also piecework, is to assess the value of various tasks, assign those tasks to a group, and let them divide up among themselves the value assigned. This is often done, again, on a basis that discriminates against women in that each member of a team is given a work classification that determines her or his share of the collective task. In a tea-growing brigade in the mountains of Zhejiang, Arthur Wolf collected the workpoint classifications of 30 men and 34 women. The average age of the men in the sample was thirty-four years, the average workpoint rating was 9.2 workpoints per day. The average age of the women in the sample was thirty-six years and their average workpoint rating was 5.7 per day. The new family responsibility system now being instituted throughout China was just getting underway in the commune I lived on in Shaanxi. A certain amount of land was allocated to each family according to the number of able-bodied workers they could muster. They were obliged to produce from it a set amount of cotton in exchange for a set number of workpoints. If the family did not meet the quota, they were penalized by a reduction in workpoints; if they produced more than the quota, they were rewarded with a percentage of the profits. An added bonus was permission to grow rapeseed on the land in the off-season and to keep the entire crop except for the stalks, which were to be turned over to the collective's livestock units. Although the system was just going into operation during my visit, labor-workpoint exchanges were already being bartered among those who had more of one and needed more of another.

None of the brigades I studied was entirely dependent on agriculture for income. They all had small or medium-sized enterprises and many of them had some or many workers who earned their living in commune or state industries. The ways in which the brigade shared in the income earned from nonbrigade activities were varied. In Jiangsu, for example, the commune in which I interviewed was located on the edge of the Grand Canal, not far from the city of Yangzhou. Large tracts of their land had been appropriated by the state to build factories—some fairly heavy industry, such as a shipbuilding yard, and some light industry, such as a button factory. To compensate for the loss of land, the state allotted a certain number of jobs to the commune. This original batch of workers was given an urban registration so that they, but not their families, were no longer members of the commune. They bought their grain allotments and other scarce supplies through state stores. Other people work in the factories "on loan," some of them for years at a time. These workers remain full members of their collectives and support their production teams in a variety of ways. Some of them are required to turn over a percentage of their earnings to the team, making them eligible for the team grain allowance and other team benefits. Others receive only a small amount of their salaries for daily expenses (assumed to be greater than that of a farmer); the remainder of the salary is then paid directly to the team, which pays them at the end of the year like any other member of the collective, basing their share on the average earnings of agricultural workers of their age, gender, and strength. Each team makes its own decision as to the amount outside workers must contribute to the collective.

Theoretically, every brigade organized its enterprises from its own capital accumulation and natural resources, but there is clearly a good deal of politicking required at the county and pro-vincial levels. All the brigades I worked in were model brigades, although only one, in Shandong, was heavily subsidized by sources outside the commune. Permission to start an enterprise must be obtained from the county authorities, and it is hard to believe that model brigades were not more likely to get such per-mission for new enterprises. Enterprises organized by the brigade (or in a few cases, the team) pay workers in workpoints, usually by taking the average earnings of an agricultural worker in their age, sex, and strength categories for the base. The most prized jobs are those outside the team and brigade that bring urban reg-istration, for this gives at least some reality to the dream of one day moving permanently into a city, but any of the nonagricul-tural enterprises are preferred to the drudgery of field labor.

Just who works in the local level industries is not exactly clear. Phyllis Andors, using data from her visit to Hebei in 1979 and from the Chinese press, says that young women are an important part of the labor force.[6] Marina Thorborg, who did a detailed analysis of the published record, appears to concur.[7] The data pre-sented in Table 2, collected by Arthur Wolf and me in 1980–81, suggest otherwise, though this broad picture may be too great an oversimplification. Moreover, for women in particular, the desig-nation "farm work" is very misleading, since in some areas women may work only a few days a year during the harvest season but still call themselves farm workers. Nonetheless, putting together all those who said they participated in collective agriculture, whether for a few days of the year or almost daily, it is clear that in all the communes for which I have data, women are far more likely to be engaged in farm work than they are in other rural enterprises. When one looks at the type of work men are likely to do, one sees a very different pattern of activity, most particu-larly in Jiangsu, where only 11 percent of the men in the families of the women we interviewed were engaged in agriculture. The reader should also note that there is a great deal of variation from area to area, owing to factors as diverse as the extent of economic development and the cultural-historical attitudes toward women.

Table 2. Employment in Farm Work and Rural Enterprises by Sex

Site[a]	Women			Men		
	Number	Employed in farm work	Otherwise employed	Number	Employed in farm work	Otherwise employed
Fujian	77	68%	32%	103	54%	47%
Jiangsu	92	64	36	82	11	89
Shandong	147	59	41	195	37	63
Shaanxi	144	81	19	173	64	36
Sichuan	73	88	12	104	56	44

[a]I use the names of the provinces in which my field sites were located because they are easier to remember. I do not mean to imply that these data are representative of anything beyond the sample described in the text.

Because of these complexities, one has to consider the data commune by commune to get a clear picture.

The brigade in which I worked in Fujian ran seven small enterprises, and its members had access to others run by the commune of which they were a part. The brick kiln, one of the most common rural industries throughout China, had 27 employees of whom only 8 were women. The next largest brigade enterprise was the sawmill. This employed 11 people, only one of them a woman, who had the job of writing receipts for the amount of lumber sold or distributed. She was decidedly underemployed because the mill was primitive and production was low. Two barbershops employed 10 people. I did not interview any of them, so I have no idea whether any women were employed there. The tailor shop had 6 employees, only one of whom, the manager, was male. The rice husking mill was also managed by a man, and it had 3 female and 2 male employees. The noodle shop had 7 workers but I do not know their sex, and the farm tool repair shop had only 2 employees, both male. The brigade and one of the teams within it had built mushroom-growing sheds (classified as agriculture by them, but run more like enterprises), which employed women, but were, of course, managed by men. There were also 3 women primary school teachers, a nursery school worker, 2 young women who were doing embroidery at home on a putting-out system from a commune factory, and a young woman who handed out slips of paper in the clinic. Nonagricultural male occupations at the brigade level included the 2 doctors at the clinic, the man who managed the canteen, 2 men who took care of the water buffalo and oxen, various team and brigade accountants, tractor drivers, and a few entrepreneurs, including a man who played at funerals, a man who set up a sewing machine in the market to mend clothes and hem garments, and a man who sold vegetables out of his private plot.

Another large number of my informants' family members, some 44 people, worked for cash outside the brigade, either for the commune or in state factories. Of these, 9 were young men in the army (only 2.6 percent of the 4.2 million members of the People's Liberation Army are women),[8] 10 were women, and the remaining 25 were men. In other words, only 23 percent of those who held the prized nonbrigade, or nonteam, jobs in my sample were women, and less than a third of the nonagricultural jobs held by my informants were held by women. A careful examination of the responses of women who identified themselves as agricultural workers produces an even more dismal picture of women's involvement in productive labor. Twenty-six of the 52 women who were engaged in farm work indicated that they only worked during the busy seasons of harvest and planting, a statistic that is poorly matched by the 55 men identified as farm workers, of whom only 2 were considered "busy season workers."

The situation in my Jiangsu field site was the opposite of that in my Fujian site. Wantou Commune, as I mentioned earlier, lost a large piece of its land to the state for industrial development. I was told by the head of the commune before I began my research that the remainder of the land was worked primarily by the women members of the commune. Traditionally, women in this area worked in the fields although they were not solely responsible for agriculture. In Table 2, the figures for men are probably more indicative of the current situation than are the figures for women. Only 9 of the 82 men for whom I have employment information worked in agricultural production. The rest were employed in state industry or brigade enterprises. Arthur Wolf, who interviewed in another brigade in the same commune, found similar but not identical patterns. Women in his brigade were even more likely to be doing agricultural rather than industrial work, but men were also more likely than my sample to be in agriculture, 28 percent to my 11 percent. The variation seems to depend to some degree on location—that is, how much of one's land was affected by the state's factories and shipbuilding yard. There was also a good deal of variation within the commune in the number and success of their nonagricultural enterprises. Cadre from my two brigades listed for me the enterprises they had developed and the sex of the employees. These data are presented in Table 3 and indicate some of the difficulties of trying to generalize from the experience of only one or two brigades. In Tianzhuang Brigade, only 19 percent of the enterprise employees were women and even that figure would have been much lower if one of the enterprises had not been that of making cloth shoes, a traditional female occupation. On the other hand, 40 percent of the Zhoujia Brigade enterprise employees were women. The same cadre who gave me these statistics also said that 70 percent of the agricultural workers for this brigade were women. Zhoujia was also the poorest brigade in the commune, its workpoints being worth less than one-third those of Tianzhuang Brigade.

As I indicated in Chapter 2, the Shandong brigade in which I worked was the least representative of rural life of any I studied. Since Arthur Wolf and I were both given false statistics by brigade officials, it is hard to evaluate the extent of the opportunities available for women. We were told that only 26 percent of the brigade's income came from agricultural produce and livestock, but little else was in evidence. Aside from a pig farm, a chicken farm, a rabbit farm, a plastic bag factory (employing 19 workers) and a canvas shoulder bag factory (employing 38 workers), there were no other local industries reported. We discovered in the process of our interviews a felt factory—not listed by the cadres—that employed 19 of our informants' family members (9 women and 10 men). Even so, I suspect that a good proportion of the nonagricultural income to the brigade was provincial subsidy of some sort.

In Shijiazhuang, I found that 66 of my women informants and their female relatives were employed to some extent or another

Table 3. Employment in Rural Enterprises in Two Brigades
in Jiangsu by Job Description and Sex

Job location or description	Total employees	Percent women	Percent men
Tianzhuang Brigade			
Machinery to wrap candy	250	1%	99%
Cloth shoe workshop	60	70	30
Building unit	25	48	52
Hotel and restaurant	30	33	67
Bike repair shop	6	0	100
Tailor shop	10	80	20
Tractor driver	20	5	95
TOTAL	401	19%	81%
Zhoujia Brigade			
Oilcan and dustpan factory	130	30%	70%
Shoe brush factory	20	30	70
Writing brush workshop	14	71	29
Paper box factory	22	73	27
Noodle factory	3	67	33
Handbag factory	11	64	36
TOTAL	200	40%	60%

in collective agriculture, and only 48 of the males. Another 20 women worked in the chicken farm and another 24 of the men worked in the pig, chicken, rabbit, or horse barns. An unusually large number of officials, 15, all men, turned up in my interviews. These did not include team leaders, also all male, whom I classified as agricultural workers. Sixty-one women and 123 men derived their income from nonagricultural sources. Twenty-three of these women, mainly unmarried teenagers, were employed in the shoulder bag factory, a newly formed enterprise that I was told drew its workers from the last two graduating classes of the middle school. (It should be noted in passing, however, that the three newest employees were women recently married to sons of brigade officials.) The next largest group employing women (6) was the building unit that also employed 20 male family members of my informants. Twenty-six of the men, but only 7 of the women, worked in commune or state enterprises in the area. This was the only commune I studied in which the brick kiln, a high-paying enterprise (also not mentioned by the leadership), apparently hired only men.

Fenghuo Brigade in Shaanxi, my last field site, was organized into twenty-eight work groups, the first twelve of which were cotton and wheat teams, that is, strictly agricultural labor. At some point these were also residential units, but nearly all families have now been rehoused in new brick row houses. The other sixteen groups are composed of the brick kiln group, scientific research office, clinic, machinery repair shop, nursery-kindergarten group, piggery, the forestry group (a combination of three groups: workers from the pear orchard, the mixed fruit orchard, and the vegetable gardens, which are under the trees in the orchards), the guesthouse employees, teachers, the sanitation group, the irrigation group, the basic construction group, the brigade office, and the livestock group. Table 2 showed that 81 percent of the women among my informants and their families worked in agriculture, almost all of them in the wheat and cotton teams. The men's agricultural contribution in this table is somewhat misleading in that their work units are far more likely to be in the more prestigious and better-paid forestry groups, scientific research unit, piggery, and so on. The best-paid women were the eleven who worked in the brick kiln at piecework. Only five of the men in my informants' families worked in the brick kiln. Because of its location, only 23 of my informants' relatives worked for non-brigade enterprises, and of these only 5 were women, one of whom got her job when her father retired. For most women in Fenghuo, the jobs are hoeing, weeding, and harvesting under the watchful eyes of male team leaders. As in all the other brigades I studied, there were in Fenghuo no female team leaders, nor could anyone recall that they had ever had one. The epigraph with which this chapter opened fairly sums up women's work in Shaanxi.

The last line in Table 2, for Sichuan, is based on field research in which, unfortunately, I did not participate. (Arthur Wolf kindly collected some basic data for me.) Women in the Sichuan brigade were almost completely confined to working in the fields. This may have been due in part to the fact that many of the

younger men in the brigade were working on construction projects in Tibet, but the major factor was probably the same one
that keeps women out of "technical" work elsewhere in China—
the presumption that they are incompetent.

What effect did these many inequities produce in the compen-
sation women received for their work? The data in Table 4 indicate quite clearly that the effect was major. The first section of
the table lists the average yearly income of individuals whose
earnings were in the team or brigade and were reported to me by
them in workpoints. I converted them into yuan per year to allow comparisons with the second section, which lists the average
yearly income of those who worked at the more desirable and
better-paid commune and state jobs. The workpoint calculations
were fairly complicated in that each team has a different yuan
value for its workpoints, depending on the profit-and-loss ratio of
that team for the year. For those paid in yuan, the calculations
involved no more than converting wages reported per month to
per year.

For those compensated in workpoints, men were better paid
than women in all five areas, in some cases much better. It would
require a sample many times larger than this to be able to pinpoint the precise causes for this imbalance, but it is not difficult
to describe those causes. As we have seen, women are more
likely to be laid off during the slack season. In Fujian, women
took turns working, but the men worked every day. I asked women
why, and one told me, "Men are the main workers in a family, so
what would happen if they didn't have work? The team thinks it
is a waste of workpoints to pay women." Some women lose several paydays each month during their menstrual periods. Even if
working full time, they may lose one or more workpoints each day
because they must cook the morning meal so that the men can
come home from the first work period, eat quickly, and return to
the fields. Supposedly their day's work begins after breakfast, but
they usually have been up and at work on domestic chores before
the men. Women who are nursing or who must leave work to
prepare the evening meal are also docked workpoints.

Aside from fewer work days and fewer hours in the work day,

Table 4. Average Yearly Wage by Source and Sex: Rural

Location	From team or brigade (workpoints converted to yuan)				From commune or state (in yuan)			
	No. of cases	Women's wage	Men's wage	Women's wage as pct. of men's	No. of cases	Women's wage	Men's wage	Women's wage as pct. of men's
Fujian	25	¥ 122	¥ 276	44%	30	¥ 331	¥ 525	63%
Jiangsu	108	283	327	87	205	337	482	70
Shandong	278	389	558	70	31	414	524	79
Shaanxi	285	279	420	66	18	407	570	71
Sichuan	138	142	235	60	36	252	855	30
Beijing					105	570	729	78
Shaoxing					131	538	679	79

women are paid less for their work than men are. Until the mid-1970's, printed reports of wage discrimination appeared in the media all over China. In her review of a difficult literature, Marina Thorborg cites some all too familiar cases. "In one people's commune in Kansu Province in order to enforce equal pay for equal work, the actual work performance of a women's team was measured against a men's team, both performing the same type of work. Because the female group on the average accomplished more work and of better quality than the male, they were awarded the equal amount of labor points as men but not more."[9] She described another case from the papers with a less happy outcome: "In a commune in Chekiang . . . a woman commune member who had picked 40 catties of peas was given 5 work points, while a man who had picked 32 catties was awarded 10 work points. When the woman complained, she was accused of 'putting work points in command.' Frightened by these accusations, she had to accept being grossly underpaid. The same happened to women in Shensi . . . and in Hopei. . . . Women demanding equal treatment were told that they 'practiced economism.'"[10] In only one commune I worked in was workpoint discrimination still this open and obvious. Able-bodied women were paid 6.5 workpoints for a day's work and able-bodied men were paid ten workpoints for the same day's work. Piecework was used for some tasks, particularly during the busy planting and harvest seasons in order to encourage women to come out to work. Afterward, when their labor was no longer needed, the suitable work for women was usually paid on a day-labor basis. Other communes were no less discriminatory but had developed, perhaps to preserve their model status, subtler ways of disguising their unequal pay scales. Most commonly, workers were ranked as to their strength and skill: the most valued male workers were categorized as twelve-point-a-day workers, while the best women workers rarely ranked higher than nine-point-a-day workers. Although work was all on a piecework basis, the ranking of a worker determined her or his share of any piecework assigned to the group.

Another common ploy was to devalue tasks usually assigned to women and rate highly those considered male. This had been almost institutionalized in one brigade where the male workers had been taken out of the work teams and assigned to technical groups with higher yuan valuations of their workpoints. As a result, when they participated in collective labor with women, they might receive the same number of workpoints, but those workpoints were worth considerably more at the pay-out at the end of the year. If men and women were assigned to do piecework together, the inequality was even greater. As the head of this particular brigade explained it, "If a group is doing a task on a piecework basis, their individual shares of workpoints are based on how well they work and on their grade point ratings. For instance, those in the top grade point ranking earn twelve workpoints a day and will get more." I asked how many women were in that ranking, and he said, "Eight or nine." Then I asked, "How many men?" "Around eighty." "Why," I asked, "so many more men?" "This grade is for technical workers, those who can drive trucks or direct the work in the orchards or manage the brick kiln or repair machinery. These are not appropriate jobs for women." I pointed out that there were women drivers in the city and my host began to look a bit flushed. He answered, "That is not the tradition here. Besides, who would take care of the children and cook while they were away?" To the delight of the women present (and the dismay of my Beijing handlers), I said that if a man could learn to drive a car he could learn to cook, with help. The brigade leader did not join in the laughter, but told me firmly, "That is not the custom in the countryside. If a woman drove a truck, she would be working among men and people would gossip. It would be bad for her." He made little attempt to conceal his irritation and abruptly turned to another topic.

Job assignment is a major source of discrimination in both city and country. As Table 4 shows, both men and women who work for commune or state enterprises have significantly higher yearly incomes than their relatives working in collective agriculture. For women the difference averages 1.43 times more (over the five field sites), and for men it averages 1.63 times more. However, these are differences within gender categories. Whatever the source of their income, men retain an absolute superiority of pay. In fact, in two out of five sites, male farm workers are better paid than women working for commune or state enterprises; the ratio of summed earnings of women yuan-earners to men workpoint-earners in the five sites is 1.04.

Table 4 also has some interesting information about the economies of the various communes listed. Although the Fujian sample is extremely small, owing to error and oversight, it is, I think, a fair reflection of the brigade's position in relation to the others. We were the Fujian commune's first foreigners, and the commune may also have been fairly recently elevated to this status. Earnings were low. The quite high male yuan earnings were the result of its very rural setting. The men who earned yuan were by and large not commuters but men who worked in distant cities and came home once a week. They were not factory workers but well-paid drivers and technicians. The Jiangsu site, on the other hand, was surrounded by factories, and its yuan-earning men were plain factory hands who received average salaries. The Shandong data fit well with my suspicions about its income sources. Although Shandong is in one of the poorest areas in China, the agricultural income there, for both men and women, is the highest. Very few women earned yuan, and the men who earned yuan were again men who commuted to An Qiu, the county seat, or farther and were skilled workers of one sort or another. Four of the five women who earned yuan in the Shaanxi site lived and worked in Xian, some four hours away by bus, and returned home once a month or so. The majority of the male yuan-earners also lived in Xian, although a few lived in the nearby county seat and some were well-paid commune level officials. The very large yuan earnings for men in Sichuan come from the younger men who are working on construction projects in Tibet and Xinjiang. Although they may only get home once a year, they contribute to their brigades and are considered full commune members. The few women who earned yuan in Arthur Wolf's Sichuan site were considerably less well off. One was a teacher, one a substitute teacher, one worked in a commune oil press, and two were impoverished widows who earned such income as they had by hawking cigarettes and other items on the streets. Other than this, *all* the working women in the Sichuan sample worked in agriculture. I include the Beijing and Shaoxing data in Table 4 to give some sense of the material differences that exist between rural and urban life. This is still an understatement, however, of the real gap, in that my rural collectives were all prosperous model brigades with considerably higher incomes than could be found elsewhere in rural China.

Just as stated policy in China is aimed at the removal of inequalities between rural and urban living standards, so is China on record as wishing to eradicate the gender inequalities in all aspects of society. Neither is an easy task, but I fear the latter may be the more difficult. Long before Liberation, in Yenan, the Party had trouble with local level male cadres over the issue of women working outside the home, and it learned even more convincingly during land reform that if they didn't get the local cadres behind an issue, they could not hope to get the masses behind that issue. Mass reeducation depended on local cooperation. In general, local cadres have strong misgivings about equality for women. Work and workpoints are divisive topics in the rural areas, the one being wide open to divergent evaluations and the other still being considered a concrete statement of an individual's personal worth. Motivation to work remained, in 1981, a serious and potentially disastrous problem in China's collectives, and cadres see equal pay for working women as detrimental to that motivation. It is not simply that men wish daily confirmation of their alleged superiority, although that is certainly a factor, but that men see in the increase of workpoints granted to women the devaluation of all workpoints and hence an absolute loss in income to themselves. Some cadres are willing to argue against this attitude by saying that the increased productivity resulting from women's increased motivation to work will enhance rather than reduce the value of workpoints. But many other cadres are quite as certain that increased participation by women will not make a bit of difference, and furthermore that the loss of enthusiasm by men will actually reduce production. No matter how many directives come down from Beijing or how many editorials appear in the provincial Party paper, the issue of equal pay for equal work remains unresolved. When I tried to question a woman cadre in Fujian about the workpoint issue, she at first attempted to get round the question by saying it was a commune decision and that men were stronger workers. "Are women then poor workers?" I asked. "No," she answered. "Even if women do the same job as men, the men get 10 workpoints and the women get 6.5 workpoints." When I put the question directly, "How do you feel about this policy?" she replied at length: "The decision has been made and there is nothing to be done about it. That accountant you met yesterday works very hard and puts in long hours. All agree, even the men, that she should be paid more, but because she is a woman it is impossible. Last year someone from the county Women's Federation came out here and argued for half a day that women's workpoints had to be raised. We did it, but as soon as she was gone, the men expressed their anger and changed it back."

I had another very frank interview with a woman cadre from a different area. When I brought up the issue of workpoints, she groaned. "The equal pay policy is difficult to establish here where the general attitude is that a woman is merely a woman. But the main problem is with the team and brigade leadership. They

don't want it. X Brigade in the next commune is more enlight-
ened on this issue. They point out that the birth limitation program cannot possibly succeed unless women get equal workpoints because you can't expect people with two daughters to
willingly be sterilized if they know those two daughters cannot
support them as well as one son would in their old age. In that
brigade women have higher workpoints than here and for some
jobs they get the same as men." "Do women ever rebel?" "Sometimes. When the commune holds a meeting, both men and
women representatives attend from the various brigades. The
men get 10 workpoints for the day's meeting and the women get
6.5 workpoints. Finally, one day some of us stood up and said,
'We sit here all day long doing the same thing as you are doing
exactly. Why should we be getting only 6.5 workpoints for your
10?' Those of us who were brave enough to speak out now get 10
workpoints for meetings—that is about one-third of the brigades." "Will women ever go on strike and refuse to work?"
Laughter. "No, they wouldn't dare." "Then how will change
come about? Will it be voted in each team or will it be decided
by the leadership?" "The team leaders decide who gets how many
workpoints and then they give the list to the people to discuss in
public meeting." "What can women do to change this?" "Abso-
lutely nothing. Men are in charge. If the men's minds are not
liberated, it is hopeless. I once asked the Party Secretary from
X Brigade to come over here and talk to our Party Secretary.
They got the brigade leaders together and talked to them, but it
was of no use. The others say to me, 'Your brigade is the advanced brigade in this commune. When all the teams in it give
equal pay to women, we will talk again.' That was the end of it."

Aside from the comments of these two women, I found it very
difficult to get other officials (who were nearly always male) to
admit that there might be any inequality in payment. When they
did, it was usually explained away as the result of women having
other responsibilities (domestic), hence working fewer hours.
When I raised the equal pay issue with the women themselves,
there was even less openness—which is not surprising in view of
the fact that there were always Beijing officials attending our in-

terviews. Mainly they told me that they worked less and therefore were paid less. And when I asked why they worked less, they
said there was less work to do that was suitable for women, or
that there was less work to do and it had to be given to men because they needed it to support their families. There was also an
unlikely number of women who said they no longer participated
in collective labor as much as they used to because of poor
health. Those women who agreed that men got paid more than
women for the same tasks said they were not resentful of it: "Men
ought to get more workpoints than women. They are stronger
and do the harder work, like carrying manure to the fields." The
forty-year-old woman who said this was one of the many women
in her team that I had been observing for the several days previous to our interview carrying heavy loads of nightsoil, two pails
to a pole, to the vegetable garden. There was no irony in her
voice, but she must have realized when she chose her example
that I had been observing this scene on my way to other interviews. With a good many women, however, I had no doubt as to
their sincerity. They accepted the lower evaluation of their contributions to be the direct result of their lesser strength and skill.
It was as if the new constitution had not been written.

My question was, I think, more fully answered when I asked a
different series of questions about whether women would like to
work more if there were more work available. A frank no to these
questions would have been politically unacceptable, but as with
so many of my questions, the women got their attitudes across in
other ways, as well as the reasons they held them. Poor pay was
one of them. Thorborg quotes the kind of pithy summary I heard
a lot of: "Men and women do the same work but do not get
the same pay; even if we removed Tai mountain we would get
7.5 points (compared to 10 for a man), so who would like to
sweat?"[11]

Women in China are no less astute than the farm women I
lived with in Taiwan. Political inexperience may have blinded
them to the importance of struggling for equal rewards in recognition of their equal contributions, but their practical experience
allows them to see all too clearly that collective labor puts them

at an economic disadvantage. When I first recognized this, during an interview with a woman in her early fifties, I felt very
foolish indeed. Comrade Wang had been telling me that she quit
collective work a few years back after she had been assigned to
the vegetable group, a corps of older women in her production
team who are paid by the day at a low rate. She said that age and
failing health were the motivating factors. We then began to talk
about her family's economics, and she told me about the four pigs
she had raised, the amount she earned for selling their manure to
the brigade, what she got for her chickens that year, and how
well she had done in eggs. I casually totted this up in the margin
of my notebook and suddenly realized that she had earned nearly
as much as the average yearly wage in her brigade of *two* able-
bodied young male workers. I blurted this fact out, and she gave
me one of those sympathetic smiles Chinese farm women save
for ignorant foreigners. The attending cadre looked uncomfortable, and I had enough wits left to move on to another question.
The lesson learned, however, is a curious one, and I think in the
long run a very worrisome one for women's progress in socialist
terms. Table 5 shows that a large proportion of a rural household's income comes from the sale of sideline products, such
as pigs, chickens, and seedlings. This income varies from area
to area; in my samples, it ranged from 23 percent in Jiangsu to
48 percent in Shandong. Of equal interest in Table 5 is the clear
evidence that in all but one of my field sites, sideline products
produced more income than the average yearly earnings of an
adult male. These findings would not surprise the local cadres,
one of whom in Fujian volunteered the information that "around
40 percent" of the household income in his brigade came from
these noncollective sources.

Another way to look at these data is presented in Table 6. In
the countryside, agricultural workers are not paid weekly or even
monthly. At the end of the year a household's accumulated
workpoints—that is, the combined total of all the members
of the family who engaged in collective labor—are balanced
against the household's debt to the collective, including their
yearly allotment of grain, cooking oil, vegetables if they do not

Table 5. Proportion of Household Income Coming from Sideline Products

Measure	Fujian[a] (N = 5)	Jiangsu (N = 36)	Shandong (N = 22)	Shaanxi (N = 41)
Percent of income from wages or workpoints	57%	77%	52%	76%
Percent of income from sideline products	43%	23%	48%	24%
Average sideline product income per household	¥638	¥396	¥1,148	¥328
Average yearly wage for a male	¥276	¥327	¥558	¥420

[a] Although in Fujian I have only five cases with complete income data for all household members as well as complete information on their sideline income, the average sideline product figure for Fujian is based on 36 cases.

Table 6. Proportion of Cash Income from Sideline Products

Measure	Fujian (N = 28)	Jiangsu (N = 18)	Shandong (N = 30)	Shaanxi (N = 46)
Percent of cash income from end-of-year pay-out	18%	54%	59%	75%
Percent of cash income from sale of sideline products	82%	46%	41%	25%

have private plots, and so forth. After these items have been deducted, the balance is converted into cash and paid to the head of household, nearly always the senior male worker.* It is the only cash the family sees (and often it is only the senior male who sees it). But there is one exception: sideline products are usually sold for cash. Since this is a way in which women's contribution to the household budget is made manifest, I have in Table 6 laid out the comparison between the two sources of cash. The contribution of sideline products ranges from a low of 25 percent in Shaanxi (where pigs were the only sideline) to a high of 82 percent in Fujian.

*Many of my informants reported a zero balance at the end of the year, and several admitted to being in debt to the collective for several years' running. In poorer collectives, this was undoubtedly much more common.

Whether or not officials are conscious of the large proportion of a household's income that is produced by women, older women at that, is unclear to me. The women certainly make no bones about it. A few old men may be involved, but very few. For example, of the 33 women I asked in Fujian about who took care of their pigs, only one said a man in the family (her father-in-law) did it. In Shandong, 4 of the 28 women I asked mentioned help from elderly fathers-in-law. No men were mentioned in Jiangsu. Sons and husbands might be called in to do some of the heaviest jobs, such as spring plowing of the private plots or shoveling pig manure out of unusually deep sties, but in the main, sideline activities are classified as women's work, household chores. If women's interest in collective labor is as ambivalent as I believe it to be, China might be well advised to take a closer look at what socialism offers rural women. When rural organization provides unequal rewards for collective labor based on gender and continues to assume that women are and should be primarily concerned with their families, family responsibilities will naturally assume a higher priority in their eyes. When those family chores also produce an income for the family that is considerably greater than a woman could possibly earn working within the collective, farm women are not likely to be motivated to "put society's needs first."

During the Great Leap Forward, when women's participation in collective labor was at its height, socialism seemed to have a lot to offer women in the rural areas. Brigades organized dining halls, nurseries, and mending units to free women to participate with the same ease as men, and praised them for doing so. They were to be first workers and second wives and mothers, in the way that their husbands were first workers and second husbands and fathers. Unfortunately, ideology exceeded capacity, and the Great Leap did not make it over the economic hurdles brought on by bad planning and even worse weather. The facilities that allowed women to put aside domestic concerns were the first to go, but as Thorborg has said, women were expected to remain on the job because they were getting equal pay and exercising positive revolutionary thinking.[12] Positive revolutionary thinking does not keep toddlers left alone all morning while mothers work in the fields safe from serious accidents, and we have seen how far the equal pay provision went. The burden of domestic responsibilities was the one most often mentioned by the women I questioned about working more if more work were available. I recognized that on one level they were saying they could earn more staying at home, but on another level they were saying that as long as their role in society was defined as wife and mother, not farmer, that was what would come first.

When I asked young mothers if they would rather work in the nearby factory or brigade enterprise than in the fields, they nearly all said that factory work would be impossible because they needed flexible hours to take care of their children and chores. A Jiangsu woman told me, "The reason farm work is better for women is that the hours are irregular. During harvest or planting you might have to put in long hours, but you can catch up with the household work in the slack season. Also women do most of the work on sideline products. It would be hard to keep factory hours and do the rest of the work after." Others answered like a Shaanxi woman who said bluntly, "Women have household chores. The factories don't want married women." But most women found even regular agricultural work a strain. For example, when I asked another Shaanxi woman why there were so few men in her work team, she made little attempt to conceal her resentment. "Every team has fewer men than women now because the men are all in the special groups or in the orchards or machinery group. They just come to the fields to do the plowing or to tell us what to do. They are all in special groups that work farther from the village. They have to take turns staying overnight to guard the crops. Women have so much to do at home that they can't do this. Our burdens are heavy. We do all the chores at home and work in the fields besides." A woman from another part of China told me, "Men have no worries. Women have everything to do—cook, wash clothes, feed the pigs and sheep, clean the house. Men are very busy outside too, but when they come home they can rest. Not women."

I have page after page of comments like these, but when I

asked women point-blank whether they would rather stay at home or work in the fields, I did not get a uniform set of answers. The younger and/or more politicized women gave me slogans about being good commune members, but even the more typical women with young children were not really eager to stay at home. The reasons given ranged from the monotony of household tasks that were never finished but had to be done again and again to the irritation of having children hanging on one all day. Women with mothers-in-law at home to care for the children and the domestic chores were the most interested in participating in collective labor. Clearly, for them work away from home offered some status in relation to the older and more established woman in the household, and also escape from her control. No one could criticize them for neglecting their domestic duties since someone else was responsible for them, and all the commune rhetoric was on their side.

Although there were many, many exceptions, rural women are expected to retire from active participation in collective labor at about fifty years of age. Those who work longer usually have no surviving children to support them. For example, Arthur Wolf interviewed two childless widows in their middle sixties in one brigade who were still considered able-bodied and were expected to turn out for work, even though they were prime candidates for the *wubao* system.* Most women retire much earlier; in fact, the general rule seems to be that a woman withdraws from her collective's labor force as soon as she has a replacement, either in the form of a teenage daughter or a daughter-in-law. At least that is the way it is usually explained. In view of the major contribution women make in sideline activities and the lack of experience newly married women have in such matters, there is a distinct possibility that the decision to retire is a negotiated withdrawal between the family and their production team—possible for women members but not for men, a gender discrimination that I tend to lose sight of from time to time. One day in Shandong

---

*The *wubao* (five guarantees) is a team-level welfare system designed to assure childless people of care in their old age. It is discussed in more detail on page 196.

when I was being a bit too sympathetic for a good interviewer with a woman who had been complaining of the double burden, she turned aside from her lament to comment that women at least could take time off work if they needed to and men did not have that prerogative. The same is true of retirement. In the rare case in which a son-in-law is brought in to marry a daughter, he joins the male production team, but that does not give his father-in-law the same right to retire from collective labor that a new daughter-in-law affords her husband's mother. It is assumed that a man will continue to work until he is at least sixty-five years old. Many men continue to work as long as their health will allow, doing lighter chores for lower rates of pay as the years go by.

To conclude this chapter on rural women's employment, it might be useful to look at the lives of these women in comparison with the lives of women in the cities. For urban women, their jobs are now an unquestioned part of their lives. Every young woman assumes that eventually she will be assigned a job and allowed to get started in her life as an adult. Rural women have no such commitment to the work world, for it has thus far shown no commitment to them. Out of political fervor some rural young women develop a solidarity with the collective that gives them satisfaction even with doing second-class work for second-class pay as second-class associates. Most, however, see their mothers and sisters being called upon to labor when the men need them and sent home when they do not; they have little opportunity to develop a sense of involvement with, let alone responsibility toward, the collective. They follow orders, quote the current slogan, and worry about getting dinner cooked on time. Some of them may resent having to work in the fields, but few of them would admit it. Urban women are far less likely to even feel such resentment because their roles have been expanded to include the eight-hour work day. What urban women resent is the *second* shift that is their lot after the work day is over, particularly if their husbands make no effort to help out.

Certainly, as we have seen, rural women complain a great deal about the difficulties of working all day in the fields and also fulfilling their domestic responsibilities, but they express and experience far less role conflict than do urban women. They are first and foremost wives and mothers, and if agricultural work interferes with the satisfactory performance of those domestic roles, they take time off or withdraw completely. Male team and brigade leaders expect this of their women workers, though they may complain about it; and women expect it of other women. In the cities, women work; in the country, they help out. As Thorborg reports, "In a special dispatch in English on Women's Day 1965, Chinese women workers were said to enjoy equal pay for equal work, while peasant women 'were adding to the family income.'" [13] Again, as we have seen, they may be the source of a large share of that family income, but it is earned within their roles as wives, mothers, and caretakers of the home—*nei ren*.

And there is considerable satisfaction on the part of women with that role. To my surprise, in each of the six field sites I worked in at least one woman (and usually more) made a snide reference to male incompetence. As a woman in her mid-forties expressed it, "*All* they can do is work." Another woman said, "I can manage on my own, but he would be in rags in two weeks and starve to death in a month." I asked a woman in Jiangsu if she would rather have a nice clean factory job or work in the fields. "No, I prefer the farm work. If I need something, I can just sell a chicken or some vegetables, but factory workers don't have any flexibility. Besides, I can see workpoints getting more valuable as we improve our methods. Factory workers get salary increases when somebody decides to give them to them. But really, how would I have raised all these children [four] if I had worked in a factory? I had no mother-in-law to help me." I asked this question of a good many women and those who were married nearly always chose farm work as preferable. Their reasons were always the same: you cannot take care of children and manage the household tasks as well if you don't have flexible hours.

Which is not to say that women do not smart under the inequalities they are forced to tolerate by the leadership and the narrowness of the role defined for them. They do. They also are aware of how much better their life is than that of their mothers or their own before Liberation. Some, on a conscious level, are willing to "make progress slowly." Like farm women in Taiwan, they are prepared to take the material available to them and work with it. A woman in Shandong delighted me with her twist on the usual apology for male superiority. When I asked her the question about factory work, she said, "Men are stronger so they should stay home and do the farm work. Let the women go work in the factories. I am making my daughter stay in school so she can get a good job. Men make more workpoints anyway so let them work in the fields. My daughter should work in the factory."

◇

FIVE

Being and Becoming
a Proper Chinese Woman

Why do you think girls are easier to raise? "They are not as precious as sons."
— *Middle-aged woman from Fujian*

What is women's proper work? "They work in the fields, raise the children, take care of the pigs, do the washing, cook, and mend clothes." What is men's proper work? "They go to work."
— *Woman from Jiangsu, age 28*

Men are more capable than women and can contribute more to society.
— *Woman factory worker in Beijing, age 27*

It is almost impossible to get a Chinese woman to describe for you the attributes of a proper woman. She immediately translates your subject into proper wife or mother or daughter-in-law, and if you object, she tells you about a good daughter. I interviewed only a tenth as many men as women, but they all responded to such questions with descriptions of their occupations, politics, personalities, or physical prowess. Women spoke of their relations with others. Indeed, one woman came close to defining the problem as well as a proper woman for me when she said, "To be a woman means you must always be doing things for other people." My purpose in asking such a question was to discover what exactly Chinese parents were socializing *for* in their female children. In order to arrive at an answer, I have had to cull my interviews for what amounts to lists of adjectives. By looking at all the comments made about good wives, mothers, and daughters, I came up with a fairly uniform set of characteristics expected of all women, whatever their particular point in the life cycle. Women are expected to be quiet, obedient, well-behaved, nurturant, hard-working, timid stay-at-homes. Women might describe with shining eyes and amused shakes of the head the brash, naughty, imaginative exploits of a young son, but of a daughter they observe simply (although no less fondly) that she is a good girl. Parental expectations are not often disappointed. When I asked women whether boys or girls were easier to raise, 81 percent, if I exclude the Shaanxi sample, said girls were far easier to raise (see Table 7).* The exception, Shaanxi, is odd: nearly every woman who said boys were easier to raise mentioned the nuisance involved in combing girls' hair and keeping them in clean clothes—a matter, I was told, that was of considerably more interest to girls than to boys, for boys would just pull on any old clothes and leave the house. But in speaking of why girls were easier to raise than boys, other mothers said this was because, unlike boys, they didn't run around and get into trouble. Two mothers in Beijing described good daughters as children who studied hard, listened to their parents, and stayed at home. The second mother added, "She does chores." A mother in Jiangsu told me, "Girls don't go out as much as boys. They like to watch you do things and then imitate it. Boys just run away and play."

In other words, boys are easier to raise because they just pull on any old clothes and run off, but girls are easier to raise because they stay at home and learn to do chores—an interesting paradox. Parents are particularly concerned about what the boys who go out might bring back home with them. A Shaoxing mother explained, "A good boy is one who listens to his parents, studies hard, and doesn't go out and bring trouble home with him." A Beijing mother said, "Boys don't need to do extra chores. Mainly they mustn't fight." Another mother told me, "Boys cause their parents much more trouble than girls. Especially over the fighting. Parents come to the door to complain." All these comments were familiar to me, for I had heard them time and again from mothers I talked with in Taiwan.[1] Aggression in China is a bad thing, and keeping children from getting mixed up in quarrels with other children is a source of much anxiety to mothers.

---

* A great number of women on this and on similar questions answered, "The same, the same." I have not included these figures in my counts because sometimes they meant that boys and girls were equally easy to raise and sometimes they meant they were unwilling to entertain the question.

Table 7. "Which Is Easier to Raise, Boys or Girls?"

Site[a]	Number of respondents	Percent who said boys	Percent who said girls
Fujian	10	30%	70%
Jiangsu	23	22	78
Shandong	12	0	100
Shaanxi	23	78	22
Beijing	30	33	67
Shaoxing	29	7	93

[a]I use the names of provinces in which my field sites were located because they are easier to remember. I do not mean to imply that these data are representative of anything beyond the sample described in the text.

Nor were there any surprises when I asked Chinese mothers whether boys or girls were more quarrelsome. Like their Taiwanese counterparts, they told me that boys were the biggest worry: 87 percent of the mothers said that their boys were the most likely to get into fights (see Table 8). "Boys are always going outside the house to fight and they are afraid of nothing. Girls don't go out that much," said a Beijing mother. A Fujian mother told me, "Boys are naughty and active; girls are tidy and good-tempered and obedient." Many mothers gave more thoughtful answers. A middle-aged woman in Jiangsu said, "Their style isn't the same. The boys end up hitting each other and girls argue. Girls have secrets and whisper behind each others' backs." A nineteen-year-old Beijing girl confided, "We are born with narrower hearts. Boys forgive more easily and are more generous. Girls stay angry longer." A kindred spirit in Shandong said, "Girls get into arguments and are fussy and shout a lot. Boys don't." The consensus seems to be that boys are more likely to be involved in physical aggression and girls are more likely to get into arguments, make nasty cutting remarks, and sulk. Once they have slugged it out, boys forget the incident (if adults allow them to), but girls do not, keeping in their "narrow hearts" the slights and slurs that they have received.

What do parents do about naughty children? I expected this to be a touchy question. When I first began asking women in one rural setting who quarreled most among their children, I was quickly assured by a cadre that Chinese children didn't quarrel, a remark that produced spontaneous laughter all around. I expected much more cautious responses when I asked how parents disciplined their children. A good deal of propaganda has come out of various government departments on the proper methods of training children in the new China. Beating children is considered feudal. Therefore I didn't even bother to ask about punishment in heavily politicized places like Shandong, nor was I surprised to find a preponderance of mothers in my two urban sites saying that they lectured their misbehaving youngsters or "taught them the principles." Fifty-eight percent said they considered this the best way to correct a naughty child. But I *was* surprised to find that as many as 30 percent of the urban sample also admitted to hitting their children. Rural women were even more outspoken on this topic. The Chinese dearly love slogans, particularly those that indicate oneness with the masses. The phrase *tu fa shang ma*, "using the local method to mount the horse," suggests that one should depend on local resources to get the country going, or, another interpretation, one should not ignore the old methods used by the masses. Many country women told me that they were aware of other ways of getting their children to behave, that they tried to teach them the principles, but mainly they relied on *tu fa*, local methods. In general, a cadre explained with noticeable embarrassment, that means they hit them. In

Table 8. "Which Quarrels Most, Boys or Girls?"

Site	Number of respondents	Percent who said boys	Percent who said girls
Fujian	21	91%	9%
Shandong	4	100	0
Jiangsu	15	93	7
TOTAL	40	93%	7%
Beijing	29	79%	21%
Shaoxing	17	88	12
TOTAL	46	83%	17%

fact, 56 percent of the rural women I interviewed said this was how they dealt with the problem. This sizable rural-urban difference (56 percent to 30 percent) cannot, in my opinion, be satisfactorily explained in terms of greater access to state propaganda, although that surely has some relevance, or in terms of more sophisticated urban dwellers telling the foreign researcher what the state wants her to believe. The reasons are more complex.

As we shall see in a later chapter, the family limitation program in urban China has been fairly successful. In the cities, housing constraints have added to the pressure for smaller families with dramatic results. Other factors affecting the urban family include the high urban employment rate for women and the number of urban children who grow up in nursery school environments or in the care of grandparents or other persons not related to them. Parents with only one child who see that child only on weekends or for a few hours in the evenings tend to be lavish in their affection and attention. If the primary caretaker is a grandmother, the child is even more spoiled, simply because, as one grandmother told me, "I never hit my son when he was small and I like my grandson even better than my son, so how could I hit him?" The problem of the spoiled only child—male and female both—is a frequent topic of conversation in urban China. Most people assume that the problem will get worse rather than better, but they also think that it will have no effect once the children are grown. Not unlike Americans, Chinese parents seem to assume that the schools will solve the problem while at the same time they and the state admonish the schools not to use "feudal teaching methods," meaning physical punishment. Teachers, who suffered greatly during the Cultural Revolution, are reluctant to take any actions not specifically sanctioned by a superior. From parents they are receiving messages inconsistent with traditional attitudes toward education in which parents handed their children to the teachers with the instruction that they be beaten as often as necessary to produce a good scholar. "Now," a Beijing teacher told me, "families with only one or two children who are raised by the grandparents are causing many problems. Parents come to the school and ask us to be gentle with the child because it is the only one they have. What are we to do?" And the parents point out that the problem is not merely the stereotypic spoiled only son. A Shaoxing mother said, "In the past, the boys caused much more trouble than the girls, but now, with only one allowed, they are all spoiled. The girls may even be naughtier than the boys."

In the rural areas, the single-child family is not yet commonplace, nor are nursery schools, grandparent-raised children, or spoiled girls. During the busy season, mothers may be working long hours in the fields, but the rest of the time they interact regularly with their children and seem to be as likely as ever to slap a child who is being difficult and hug her when she wails in distress. Boy children may be pampered more than girl children, but they always were. Within the domestic unit, the hierarchy of respect between adult and child as well as between male and female is virtually unchanged. Rural mothers have more interaction with children than do fathers, but fathers are the ultimate authority, which mothers often threaten to bring down on recalcitrant children. A Shandong woman described the parental roles this way: "Mothers must see that their children are healthy and warm and well fed. Fathers have no responsibility beyond providing them with an income. Fathers raise children with money." Many, many rural mothers told me, half laughing, that they yelled at or hit their kids so much that the kids ignored them, whereas the father had only to say one word and the children mended their ways.

The influence of the rural-urban differences in child-training practices on children's school careers may be as important as the difference in sex. Girls, both rural and urban, are kept closer to home (or as their parents see it, choose to stay at home), and as a result get a stronger dose of socialization than their brothers (i.e., are naturally more obedient from their parents' point of view), see less and learn less about how their social environment works (that is, are timid, their parents say), and don't get into physical quarrels with peers (are well behaved, their parents insist). For a Chinese teacher such might be the ideal characteristics of a docile if uninspired student, and in a rural school the

differences in classroom behavior between boys and girls are ob-
servable but not remarkable. The difference between rural children and urban children, regardless of sex, is more dramatic.
Compared with rural children, urban children are more competent in that they come to kindergarten or the first grade from far
richer intellectual backgrounds. Urban parents try to get their
children into nursery schools as soon as possible (usually as soon
as an opening occurs) in order to provide this superior environment. I was often told that it was "better" for children to be in a
nursery school because they learned more things, whatever other
reservations the parents might have about their physical care
there. But there are not enough places, and the nursery schools
that do have places are not always in a location possible for parents who work in different factories or even different cities.
Those who must leave their children with grandparents or others
are keenly aware of their children's handicaps and make such
efforts as they can to compensate.

Certainly, anyone who visits the nursery schools attached to
showplace factories is impressed by the advantages they hold
over the drab, cramped quarters of most homes. The average
citizen's child has little space in which to romp, few toys to play
with, and few if any picture books to daydream over. By Western
standards, the nursery schools are not a children's paradise, but
they usually have bright objects around, a few well-used toys,
and lots and lots of companions. Besides games, caretakers teach
the children little songs and dances, some of which (if they are
on the tourist route) can be quite elaborate and include colorful
costuming. Large factories may house as many as 600 children,
ranging in age from fifty-six days to six years. Most children are
brought in each morning when the parents come to work and are
taken home each evening. One of the delights of the Beijing
street scene is the exotic assortment of bicycle sidecars parents
have devised to transport their children to and from school in a
harsh climate with poor transportation facilities. Some children
are left at the nursery school on Monday morning and taken out
on Saturday night. Purely in terms of physical care, I would have
to agree that the 500 children who were housed in the nursery

school of the Beijing No. 1 Machine Tool Plant I visited in December 1980 were far better off than they would have been in the crowded, drafty homes of parents who worked eight hours a day, six days a week. They lived in big airy rooms that caught the morning sun, and had milk morning and afternoon and three nourishing meals every day. There appeared to be a good ratio of attendants to children. My visit was unexpected, and I was amused on opening the door to the toddlers' room to find ten little bottoms squatting over ten little potties while a motherly looking woman encouraged with appropriate noises. It was also heartening to see how automatically the nursemaids in the infants' ward moved to pick up a baby when it began to cry.

Most nursery schools are not in showplace factories, however, and few have the qualities of the one described above. A constant complaint of women in Beijing is the lack of child care facilities in convenient locations, and a constant concern of officialdom is the lack of space to house, and lack of competent workers to run, neighborhood child care facilities. Nursery school work is not a popular occupation among young women, and after the state invests several weeks or months training them in nutrition, health care, and child handling, a disappointing number use every trick they know to transfer to other jobs, preferably as factory workers. It is, of course, not an insoluble problem, but so far the state has been unwilling to invest the money in wages and the energy in propaganda to make the occupation more attractive. The obvious feminist solution of assigning half the positions to men is unthinkable. As a result, many of the smaller nursery schools are little better than warehouses where children are stored for the day or the week. All of them are grossly overcrowded by American standards. Even so, the children are safe, enjoy each others' company, and have three hot meals a day. Nor are parents likely to complain too much when the waiting list in every other nursery school is very, very long.

I asked several urban women how they felt about leaving their children in these schools all day, and whether they thought it would be better for the children if they stayed at home with them. I also asked the same kind of question of women who left their children in the care of their own or their husband's parents. No one was very frank on the subject, and all the answers were pretty much alike, but those who had grandparent caretakers seemed more confident. In general, they said they really didn't know anything about taking care of children and grandmother had a lot more experience. A surgical nurse whose child was in day care said, "I was trained in medicine, not child care. They are trained in child care." When I asked about the psychological effect on the infants, the majority of the women seemed puzzled and some explained that at that age (until two or three) children don't care much who is around as long as they get fed. However, a woman doctor who has had some exposure to Western psychology was quite insistent about the beneficial results of institutional child care and repeated a few times too often and a bit too shrilly the fact that she had never taken care of any of her three children, and when she was very busy had sometimes left them in the nursery for a month at a time. Another woman confided that she preferred her present arrangement, leaving her son with a retired couple on a daytime basis, because he was the only child they took care of and she knew they wouldn't let him cry.

When I talked to first grade teachers about the differences between children raised at home and those who spent their days (or weeks) in nursery schools, I thoroughly expected them to tell me that the nursery-raised children were easier to deal with. To some extent this was true in that the children were used to regular hours on someone else's schedule, but I was surprised to learn that there were some disadvantages. The transition from nursery school to kindergarten is not too difficult: the children's activities are somewhat more scheduled in kindergarten and a series of graduated learning tasks are introduced. The children and their parents, however, think of kindergarten as "school," and it is here that the problem begins. When they finally enter the first grade, the children assume they know how to behave in school and they continue to exercise the "freedom" allowed in kindergarten. In rigidly structured Chinese classrooms individualistic behavior is even more frowned upon than in kindergarten. What is worse, according to a Beijing teacher, the kindergarten children are not "afraid" of the teacher and do not realize that they must obey her or his commands immediately. This misconception combined with the new indulgent parental attitudes has served to make the teachers' lot a difficult one.

During the Great Leap Forward, production brigades and teams hurriedly formed nursery schools in order to free young mothers for full-time participation in agricultural production. One of the high points of every visit to showplace communes on the tourist route these days is the trip to the nursery school where adorable children with bright bows in their hair perform intricate dances to entertain their foreign friends. (After one has been through a dozen or so of these delightful experiences, the surface charm fades and questions about exploitation of children begin to cross one's mind.) As one goes deeper into the countryside, both the quality and the quantity of child care facilities drop sharply. Even in the model communes, child care was provided only during the planting and harvest seasons. In at least two of the collectives studied, the child care centers appeared to be set up for my benefit. One, located in an area known for harsh winters, consisted of what had clearly been a storeroom. Even in late spring it was a chilly, forbidding place. About eight children had been convened. They were sitting around a plank table on little stools, quietly watching the old woman in charge of them wind up a very new plastic toy. None of the children grabbed for it or shouted or even asked to touch it. They simply stared at it and at me. The table was in front of the door and there was one window (unglazed) in the room. There was no electricity. Another brigade in another area of China had a room set aside that functioned as a drop-in center for children whose mothers were working. I never saw more than half a dozen children around, but my local assistant left her young son there every day. It was another drab and colorless place with a beaten-earth floor, managed by a couple of truly aged-looking women. Whenever we walked past, the old women would yell to my assistant's little boy and he would rush out of the house at the fastest crawl I have ever seen in a child, trying desperately to catch his mother. The nursery school in another commune I worked on was attached to the local school, and although I was assured it took "all ages," I saw no children below the age of two. I suspect that they had to be weaned and toilet-trained. The fourth collective I studied seemed to have larger quarters, but they were silent and so dark I could see little from the outside. I was not given permission to visit.

From estimates made by Marina Thorborg and from my own observations, it would appear that only a very few rural children spend any time in a nursery school, and only a small fraction of those who do find it the enriching experience that urban parents expect.[2] Most rural children whose mothers work either stay with grandparents, "play around home," or endure the "older-watches-younger" system of child care. For them, the first day of school is a vastly different experience from that of the urban child. For the urban child it involves a new room, a new teacher, and an increasing number of demands, but for the rural child it is a new world and not a very pleasant one. For the first time the children are subjected to physical and mental restraints for hours on end. The compensations are not as readily apparent for rural children as for urban children. Schoolrooms are likely to be less rather than more appealing than home, and parental support is likely to be considerably weaker.

I was not always allowed to visit schools in the communes, but even when an official visit was denied, I peered through windows and over walls. Most classrooms were bare, indeed barren. In one school I was shown a classroom all outfitted with new furniture, but when I did an attendance survey of the other classrooms, I found children sitting on rough stones (presumably from the quarry nearby) and doing their lessons on desks made of concrete slabs and bricks. On another unscheduled visit to a school I found a first and second grade housed in the shell of a building that had never been finished, a victim of changing policy on who should pay for the education of the next generation of China's farmers. I don't know where those children studied when the temperature dropped below freezing and the wind began to whip through the unglazed windows. Even in the best of the rural schools I visited—in Shandong of course—the walls were bare of the posters and brightly colored teaching aids I saw in the city schools, and there were hardly enough textbooks to go around. But for the rural children, probably the most difficult part of the learning process was sitting at a desk without moving about for long hours, learning by rote the phonetically mute symbols that are the keys to knowledge.

There are now some excellent studies of the changing policies toward education in China during the thirty years since Liberation.[3] I will not trace these policies here, other than to say that, as with many other things, the difference in the quality of education available in the rural areas and in the cities is extreme. Except for the period of the Cultural Revolution when the schools were closed down, all urban children have had access to state-run schools. Such schools have not been consistently available to rural children except in the wealthiest villages, which are also usually those closest to the urban areas. Even before the Cultural Revolution, the communes were expected to organize and support their own primary schools. The quality of education was hit-and-miss, and during the Cultural Revolution when policy encouraged the communes to use local personnel as teachers, it was more miss than hit. Control over the curriculum and the qualifications of teachers was taken away from the county education bureaus and handed to the commune hierarchy who were more responsive to political issues than pedagogical ones. As a result there were teachers who, though politically pure, were themselves barely literate and could not speak the national language. From 1958 until the mid-sixties an innovative half-and-half school system was introduced that allowed students to work half-time for the school and study half-time. In poorer villages, where parents required their children's workpoints to meet their own needs, and where there was little enthusiasm for schooling anyway, these half-and-half schools quickly foundered. If children were going to spend their free time working in the fields, parents felt they might as well work for their own families. Since these were also the areas in which state-run schools were few and far between, large numbers of rural children got no education at all. During the Cultural Revolution these schools also came under attack as being a sop for the masses while the urban elite were provided with state-financed superior schooling. The criticism was justified. Urban schools were far better than even the state-run rural schools, and all parties were aware of it.

Table 9 shows the results of the rural and urban differences in education.* Looking first at the most extreme case, those who received insufficient education to achieve literacy, we find that among people under forty, the rural residents are considerably more likely to be illiterate. (Literacy is defined as reading, but not necessarily writing. As one woman told me, "Farmers don't need to write. Reading is enough.") For the other extreme, those who managed to get some middle school education (anything beyond primary school for my purposes), the difference is even greater. About 42 percent more of the urban dwellers in my sample had middle school education than did the rural dwellers. The rural-urban difference in illiteracy is not as high as the male-female difference, however. The illiteracy rate of women in the under-forty age group is ten times as high as that of men. Even this figure is heavily influenced by the rural-urban difference in that the very high literacy rate for urban women distorts the general figure. Whereas only 4 percent of the urban women under forty are illiterate, 31 percent of the rural women in this age group cannot read or write. At the other end of the scale, of the urban women under forty years of age, 81 percent made it to middle school, but only 23 percent of the rural women in that age group had any education beyond primary school.

These figures are somewhat higher than the 70 percent literacy rate quoted by Whyte and Parish for their urban population, but my definition of literacy (see above) is probably more generous.[4] Whichever set of figures one accepts, they are an impressive achievement for only thirty years. In my sample, 97 percent of the urban adults under the age of forty are literate and 83 percent of the rural population in that age category claim at least literacy. Contrast this to the group who are now forty years and over: only

---

*These data are drawn from the families of the women and men I interviewed. Though I tried to get a cross-section of the population, I had little control over the people selected; my informants probably had more advantages on the average than the general population.

Table 9. Percent of People Who Are Illiterate, Literate, or Educated
by Age, Sex, and Rural/Urban Location

Category	Number of people	Percent illiterate	Percent who attended primary school or are literate[a]	Percent who attended middle school or above
Age 18–39				
Urban	137	3%	14%	83%
Rural	279	17	42	41
Male	194	2	30	68
Female	222	22	36	43
Age 40 or over				
Urban	124	23%	43%	34%
Rural	239	60	36	4
Male	188	21	49	21
Female	175	75	18	7

[a]"Literate" includes people who can read but cannot write.

77 percent of the urban dwellers in that category and only 40 percent of the rural dwellers achieved literacy. For women the comparison is particularly striking: 69 percent of the women under forty in my rural sample were literate. Although far fewer rural women than men were getting middle school educations, this 69 percent is still a great improvement over the 7 percent literacy figure for rural women forty years and over; also, not a single woman in my older rural sample had any education beyond primary school.

In sum, urban women are now as likely to be literate as are urban men but somewhat less likely to get through middle school. Data from the rural areas is not as encouraging. Great progress has been made in achieving literacy for women, although not as great as that for men, but women who wish to go beyond simple reading and writing have been less fortunate. In the countryside, middle school or other technical training remains a male monopoly. Why? Are girls discouraged from higher education? By whom? Their parents, their teachers, or the system itself? Do they do less well, and if so, why? Are the entrance exams scored or weighted in a discriminatory manner? Do girls drop out because they are uninterested? My data do not give me answers to all these questions, but I was surprised at how open women were about sexual discrimination in education. Rural and urban informants differ widely in their attitudes toward education and toward the value of educating women, but all women labor under the same social and psychological handicaps with regard to education. Urban women, nonetheless, have advantages in terms of lower costs, higher expectations, and greater ideological support than their rural sisters. In answering questions about how much education they hoped their children would achieve, rural and urban women often looked at different parts of the educational scale—that is, middle school was the grandest goal for rural women and college for urban mothers, but they placed their sons and daughters in the same rank positions on it. Typical statements from city mothers were like this one from a forty-five-year-old mother of four: "Of course it is more important to send the boy to college. Men can do big things and women cannot." This is matched by the statement of a Shaanxi farm woman, made in a discussion of the same topic: "Girls are cuter, but when they grow up, boys are more useful, stronger." I was amused at the response of a male farmer to my questions about educating girls. In pre-Liberation days, men felt required to give their daughters the best they could manage in the way of a dowry because, aside from making her entry as a stranger into her parents-in-law's household easier, it enhanced a man's reputation in the community. When I asked this particular farmer just why he thought it was a good idea to send his daughters to school, he gave me the same reason: "It gives you a good reputation in the community if you let your daughters study." It showed that he could afford it and that he was "modern." (Of course, other men might not share his opinion, just as some men in Taiwan had muttered that only fools threw away good money on their daughters' dowries.)

Country people and city people also see a different set of advantages in educating their children. In the better-off villages where I worked, the farmers knew about "scientific farming" and knew that in the future the illiterate farmer was going to be at a disadvantage, in fact already was. Urban parents accepted pri-

mary school as a necessity for their children if they were to survive in the modern world, and middle school was a basic financial investment. When they looked at their own progeny and the
personal advantages and disadvantages in educating them, they
calculated shrewdly: in the country, educating a girl seemed to
many parents a waste, but educating a boy might enable him to
take a leadership role in the community that would eventually
bring face and fortune to the whole family. The boy might even
be lucky enough to get a factory job, whereas a girl would bring
nothing to the family in the long run and probably not much in
the short run. Rural women are not likely to be sent to factory
jobs and even less likely to be given leadership roles. As one Fujian woman explained, "If you educate a daughter she might go
out and work and send money home, but then she would get
married and you would have wasted all that money to benefit another family. We have to depend on our sons. Educate them."

Urban parents are less likely to make such frankly economic
statements, but the results are not so very different. A middle-
aged Beijing mother said to me, apologetically, "Maybe I have
feudal ideas, but it seems to me the boys are mine and the girls
belong to others." Another Beijing woman gave an evasive answer to the direct question, but as the interview session went on
it came out that the family had sent the son to college but had
taken the daughter out of primary school after the fourth grade
because it needed another income. In China, the cost of an education is not so much the money necessary to pay for fees, books,
and paper, as it is the loss of an income to the family. Thomas
Bernstein, who interviewed emigrés in Hong Kong, some from
less well-to-do villages than those I studied, was told that teachers found it difficult to keep their students in school because parents wanted them to bring in workpoints as soon as they were
able.[5] The domestic labor of girls becomes valuable at a much
younger age. A thirty-eight-year-old farm woman in Jiangsu be-
wailed the fact that she had no help in the house: "It would be
better for me if my oldest son were a girl. I can't make a son help
me with the chores the way I could a daughter. Boys just run off
and play, but a daughter can't do that."

It is not easy to document these sex differences in numbers. The 1981 *Statistical Yearbook of China* reports that females constitute 44 percent of the population of primary schools, 39 percent of the population of the regular secondary schools, 33 percent of the secondary specialized schools, and 24 percent of the institutions of higher learning.[6] I regret that I did not recognize earlier the importance of surveying the classroom population in all my research sites. As a result, I have accurate school attendance data for only two places, Shandong and Shaanxi. Schools I visited in Beijing seemed to have more or less equal enrollments, and I did not visit any schools in Shaoxing. On one of the other communes I studied, I was told frankly by the official giving me the "brief introduction" that there were about the same number of girls as boys in the primary school, but more boys in the middle school. With no self-consciousness at all, he explained that girls were simply better at other things, such as cooking and feeding pigs, so their parents preferred to keep them at home. Besides, he said, they marry into other families so people are reluctant to waste too much money educating them.

In a brief tour of the brigade school in my Shandong site, I noted twice as many boys as girls in a classroom, and although the principal assured me there was an equal number of boys and girls in each grade, I later returned to do a room-by-room survey (see Table 10). After my survey, I again sat down with the principal and the school's Party Secretary. Up to the third or fourth grades, they told me, girls usually were at the top of the class, but by middle school the top five students were always boys. When I tried to get their opinions as to why this happened, they seemed not to have thought about it. I fear it is something they accept as so "natural" that they had never considered it a problem. But as Table 10 shows, the differences are indeed large, and, according to the principal, consistent. In the seventh grade, there were less than half as many girls still in school as there were boys. This school, incidentally, was in the process of changing back from the 5-2 system (five years of primary school and two years of lower middle school) to the 6-3 system (six years of primary school and three years of lower middle school) used before the

Table 10. Percentage of Students in Classrooms by
Grade and Sex, Shandong and Shaanxi

	Shandong			Shaanxi		
Grade	No. of students	Percent boys	Percent girls	No. of students	Percent boys	Percent girls
1	31	52%	48%	37	38%	62%
2	33	58	42	33	42	58
3	34	50	50	34	56	44
4	33	42	58	31	58	42
5	42	50	50	37	51	49
6	34	47	53	106	53	47
7	40	65	35	66	62	38
8	39	64	36	43	70	30
9				43	70	30
10				73	86	14

Cultural Revolution. They expected to be back to the full nine-year course by 1983. Students who fail the examinations for middle school are allowed to spend another year in the fifth (to be sixth) grade and try again. The principal said, "And if they fail again, they are out," but the Party Secretary quickly said, "If there is any hope that they might pass, they would be allowed to try again." In the year preceding my survey, forty-two students had taken the exam to go on to senior middle school; twenty-two had passed, of whom six were girls. When I asked how many girls had taken the exam, they were unable to tell me.

In my Shaanxi field site, the school was also still on the 5-2 system, and I was not told of any plan to return to the pre-Cultural Revolution system, but I would be surprised if they did not. This brigade also "houses" the commune's senior middle school. Dormitories and many of the classrooms are in caves in the cliff above the village, making a very impressive backdrop for a village that has lost its original style to modern row houses. Once again, my own counts of children did not match those that had been made for me by the school officials, either in representation of sex or total count. Since it was harvest time, and young men do much of the cutting and threshing, it seems likely that the number of middle school males was lower than usual—which would make the real imbalance in the upper grades (less than one-third female) even greater than the figures indicate. The major discrepancy in the tenth grade (girls representing only 14 percent of the enrollment) also is influenced by its multiple function. Young people who are preparing for the college entrance exams will enroll in this class and attend irregularly or when certain topics are being taught. Some of these "tenth-graders" looked to be at least twenty years old and were clearly making up for schooling lost during the Cultural Revolution. There were quite a few more girls in the first and second grades at Shaanxi than boys, and many of the girls in the first grade were several years older than the boys. Parents in Taiwan and elsewhere in China told me that they sometimes keep their daughters at home until a son is ready to enter school, so that the girl can accompany him and take care of him. Girls were also kept at home to help their mothers until another child was old enough to be useful or a daughter-in-law entered the family. When I asked the principal about the all too obvious sex imbalance in the upper grades, he told me that girls seemed to be unable to learn beyond a certain point and dropped out. He also volunteered, however, that at this age parents began to pile on extra chores at home and many girls simply couldn't get the time to study, so they gave up. I might note that in this village there is a cadre family that had five sons and two daughters, ranging in age from twenty to forty-two years. Neither of the two daughters had "been through the schoolyard gate," as the local saying goes, but three of the five boys had gone to college and the other two had completed senior middle school.

The principals at Shandong and Shaanxi and many of the teachers I talked to all betrayed an attitude that is deeply embedded in the Chinese value system—that older girls are not as smart as younger girls, and women in general are not as smart as men. They used many words to mask or qualify that belief, but the belief was still there, and even the society's intellectual sophisticates find it hard to deny. Urban workers assume it. As a Beijing mother of four told me, "Boys are quicker and smarter and get more out of it—that is why you send boys to college and not girls." Another urban mother said, "My second daughter is trying very hard to pass the college entrance exams. Whoever gets the best marks can get to college now. She studies night and day, but she doesn't make much progress. My son does nothing but play and he does very well in school."

The belief in the superiority of male intelligence was so obvious in my first set of interviews in Beijing that I inquired about intellectual differences in all my interviews, and got some surprising and interesting rural-urban differences. Our stereotypes about life in the countryside lead us to expect that whatever the issue, the more conservative stance will be found the farther you travel from the urban centers. The data in Tables 11 and 12 appear to contradict this assumption. Urban women are much more likely than rural women to say that male children are smarter than female children. Rural women are less consistent, and 11 percent of them in my samples were bold enough to say that men are not as smart as women. From less easily quantifiable comments that will be discussed below, I think these rural figures would have been even higher in favor of women's superior intelligence if the cultural requirements for accepting male superiority were not so strong. In other words, I think more rural women than were willing to admit it think men are not so bright.*

Some women in Jiangsu and Shaanxi insisted on a peculiarity in children's intelligence that I had heard about in other field sites but had not paid much attention to. It was also mentioned by educators. When they are little, girls are smarter and quicker, but when they "get older" the boys are smarter. (See Table 11.) I put the "get older" in quotation marks because it means something more than just chronological age. It was always stated with that curious combination of intonation and body tension that alerts one to the fact that a Chinese informant is alluding to something slightly sexual, slightly embarrassing. In this case, the allusion is to puberty. Once a girl reaches puberty, her intelligence becomes "unfocused"—a metaphor used by teachers and

---

*The word used here was *congming*, intelligent, clever, bright, wise—and considerable attention was given to finding the appropriate translation when I had to use an interpreter in other dialects.

Table 11. "Which Is Smarter, Boys or Girls?"

Site	No. of respondents	Percent who said boys	Percent who said girls	Percent who said younger girls and older boys
Fujian	18	72%	28%	0%
Shandong	11	82	18	0
Jiangsu	36	42	22	36
Shaanxi	38	63	26	11
TOTAL	103	59%	24%	17%
Beijing	16	100%	0%	0%
Shaoxing	34	91	9	0
TOTAL	50	94%	6%	0%

Table 12. "Which Is Smarter, Men or Women?"

Site	No. of respondents	Percent who said men	Percent who said women
Fujian	22	95%	5%
Shandong	14	93	7
Jiangsu	32	86	14
Shaanxi	36	89	11
TOTAL	104	89%	11%
Beijing	10	100%	0%
Shaoxing	31	97	3
TOTAL	41	98%	2%

farmers alike. Instead of concentrating on her schoolwork, her mind flits about, thinking of clothes and, oddly enough, domestic tasks. She no longer seems to put all of her intellectual energy into her schoolwork, whereas boys are just the opposite. They play as young children and then when the work gets harder in middle school they focus their energy on it, ignoring all distractions, and pull far ahead of the girls.

Besides the problems brought on by puberty, girls were also assumed to start out with less intelligence. I asked a teacher in a Beijing key school (those schools from which China's future leaders are to be drawn) whether she thought girls or boys were easier to teach. "Girls pay more attention to their teachers, but boys are smarter. Girls memorize and recite back everything the teachers say to them, but the boys are more creative with what they learn. Girls are better students in primary school, but by the time they get to middle school, they can't compete." Children pick up this kind of gender-defining information very early, and I found it particularly dismaying coming from teachers, even nursery school teachers. I asked a nursery school teacher whom I admired for her warmth and wit in dealing with the children whether she thought men or women were brighter. She laughed at the absurdity of my question and said, "Of course men are smarter. They think faster and are more inventive. In China all the inventors are men." "Do you think they are naturally smarter or just get better educations?" "In my family and in my natal family, by the time the girls have figured out *what* to do, the boys have got it all done."

Farmers may have some doubts about the usefulness of education for themselves and their progeny and may in fact have a very realistic understanding of how few doors it actually opens for them, but they retain the ancient respect for it in the abstract. Urbanites, even after all the anti-intellectual campaigns they have witnessed and/or endured in the last three decades, still see education as the path to a brighter personal future. One might expect, given the fact that education has more relevancy for the urban worker, that educators in the cities would be men, and that in the countryside women who can't do much else would handle the basic educational needs of the young. In fact, the opposite is the case. In the cities, men, as in the West, are more likely to be school administrators, but the classroom teachers in primary schools are usually women, even in the high-status key schools. In the countryside, the vast majority of the classroom teachers are men. In the schools I surveyed in Shandong 20 out of 23 teachers were men, and in Shaanxi only 6 out of a staff of 39 were women. This is not as contradictory as it might at first seem. In the cities the primary grades are women's work in that they are handling children and the things being taught are not complex. In the countryside, the things being taught even in primary school are far removed from the everyday world of the farmer and must be entrusted to men, who are known to be more competent in such affairs. However impractical education may seem to the farmer, it is still serious business and still a high-status, hence male, concern. This makes the lack of role models yet another impediment in the educational careers of girls.

Socialization does not end with childhood, particularly not in the People's Republic where an endless series of programs to re-educate the masses flows out of Beijing. From the outset of the revolution in China, adult socialization or resocialization has been an important implement in the Party's toolbox. Certainly the early campaigns had a critical influence. The initial land reform effort would have failed without effective and unflagging propaganda to support it. The class struggle might never have been resolved to the point of allowing for the next step, successful collectivization, without careful and well-planned educational campaigns. But how much influence did these campaigns have on women? At least once in each field site I tried to replicate the "speaking bitterness" accounts that tourists and scholars alike have been treated to in the last decade in China. I usually picked an articulate woman who was not an official, former official, or relative of an official. Toward the end of my regular series of questions I would begin asking her about various campaigns I had read about or knew to be major affairs, such as the marriage reform campaign of 1953. I was stunned to discover that many of these women had no idea what I was talking about. One otherwise very good informant struggled with my questions about the marriage reform campaign for fifteen minutes and finally said in despair, "I just didn't pay much attention to what was happening then. I was busy . . ." Another equally cooperative woman said, "I was a child then." I pointed out that she was twenty-two and married, and she responded, "Women didn't go out much in those days."

To my dismay, the week after I settled down to interview in one commune, I was invited to attend an award ceremony that was the culmination of a "good daughter-in-law, kind mother-in-law campaign." I was dismayed because this was a topic I would be interviewing about in the weeks ahead, and the natural inclination of my informants to give me "good" answers would be exacerbated by the ready availability of fresh slogans. As it turned out, I had nothing to worry about. None of my informants seemed to see the relevance of my questions about the nature of relations between mothers-in-law and daughters-in-law to the things they had been hearing over the public address system or in meetings. On the day of the award ceremony I was seated on the stage with other dignitaries such as the Party Secretary of the brigade and commune and discovered for once that this was to my advantage: I could observe the audience and their reaction to the lengthy speeches. The hall was festooned with colored banners and posters illustrating the self-sacrificing women —*both* mothers-in-law and daughters-in-law in new China—and the public address system blared martial music. The place was packed with women and children and the din was horrendous. When the first speakers got up to describe what good deeds they had done to merit their awards, the music was turned off, but there was little if any diminution of noise from the audience. Children continued to race up and down the aisles, women chatted amiably with their neighbors, and grandmothers settled comfortably back in their chairs to knit, sort beans, or in some cases doze. Little effort seemed to be made to quiet the audience, although one of the women I recognized as a brigade official made some of the more rambunctious children go outside to play. When the women who had been selected as the most virtuous filed up to receive their awards (tin wash basins with big ceremonial paper flowers attached), there was applause, and when the commune Party Secretary got up to speak there was a considerable drop in the sound level, but by no means did "a hush fall over the room." He concluded his speech with the hearty wish that the spirit and enthusiasm witnessed here might spread to the other brigades as they too took up the campaign to improve family relations. There was no trace of sarcasm in his voice. When I asked later how they got such a big turnout, I was told that attendance was required. I did not pursue the matter, but I felt I had a better understanding of the influence of campaigns on women.

One of the banes of rural life, at least on all the communes I lived on or visited in China, is the public address system that interrupts one's morning sleep, one's afternoon nap, one's peace of mind and good temper. A trumpet sounds for a good five minutes at dawn and is quickly followed by brisk martial music and the shouted commands of a drill instructor who counts out the duration of a wide variety of calisthenics. My hosts seemed unaware of the irony of this routine in a rural village during harvest season, where every man, woman, and child drops into bed every night exhausted with physical labor. On the other hand, I never once saw anyone doing exercises in response to the drillmaster's commands, though I was told that the boarding students in the middle school on my Shaanxi site were expected to do calisthenics at this hour. During the day, the public address system would send forth announcements and notices, such as calling individuals or small groups to meetings, announcing changes in work sites, informing the citizenry of emergencies such as a fire on the drying grounds; it would also give weather and other news (taken from the radio), play music, and broadcast long speeches about whatever the current political issue under study might be. The endings of these speeches, with all the slogans, were sometimes repeated many times over. I certainly never observed groups of people gathered around a loudspeaker taking it all in—though in times of crisis this might indeed be the case—but the system was virtually inescapable and some of the messages must have been absorbed. When I asked a Women's Representative how the family limitation program was presented in the villages, she smiled mischievously, pointed at a loudspeaker, and said, "Da-de, da-de, da-de." Obviously this was not the only way, but it was one that was hard to avoid.

Propaganda in China is about as subtle as a cannon. Little attempt is made to provide realistic situations, common-sense discussions, or simple arguments. Language is flowery, villains are villainous, and heroes are unflawed. Expectations or "targets" are set hopelessly high and results are inflated beyond belief. Nonetheless, information is provided to women as well as men. Some information may be of limited interest to a particular individual, but it is available to all. In the old days, women were truly ignorant, impressed by the mysteries of writing and the exclusively male events that took place in the lineage hall or the distant market town. However inadequate a woman might find her husband, she knew that he had access to information (perhaps esoteric but all the more impressive) that was forbidden to her. This is slowly changing. There is a process of masculine demystification going on in rural China that I do not wish to overemphasize but feel should be recognized. Except for those few men who hold commune-level leadership positions or work outside the collective, there is little information about events or the rules that govern them that women cannot obtain in their own right. Women are not allowed to participate in decision making or occupy most leadership positions, but because the propaganda on the radio says they *can* do these things, they are less impressed by the fact that only men do them. Perhaps these important things of the men's world are not so important after all.

Traditionally, Chinese women have been subversives in a male supremacist society, acquiescing on one level to the superiority of their masters and undermining their power on another level. Rural women have been more competent at living these contradictions than their urban sisters, who were more nearly the victims our stereotypes hold them to be. It is for this reason—the conviction by a fair number of rural women that women are as a class smarter than men—that the findings in Tables 11 and 12 do not seem particularly surprising. In the new society, urban women have been told that they can do anything a man can do, and whether or not they believe it they measure their performances at work against those of men. The propaganda downgrades or ignores their other duties, housework and child care, so that when they fail to meet the standards of male performance, they cannot point to these most essential activities in explanation.* They are simply less capable.

---

*Marilyn Young in commenting on this book in manuscript pointed out that only when the state wishes to retire women from the work force do "good socialist housewife" campaigns demand respect for women's other duties.

For rural women, however, work has not changed as dramatically as it has for urban women, although it certainly has changed. Rural women are expected to do far more than women of previous generations, and as I described in the last chapter, in one of the field sites I visited women had almost completely taken over the agricultural activities of the commune, freeing the men to work in the more lucrative factories. The reader should note that Jiangsu, the site where women farmers predominate, is also the place where women were the most generous in their evaluations of their gender's intelligence. One of the Jiangsu women who insisted that men were not as smart as women explained, "Generally women are smarter, but some men are smart too. Men may be clever with outside affairs, I don't know about that, but they are really dumb about family affairs." This woman's husband lived and worked in Shanghai and came home only once a year. Another Jiangsu woman farmer agreed with the majority that men were smarter, but wanted it on record that women were more capable. "Among farmers, women are more capable. They can do everything—both indoors and outdoors—but men can only do outdoor things. For example, they can't sew or mend the winter clothes. They are very dependent on women. Without women they couldn't live because they couldn't take care of themselves, but women can." Women elsewhere were not as explicit in their statements, but they laughed at the questions I had asked city women in order to elicit information about sharing of housework and volunteered anecdotes about men's incompetencies.

As for sheer intelligence, another rural woman insisted, men were not really that much more intelligent or perhaps even as intelligent as women. Men and women simply worked differently in that men (like schoolboys, the reader may recall) were free to focus all their energy on their work. As a result, they were likely to be leaders, to develop new methods, and to be interested in "scientific farming." Women (like middle school girls) found their energy divided between caring for people, managing the domestic economy, *and* meeting the collective's requirements for their labor. Her generalizations ended there, but it is clear that when conflicts occur between these responsibilities, women give

their family obligations top priority, and those obligations include sideline activities that provide a substantial proportion of
a family's living. Unlike their urban sisters' sense of failure in so
doing, few rural women saw this as anything other than the intelligent response to a difficult situation. As I said before, had it
not been unseemly for them to have said so, I suspect a good
many more rural women would have declared that women were
easily as intelligent as men. Many things in China that cannot
be openly expressed are expressed through the children. It is not
considered proper, for example, for women to wear bright outer
clothing, but they dress their children up in all the colors of the
rainbow. Perhaps it is significant that nearly a quarter of the rural
women insisted that female children were smarter than male
children.

SIX

Cooked Rice:
Marriage in New China

If you let your son choose his own wife, won't you worry that he will bring home someone unsuitable? "If he is happy, that is enough. If I tried to separate them and one of them committed suicide, it would be on my head." Does this happen very often here? "No, not here, but in the next brigade there was a case last month. The man's family came and scolded the girl for stealing their son and so she killed herself. The girl's parents demanded a full bride price to put in her coffin. They had to pay up. If they didn't, her spirit would come back and take the boy or his new wife."
—*Farm woman, age 43*

How do you choose a husband? "People must not be influenced by a person's job level, wages, or status. It is important only that both have the same goals and determination. I know a leader in my neighborhood who married a worker and they are happy. The social status of men and women is equal."
—*Beijing factory worker and Communist Youth League member*

Old people and old ethnographies usually give the same four reasons why people in China marry, reasons that can be applied to rich and poor alike. Before Liberation, marriage ritual in all parts of China was heavy with symbols of fertility. Wherever she looked, a bride was reminded of the reason so much fuss and money had been expended to bring her into her new family. She was expected to carry on the line of her husband's family, something that neither her husband nor the women born to that line could do, albeit for different reasons. Given the serious nature of China's population problem and the serious measures now being taken to deal with it, modern marriage celebrations do not lay much stress on fertility. Nonetheless, when I asked a few women why they thought people wanted to get married, all replied, "In order to have children." There are many reasons why having children is important for women, as we shall see later on, but from the perspective of the families of their husbands, children are still essential in order to carry on the family line. In three of the six places I visited, ancestor worship continued in one form or another, usually surreptitiously, but in one place quite openly. The ideology of the men's family remains strong in China even though the formal manifestation of the men's family's macrostructure, the lineage, is now forbidden.

If the reproduction of the male family was the reason for marriage most stressed in ritual, in the negotiations preceding a marriage the relations being formed between families were most apparent. Wealthy families, both rural and urban, exchanged women to strengthen political alliances, confirm individual friendships, cement business relations, or create new and potentially beneficial relationships. Even the poor and the impoverished needed the help of relatives to survive. The rickshaw puller who lived from day to day could count on at least a day's help from his wife's or his married daughter's relatives should illness keep him off the street. The tenant farmer sought anxiously to marry his daughters to small landholders or (dream of dreams) a local landlord, knowing that this might be the first step out of poverty. Go-betweens, successful ones, knew the fine gradations in the social and economic hierarchies of their areas as well as the tragedies and strokes of luck that moved people up and down them. These alliances remain important in contemporary China. At higher levels of government, daughters are still used as pawns in their father's struggle up the political ladder. The importance of these alliances at the lower levels of society are less obvious, but B. Michael Frolic in his fine book provides some examples and my own interviews are suggestive.[1] An inordinate number of the children of cadres and team leaders that I interviewed or heard about were married to other officials or to men with city registrations.

A farm family's need for labor and a mother-in-law's need for kitchen help are also reasons given for a marriage. In Shandong, families carried this reason to its logical extreme, on occasion marrying mature women to small boys. Everywhere in China, widowers remarried as quickly as they could in order to obtain much-needed domestic help. Mothers-in-law were known to thump prospective wives for their sons as they might cattle to be sure they were firm of flesh and healthy enough to withstand the rigors of farm life. Obviously this was not commonly the reason a wealthy family undertook a marriage (although it might be for a widower with young children), but it was paramount in the minds of some farm families I talked with in modern China. A young bride frees her mother-in-law from collective labor so that she may devote more of her time to sideline activities, and for a few years, until she bears a child, the younger woman will earn the most that a woman can earn in collective labor.

A fourth reason for marriage, often mentioned in Taiwan and alluded to in the rural areas of the People's Republic, is the need to provide for the comfort of one's old age, both with an income and with the care that only a filial child can provide. Prostitutes in Taiwan who feared they might not marry used to adopt daughters to support them when they were no longer able to work. An elderly farm woman in Fujian introduced me to the "grandson" she had adopted for her son (not an easy thing to do in a country where government policy limits the number of children any woman can bear); this woman's son had been born with a twisted body and damaged leg, and though these defects in no way prevented him from earning a satisfactory living for his now elderly parents, they made him an undesirable marriage candidate. (Adoption is at best an unsatisfactory substitute in that the demands of filial piety and Chinese assumptions about human nature assume that a child's true loyalty will always be to the parent who gave her or him birth, no matter how tenderly raised by the adopting parent.)

These are all rather basic and pressing reasons for forming marriages and, except for one fact, it is not surprising that an extraordinarily high number of Chinese marry at least once and some two or three times. Few women remain single. The fact that makes this surprising is that the cost of marriage in China is very heavy. In the past, families spent anywhere from a few months' to a few years' salary on the marriages of their sons and were prepared to make extraordinary sacrifices to assure their succession. To arrange the marriages of one's children was considered a primary parental obligation, as binding as that of a son to support his parents. Some of the strategies developed to fulfill these obligations in the face of grinding poverty and/or an uncertain future were brutal. The price of adopting a female child was nominal and the price of raising one was small compared with the price of obtaining an adult bride, so in many areas of China girl babies were adopted and raised by the mother of their future husbands until they were old enough to be transformed by a simple ceremony from the sister of the son of the family into the wife of the son of the family.[2] Elsewhere, as a hedge against changing circumstances or in the desire to forge an alliance between two families without children of marriageable age, two infants were joined in an engagement. Dealers and even bargain-conscious families sometimes journeyed to areas hit by a natural disaster and literally bought young women or girls as brides for sons.

The well-to-do, the small landlords, or even the workers in a settled and fairly prosperous part of China were not likely to employ these strategies to find a wife for a son. They followed routes more commonly traveled. The family looking for a bride usually had more than one prospect before they were even ready to call in a go-between. The family with an attractive, healthy girl of good reputation might well have go-betweens coming to call before she showed signs of puberty and certainly soon after. The richer the family, the closer the inquiries, and the longer the negotiations. Matching the families, socially, ritually, and economically could be a tricky business, and one in which tricks were often played by unscrupulous go-betweens, sometimes in collusion with unscrupulous parents. The negotiations and rituals leading up to an engagement and eventually a marriage have been described too often for me to repeat them here, other than to say that very rarely were the principals in these matters the young people who would become husband and wife. In traditional China the wishes or hopes of a marriageable man or woman in a wealthy family were given little more consideration than were those of the infants adopted or betrothed in the dusty villages. This is not to say that all parents callously married their children to the highest bidder. On the contrary, some parents fretted for years over the right match, but they would have felt equally lax in their obligations had they left such an important decision up to the children. They believed that they could serve their children's best interests far better than could the children themselves—and they may have been right. Daughters, in particular, had a limited acquaintance with the world outside their courtyards.

But in the calculus of rights and obligations, the younger generations in China were always the first to be sacrificed, sometimes literally, and the last to be served. Few of the strategies mentioned above would have survived had customary law required the agreement of the principals. Arthur Wolf has shown that marriage between girls and their adopted brothers brought misery to both;[3] infant betrothals are infamous as plots for tragic mismatches; the selling or leasing of any human being is oppression of the helpless. It was to these injustices and to the damaged half of humanity that suffered most at their infliction that the CCP directed its first legal statement, the 1950 Marriage Law. In its very first sentence, the "supremacy of man over woman" was abolished along with the "feudal marriage system," and a new system based on free choice, monogamy, and the equal rights of both sexes was established. A minimum age at which marriage could take place was proclaimed (eighteen years for women, twenty for men), and the equal rights of both parties to the possession and management of family property was asserted. The duties of parents to raise and educate children, as well as the duties of children to support and assist parents, were affirmed. In the most dramatic departure from customary law, both women and men were given the right to ask for divorce, and their mutual duties and rights in regard to children and property were laid out. The divorce provision, as we have seen, was a very unpopular section of the Marriage Law and was responsible for the unwillingness of local level cadres to teach it or in some cases enforce it.

The Marriage Law of 1950 in its most radical statement, that men and women have equal rights, goes beyond anything the United States has offered women. The equal property rights and the divorce provisions might also have been, for China, truly revolutionary, but in interpretation and implementation they were hedged at every step. The law did *not* seek to do away with the family, as some observers contend, but it did aim at destroying the authority of the extended, multigeneration unit that might or might not overlap with the domestic family. The basic provision mandating free selection of mates by the young is strong if naïve. It states, "Marriage is based upon the complete willingness of the two parties. Neither party shall use compulsion and no third party is allowed to interfere." This document and these two sentences in particular were apparently expected by their authors to revolutionize the social structure of China. By removing the authority of senior generations to forge and reaffirm ties between powerful groups of male relatives (lineages), the power structure within the communities would not be reproduced.

The 1953 campaign to educate the country about the content of the Marriage Law was the last full-scale effort made by the government to publicize the new rulings together. Since then, although particular items from the Marriage Law have been raised in editorials, study group papers, and the like, no further attempt has been made on the grand scale of a major campaign to publicize it as a package. Obviously, such anxiety-provoking topics as divorce endangered more important arenas of social revolution. Those few who hoped to create an entirely new marriage system felt that they had won a victory in getting the Marriage Law in place and did not comprehend the magnitude of their failure in not establishing marital and domestic concerns as proper revolutionary ground. There were, as Judith Stacey so astutely points out, many policy makers who had a much more conservative agenda in regard to marriage reform, and their goals were achieved almost by default when "personal" issues were deemed secondary to the important jobs of the socialist transformation of the economy.[4] The remainder of this chapter will be devoted to assessing what my data can tell us about the effect of the Marriage Law after some thirty years.

In the original Marriage Law, the minimum ages of eighteen

for women and twenty for men were set in order to bring an end to the marriage of children and to ensure that the principals in a marriage were of an age to make their own decisions. By 1962, when the need for population control was becoming painfully apparent, even later marriages were urged. In the 1970's, these urgings had been formalized into what were called "recommended" ages, varying not only between rural and urban areas but also among regions. When I was in China in 1980–81, in the cities the "recommended" ages were twenty-five for women and twenty-eight for men. The countryside varied a good deal, but the most common recommended age was twenty-three for women and twenty-five for men. The *legal* minimums had been raised in 1980 in the New Marriage Law, to twenty for women and twenty-two for men; I assume that the "recommended" ages were not adopted at that time simply because the government recognized that it could not enforce them in the countryside.

The data I collected from my rather select sample of women showed both urban and rural women marrying on the average within the guidelines during the recent decade (see Table 13). However, data gathered in the Chinese Fertility Survey from one million women (Table 14) do not bear this out on a large scale. Neither urban women nor rural women kept to the government's recommendations, even in the most recent decade. Women in the urban sample were a year short of the government's recommended age, and women in rural areas were nearly two years short. In fact, by 1980 the urban women married on the average just within the recommended ages, but the rural women were still averaging some months younger than the desired age. Looking back again at Table 13, we see that the pattern for men is quite different. Urban men show little change in their age at marriage until the 1960's when they jump to just under the recommended age and in the 1970's to just over it. Rural men, however, show remarkably little difference between the ages at which they marry and the ages at which their fathers' generation married. Their urban counterparts and their female mates show an increase of more than four years over the age at which their parents' generation married. In the most recent decade rural males

Table 13. Average Age at Marriage of Urban and Rural
Women and Men, by Year of Marriage

Location	No. of cases	Year of marriage				
		Before 1939	1940–49	1950–59	1960–69	1970–81
Women						
Urban	100	18.6	20.1	20.6	23.7	25.7
Rural	216	18.2	17.6	19.2	19.6	23.0
Men						
Urban	94	23.7	23.5	23.9	27.8	28.1
Rural	215	22.8	22.8	21.7	22.0	23.8

Table 14. Average Age at Marriage of Urban and Rural Women by Year of
Marriage According to Chinese Fertility Survey

Location	Year of marriage						
	1940–49	1950–59	1960–69	1970–79	1980	1981	1982
Urban	19.2	20.1	22.1	24.0	25.2	24.7	24.9
Rural	18.3	18.8	19.4	21.2	22.5	22.3	22.1

SOURCE: "An Analysis of a National One-per-Thousand-Population Sample Survey in Birth Rate,"
Population and Economics, Special Issue, 1983, pp. 100–101. (In Chinese.)

in my samples are still 1.2 years below the recommended age at
marriage.

For both rural and urban women and men in my small samples
and women in the large Chinese Fertility Survey sample, the major increase in age at marriage occurs in a particular decade, but
the decade is different for the rural and urban samples. Urban
women and men show a dramatic rise of 3.1 and 3.9 years, respectively, in the 1960–69 decade, but rural increases for that
decade are minor. In the following decade, 1970–79, however,
rural women show a 3.4-year increase in their average age at marriage and rural men show their largest increase, 1.8 years.

These data raise two interesting questions. Why was there a
gradual rise in age at marriage for women but not for men over
the long period for which I have data? And why did the sharp
upward jump in age at marriage in the rural areas occur a full
decade later than it did for the urban population? The answers to
both questions rest in the curious amalgam of politics, econom-

ics, and remnants of old tradition that regulate much of life in China. In some areas during the war years and nearly everywhere after Liberation, women's labor acquired economic value. Urban women were bringing home (and handing over to their parents) almost as much income as their younger brothers. In the countryside, women who were unmarried and still at home brought in the highest earnings women could expect in collective agriculture. Parents who were benefiting from a daughter's income were more likely to take note of the minimum and even, in time, the recommended ages for women to marry. Moreover, good economic conditions were in their favor. Impoverished or threatened families sought to marry off their daughters at the earliest possible moment both to save money on their food and to acquire whatever might be offered as a bride price. For men, there is a different dynamic involved. When times are tough, the marriages of men are delayed, sometimes into middle age, because they cannot afford the cost of bringing in a bride, let alone the expense of more mouths to feed. Times have been good since Liberation, and even though there has been political pressure to marry later, men, particularly rural men, have married as early as they or their parents could manage. It is here that traditional marriage negotiations produce an ameliorating effect on political policy. Rural parents may wish to retain their daughters and daughters' earnings in collective labor as long as possible, but they must contend with the groom's side and the marriage market. Prospective in-laws are interested in a girl's earning capacity, and they are also looking for someone who will free the mother-in-law from her collective labor obligations so that she may spend more time on lucrative sideline production. They will put pressure on the parents of their son's fiancée for an early marriage.

In one area where I worked this problem has been resolved by the increased use of an old tradition. Shandong has long been known for its custom of marrying women to men younger than themselves—something that is very much frowned on elsewhere in China. When I began interviewing in Shandong and discovered that women were still marrying men younger than themselves, I made the mistake of casually mentioning this to a local official. I was told curtly that this was no longer a custom in Shandong. Since I had by then learned that Shijiazhuang was a highly politicized place, I made no further comment, but my data indicate quite a different story from what the official would have me believe. Some 37 percent of all the marriages for which I have data on both spouses (57) show that the wives were older than the husbands by at least one year and on the average 2.9 years. Fully 50 percent of the marriages made by the two *youngest* cohorts of women were made with men considerably younger than themselves. Only 26 percent of the women in the older cohorts were married to men younger than themselves. Not surprisingly, in the two youngest cohorts, the average age at marriage for women is a full year higher than it is for men and higher than in most of the other rural samples. By making use of this old custom, parents of sons can marry them as early as they want (or think they can get away with), for they are not asking the parents of their future daughters-in-law to give up any years of their presence (and income).

The sharp upward jump in age at marriage for both sexes in the urban areas in the 1960's that came as a result of increased pressure for late marriage from the state was not matched until a decade later (and then somewhat less dramatically) by a rise in marriage age in the countryside. In cities, permission to marry must be given by one's unit, in writing, but in the countryside it comes from a harried leader of a production team who is often also a relative. In their urban study, Whyte and Parish find a statistical correlation between age at marriage, level of education, and high status jobs, leading them to believe that the latter two variables are at least as important as political pressure in encouraging late marriages.[5] They see young people delaying marriages to complete school and work their way up the college hierarchy. However, very few youths have the opportunity to attend college, so for most their education is over by their eighteenth or nineteenth year; they wait for a year or two before they are placed in a job; they work for another year or two to save money toward marriage. This puts them at about age twenty-three, well below the current average age of marriage for urban males. Women are unlikely to enhance their occupational situations much after this age, married or not. Marriage is more or less irrelevant to men's work world—*unless* by marrying before the appropriate age they indicate to the political leadership of their unit their lack of concern about society's welfare. Those who marry young are not advanced to higher-status jobs, as the Whyte and Parish study indicates; those who don't are.

China's severe urban housing problem is certainly another of the pressures, whether consciously manipulated or not, that delay urban marriages. In Beijing, newly married couples sometimes cannot find housing for a year or more, and some couples register their marriage as soon as they are engaged so that they can enter the housing lists and priority queues for rationed items of household furniture. The young woman who traveled with me through China was thirty years old and had been legally married for two years, but she considered herself single because she and her husband, who was stationed in Tianjin, were still waiting for housing in Beijing, where she was based. The state assumed she could room with relatives, since her husband was not in town, but they wanted a place to be together on weekends. Rural marrying couples, as we shall see in later chapters, are dependent not upon the government for housing but upon their parents. The pressures this brings on them to conform may be no less stringent, but often they are pressures to conform to a rather different set of principles.

Once again, in examining age at marriage, we have found major differences between rural and urban Chinese. They were present in the wage data and again in the data on education. In these earlier chapters the gender differences were so extreme that I concentrated on them, but as we turn now to look at influences on the more intimate matters of one's life, the rural-urban differences are more compelling. They reveal, I think, a complicated competition that is going on not between city and countryside but between the state and the old patriarchal family system. In the cities, the state has more or less usurped the power once held by the patriarch over the young. It is now the state that gives permission to marry, to get pregnant, to travel, to change jobs, to go on for higher education—not the father or the grandfather. But in the countryside, the state has fared less well.[6] The collectivization that was to break the power of the old lineages, or at least to co-opt it, has found itself still deeply embedded in kinship in that sometimes production teams are made up of same surname people who would once have counted themselves as members of the same lineage. This is not true of all production teams, of course, but even where it is not, there is still a strong feeling among country people of loyalty to one's own, and there is still a strong dependence upon one's own. In the countryside, the state does not provide in the same way that the family provides.

The strong divergence between city and country creates problems for the ethnographer as well as for a society struggling toward a socialist transformation. An ethnographer struggling toward a unified picture of China finds herself all too often required to tell two stories. I am again in that position. The homely topic of courtship requires two separate narratives, one for the country and one for the city. Since the urban customs will seem more familiar to most Western readers, I will begin there.

Imposing a law requiring young people to select their own spouses in a society that has always been and remains to a considerable degree sex-segregated creates serious problems for both the young people and their parents. What is considered normal courting behavior in the West is considered licentious in China. Classrooms may be integrated, but out-of-class behavior reverts to boys vs. girls. A young man and young woman observed in solitary conversation on more than one occasion can expect a lot of interest from their friends, and if they are in middle school and persist in choosing each other's company, they may be approached by a class monitor. They should not even be thinking of the opposite sex while in school but concentrating all their energies on preparing themselves to serve their country. The very idea of a high school romance is fraught with images of sexual and political immorality. Although premarital pregnancies are not unknown, most middle school students do seem to displace their sexual drives to their studies. However, once out of school their association with the opposite sex becomes even less frequent. Most of them spend a year or two "waiting for work." Some may be assigned to temporary jobs at the small workshops organized by the Residents' Committee, where the other employees are for the most part middle-aged women too burdened domestically or too unskilled to work in regular factory jobs. The average city young person at this stage has too much time and too little money. Certainly any youth in this liminal period who so much as hinted at getting married would be roundly criticized by all and sundry.

I asked a number of women in both Beijing and Shaoxing whether having a good job would mean finding a better husband. In Beijing they were split, 18 saying yes and 21 saying no. One of the yea-sayers quipped, "Yes. Being pretty helps too." Another told me that having a job was the basic condition for marriage and having a good job got you a better husband. The Shaoxing women nearly all agreed in their answers to this question. Of the fifteen women asked, only one said that having a good job had no influence on the quality of the husband one might find. While commiserating with a thirty-five-year-old woman in Shaoxing who had been shunted aside into a dead-end job in a Residents' Committee workshop, I commented that it would be better if she were sent to a factory and some younger woman assigned to serve time in her all-female shop for a while. She immediately said, "No, that wouldn't be right. They can't marry until they have a permanent job." A Beijing woman employed in a small factory making clocks misunderstood my question and told me, "Young women don't like to work in my factory because the pay is so poor and all the men get low incomes. They all want to meet young men who work in the big heavy-industry factories because the wages are better and they have better benefits." Having a good job not only makes one a more attractive marriage prospect, it also puts one in contact with more attractive marriage prospects.

Meeting young men becomes a serious problem after graduation from middle school. The Western custom of dating does not exist in China. Any woman who went out alone to a movie or for a meal with a series of young men would be considered not merely frivolous but perhaps even something more unsavory. Groups of young people can go on outings together, however, and this is one of the means by which future spouses meet. Joint activities allow semiprivate conversations that may eventually lead to discreet walks in the park.* In factories, study groups sometimes bring young people from different shops together; or there may be informal gatherings of former classmates. Still, as many people told me, the shy or serious-minded young person is going to need help. In fact, nearly every young person of marriageable age will be "introduced" to a series of prospective mates by concerned siblings, parents, friends, neighbors, relatives, and even unit supervisors. Whether it is a human universal or merely a "feudal remnant" of the Chinese belief that everyone should serve as a go-between for at least one marriage in their lifetimes, a young marriageable woman seems to attract a host of friends with brothers, nephews, classmates, or workmates who are "the perfect match."

A mother who was clearly worried about the marital future of her twenty-six-year-old daughter told me:

She is taking her time. She wants one who is both handsome and taller than she is. She is almost as tall as you are [tall for a Chinese], so she has a problem. She keeps rejecting men because they are too short or their noses are too wide or their eyes aren't set right. If his picture looks good and they say he is tall enough, then when she finally meets him she finds something else wrong. It only took me ten days to agree to mine [an arranged marriage], but this one! People keep introducing her to really nice young men and she keeps sending them away. Their jobs don't matter, just the way they look. I'm going to ignore the whole thing from now on and stop worrying about it. If she gets old she can just stay home with me. This girl! I can't be bothered anymore with her pickiness.

Beijing women have learned their political lessons so well that few would admit to arranging the marriages of their children or even influencing them, but it was clear in other contexts that

---

*Recent visitors to China say these "discreet walks" are becoming less and less sedate.

some of them were deeply involved in the matches finally made. In Shaoxing, women were franker about their involvement, with 18 out of 41 saying explicitly that they thought it better if girls received help from their parents in selecting a husband. There was an interesting age difference, however, when I asked the question in a slightly different way. The younger women were more likely to say that friends have the greatest influence on choice of spouse and the older women were more likely to say that the parents have the biggest influence. My guess is that this is a fairly realistic picture of what actually happens in the cities: girls talk among themselves and create images of the perfect husband that reflect their inexperience, and their parents help them to accept compromises with these unreal pictures and veto obviously inappropriate candidates.

Since interfering in the marriage of your children is known in the cities to be "against the law," I was surprised at the number of women who admitted intervening in their children's marriage plans. When I asked women what parents should do if they thought their daughter was about to make a bad marriage choice, 16 percent of the Beijing women and 23 percent of the Shaoxing women admitted that they more or less told their daughters to look for someone else. The story told me by a thirty-six-year-old accountant at a large Beijing nursery school is probably typical of marriages made in the 1970's. She described her husband with distaste as a *shu daidz* (bookworm) who was incompetent at the simplest of household tasks. He was the younger brother of her brother's wife and often visited their family. Both her brother and her mother urged her to accept his proposal, but she didn't like the idea because he was seven years older than she was. She didn't take any of it very seriously because it seemed a long way off, so she eventually stopped saying no.

A woman who was raised in a village about fifty miles from Beijing told me the story of her marriage, which took place in 1962:

My parents arranged my marriage. When I was a baby I was engaged to the son of another village family, but when he grew up he went to college and didn't want a village girl for a wife. A neighbor tried to arrange another match for me, but since I had been engaged already it wasn't a very good one. Besides, my mother was worried because our household had lots of adults and I had never learned to cook. She was afraid that I would really suffer in that family from my husband's wrath. But then some people told them that in the new society people could keep their daughter if they wanted, so they just quit talking about it. Then my mother's father's sister's son introduced someone to my father. I didn't like him because he was too old and he didn't have a job. Neither of us dared to speak out, though, because the go-betweens on both sides were important people. We were engaged and then married one year later.

I asked her how it had worked out. "Even though I didn't like him, the family principle required that I marry him and that we live in harmony."

By tradition, women in China are expected to "marry up" or at least "match doors." If asked directly, the politically savvy, like the sanctimonious young Communist Youth League member in the epigraph to this chapter, now quickly answer that men and women are equal in the new society or "we are all the same now." Once past this ritual, however, it seems that the rules have not changed much. A young woman clerk in a clothing shop in Beijing said, "What would a woman who worked in a bank say to a man who pedaled a three-wheeled delivery cart? Neither of them would want a marriage like that." A woman whose son had just married told me, "Men don't want to marry women who have more education or better jobs than they do. They fear these women will run their lives. They also worry that sooner or later they will meet someone of their own status and then will want to divorce them." A woman cadre, to my surprise, said, "Men don't want to marry women who are better educated than they are. They want women who are *xun fu* [docile and obedient], and they fear these women wouldn't be." Beijing women in general agree, with 68 percent of the 38 asked saying that men are reluctant to marry women who are better educated than they. The Shaoxing women were evenly split on the issue, half of them saying men would be worried about marrying better-educated women and the other half saying it did not matter. (In neither group was the age of the respondent a factor in their answers; young women and older women were equally likely to answer one way as the other.) Sixty-seven percent of my urban women who married before Liberation married men better educated than they, and only 23 percent married men with the same education. Among the women marrying since Liberation, only 44 percent married better-educated men; 41 percent married men with equal education. It is impossible with these data to sort out a change in preference from the simple fact that women are now more likely to be educated. Whatever the reasons, there is now a greater educational homogeneity between husbands and wives.

One of the major ordeals of the bride in traditional Chinese society was separation from her natal home and family. Because women could not marry men with their father's surname, and since in many areas of China all the men in a village or cluster of hamlets belonged to the same lineage and shared a surname, women were usually married into a village of strangers far from family and friends. Even when there were eligible candidates nearer home, there was a strong feeling that it was better if a bride was married far enough away that her natal family would not hear of quarrels in her marital home and that she could not easily run home whenever life became more than she could bear. Interviewing urban women on this topic produced an interesting range of answers. Some chose to talk about the state's role in postmarital living arrangements. The government has been callous about assigning husbands and wives to jobs in different cities and oblivious of the hardships that result when they see each other only once or twice a year. I was told that in recent years more "consideration" has been shown for couples in this predicament, but there were several women in both of my urban samples who had lived apart from their husbands for most of their married lives. A middle school principal told me that she counseled any of her students who came to her for advice against marrying a friend who he or she knew was to be assigned to another city. As she put it, "It is all right until the children are born, but after that it is very hard to raise children by yourself."

Other women responded to questions on the topic of postmarital residence with answers that would make sense to a young woman of pre-Liberation days. A thirty-six-year-old factory worker told me she was glad she and her husband lived on the other side of the city from both their parents because there was less *shi* (literally business, figuratively fuss). Her sentiments were echoed by a good many of the younger women, but some disagreed. "Oh, it is better if you can be near your mother. You get used to seeing your mother every day, and it is hard if you can't see her now and then." But the most interesting and most common answer was the one that gives us some insight into the continuing strength of the kinship tie, if only ideologically. "Marry someone who lives nearby. That way you can help both sets of parents as they get old without wasting a lot of time and money taking the bus back and forth." A Beijing woman told me proudly (and probably erroneously) that her son had chosen a bride in the neighborhood because his workplace was far away and a fiancée who lived nearby could come over and help her with chores. I lacked the nerve to ask where the young couple would live after marriage, but the son's factory is one of the larger ones that provides housing for many of its employees.

I asked my urban informants where they and their fiancés were living at the time of their marriages. These data give some indication as to why the state chose to ban rural-urban migration in the 1950's. Of the 49 couples who married before 1960, in only 47 percent were both husband and wife urbanites. Of the 46 couples who married after 1960, 87 percent were city-born and married city-born men. Of the pre-1960 marriages, 27 percent involved the migration of a rural woman to join a city husband, and in another 18 percent both bride and groom were migrants from the village. Four of these 49 women were city women who met and married rural men who had come to the city at some point. I heard of no urban women among the families of my informants who married into the rural areas. Farm people thought urban women too delicate to withstand the rigors of rural living, hence a bad investment, and urban women viewed rural life as grim, hard work.

In the old days, finding a city husband or a city-bound husband for your daughter was a boon to the entire family because it offered a haven in time of trouble. A woman from Shandong told me that she and her father first came to Beijing in the 1930's after a famine had taken the rest of the family. They would never have tried the long trek had not her father's mother's sister married a Beijing man many years before. She was long dead by the time they arrived, but her children gave them a place to sleep until they found work. As we will see when we turn to an examination of rural marriage patterns, parents of marriageable daughters still sacrifice many of their requirements in a mate in exchange for an urban registration. Youths who were sent down to the countryside during and after the Cultural Revolution were under opposing strains in regard to marriage. No one really knew what the future held for them. Those who believed they would return to the city did not wish to jeopardize that possibility by marrying in the country; village families who thought their daughters might be allowed to accompany a city husband home were tempted to marry them to the youths even though they were miserable providers in a village setting; young urban men's parents disliked the prospect, because they feared their sons' children would carry the registration of their mothers, not their fathers, and might forever be confined to the villages.[7]

When I was living in Beijing in 1980, the high price of marriage was furrowing the brows of many parents. Depending on the speaker, the fault lay with greedy brides, feudal parents, or mercenary grooms. All agreed, however, that the cost of marrying had increased greatly in recent years. In cash outlay, there was little difference between Beijing and Shaoxing, but the heavy political atmosphere of Beijing made people more cautious about how they labeled their expenditures. In both cities I was told that the man's side would have to spend an average of ¥2,000 to marry, and in both cities people admitted to hearing of marriages that cost ¥3,000 and more. One of the expenses for the groom's family in the old days was the bride price, a gift compensating the family of the bride for her rearing. The Marriage Law of 1950 expressly forbade the exaction of money or gifts in connection with marriage. Not surprisingly, Beijing people do not speak openly of bride price as such, or of dowry, but the quantity, quality, and category of gifts were frequently inventoried for me. In Shaoxing, the less sophisticated of the women I talked to spoke freely of the *pingli* (bride price), which averaged at that time around ¥200 but was sometimes as high as ¥400 among the workers and lower level cadres I interviewed. The pingli was not limited to cash; often it included watches, sewing machines, and bicycles.

Dowries consist of certain basic items such as clothing—from the skin out, as one woman explained—and quilts, but among the higher-level government cadres include such elaborate items as televisions, sewing machines, and even refrigerators. Each area seems to have a traditional item that must be brought, no matter how "simple" the rest of the dowry. In Shaoxing that item is a chamber pot disguised in a handsomely painted and/or carved cabinet. Elsewhere a matched set of boxes of prescribed shape and size is essential for a proper dowry; in another place a large pair of ceramic urns continues to be a necessary part of every bride's possessions.

Only one woman in Shaoxing suggested that all of the pingli did not return to the groom's family in the form of dowry; most insisted that the pingli and a good deal more went with the bride. In Beijing these were all described as gifts to the bride, and there was considerable vagueness as to the origin of the gifts ("His family, friends, relatives, who knows?"). The amount spent on the bride's dowry was usually estimated at between a third and a half of what the man's side spent. His side had to provide the furniture for their room, candy in huge quantities for friends and relatives on both sides, gifts to the bride, and finally the feast, which could be a simple family affair of two tables (eight persons per table) or the lavish affair that one woman told me was given for her daughter's wedding: seventeen tables of guests.

Just why marriage has become so costly after so much propaganda effort was put into keeping it down is a question with many answers, depending on whom you ask. One woman told me, "The young people all have jobs nowadays so they just decide together what they need to buy to start their marriage out. Those who demand money are those whose parents have become involved and are doing the negotiating." Another woman, somewhat older, was very disapproving of the high costs of weddings. Her eldest child married a few years ago, and she had not asked for any money at all. "My husband has been putting aside money for the rest of their marriages. I heard of a family who asked for ¥1,000 in pingli for their daughter. They didn't want it all in cash, but they asked for a television, a sewing machine, a bicycle, clothes, and seventy-two legs of furniture. Now how can you fit that much furniture into one room? When I first started to work, people believed in plain living, and even when my daughter got married people still believed in it. It is the Gang of Four. They taught them all to have modern tastes and want things." These are, of course, not at all the values the Gang of Four sought to inculcate, but it is currently acceptable to blame them for all of society's ills. In fact, during the Cultural Revolution no one dared to put on a large-scale wedding. Marriages were most commonly celebrated with a kind of open house, usually at the groom's workplace, where the young people served their friends, relatives, and fellow workers tea, cigarettes, and candy, and the head of the man's unit made a speech full of platitudes about serving the country.

Such modest affairs are now rare in China. Many say they disapprove of the new mode but nonetheless participate in the escalation of costs. A Shaoxing woman expressed her disapproval as well as her understanding of the reasons for extravagant weddings when she told me: "In the country they really have to have these big marriages. Country girls don't have jobs and their wedding is their only chance ever to get some clothes and maybe a watch. They really need to have bride prices and dowries to get them started, but city people don't need all this." Apparently a good many of the young people think they do. Not all, however. Some couples choose to travel rather than to have a big party with lots of gifts. It is also somewhat cheaper. A Beijing bride told me that she and her husband spent ¥700–800 for their wedding, which included a trip, a few pieces of furniture, candy to give to friends as an announcement, and a simple two-table dinner for their relatives. In Shaoxing a wedding-trip marriage was estimated at "under ¥1,000."

I do not have sufficient data to say confidently who pays for weddings, but I suspect the majority of parents feel that it is their responsibility, just as it used to be in the past. But the majority is not all, and a good many women told me of the kind of arrangement one Beijing mother had with her son: "He is getting married at New Year's. It will cost over ¥1,000. I pay for half and my son has saved the other half. They pay for the furniture, clothes, and the party. The girl's family is also giving a party, but that is up to her family to pay for." A forty-nine-year-old doctor who worked in a neighborhood clinic told me how they worked out the costs of marriage in their family:

We have a policy in our family that if the children hand over all their wages to their parents, the parents pay for the marriage, but if the children keep the earnings, they pay for it themselves—with some help from the parents, of course. This son [the second of four] has been saving his money for eight years now. We haven't cared too much for most of the girls introduced to him, but the one he is considering now looks pretty good. My son is a fine cook so he had her over for a special dinner recently. He has been to her house once too, so it is getting serious. My third son has just returned from the country and has only been working for a year, so we will have to contribute a larger share to his marriage. Naturally this depends on what the girl's situation is. If she is also poor or believes in plain living, they may have a simple wedding. I think the first year people start to work they should buy clothes and enjoy their incomes, but after that they must begin to save for their marriages.

Whoever pays, the cost is high. The average yearly wage for an urban male worker is less than ¥700. A family must spend one to two years' salary to get a wife for a son, and nearly a year's salary just to marry out a daughter, although the cost of the girl's marriage is offset by gifts from the man's side. A young urban worker without parents or with many brothers will not necessarily go unmarried because of his poverty as he might have done in the old days, but he will have to marry late, and he may have to make do with a not so desirable bride, unless he can find a woman in similar circumstances or one whose political consciousness is at a level that rejects the new marriage styles. When I asked a Beijing Residents' Committee member what happened to young men who had no money, she snapped, "Less money, less wedding," but I doubt that it is quite so simple. In the rural areas, farmers borrow against their next few years' income to pay for a child's marriage, and I suspect they do that in the cities too. Whyte and Parish, speaking of weddings that took place before 1978, suggest that "except for marriage age most aspects of the marriage process apparently have not changed markedly since the late 1950's, even though government pressure for more spartan and revolutionary weddings heightened considerably during the Cultural Revolution decade."[8] Clearly, weddings in recent years are different. State pressure for modest weddings is now barely expressed, and the consumer prosperity accompanying the new economic policies is being displayed in grander weddings with rented finery and decorated cars.

One of the sources of the traditional family's power over its junior generations lay in its control over family income and marriage. A young man could not marry without his father's approval and support, but he was not an adult until he did. The potential for gain tempted many a father to marry off a daughter to the less desirable but higher-bidding candidate. It was to these injustices that the Marriage Law was directed. But though the law says specifically that money must not be a factor in forming a marriage, it still is a factor, and a major one at that. One often hears now, as in times past, sad little stories of potential mates who turn away because they cannot afford the gifts leading up to marriage. (One also hears mothers full of anger over the amount of money a son must spend in courting activities.) Is this new extravagance (by revolutionary standards) maintaining dependency in the younger generation and hence perpetuating the patriarchal power structure? There are those who say that the opposite is true, that owing to the excesses of the Cultural Revolution the young have turned their backs on the older generation, steal from them, and refuse to assume responsibility for them in old age. This, too, may be true in some cases, but in the main, kinship obligations, at least among primary kin, continue to be important in the urban family. Though kin loyalties must now compete with loyalty to the state, they have not been destroyed. Martin King Whyte suggests that one of the factors responsible for increasingly elaborate marriages may in fact be parental concern for their children's futures. As the millions of rusticated youths return to the cities, poorly educated, jobless, and entering the marriage market at a late age, parents may be trying to improve their chances—or compensate for their handicaps—with major gifts and costly wedding parties.[9]

The question remains, then, has the Marriage Law of 1950 achieved its purpose in the cities? I would say yes, guardedly. The old authority structure within the urban family is a thing of the past. Young people play an active part in arranging their marriages however stiff and formal their behavior may look to foreigners. Courtship as we know it—dating, intimate talks, expressions of affection—does not take place until after a couple have formally promised to marry, and even in the cities this kind of interaction is still considered a preparation for marriage, not a means of discovering whether or not two people are compatible.[10] Parents may be heavy-handed at times in attempting to impose their will on their marriageable children, and it is clear that there are still many marriages of the arranged type being made in the very heart of Beijing; but the consequences of a son or daughter seeking help from her or his, or worse yet the offending parent's, workplace have been observed often enough to keep the most oppressive practices of the past under control.

Nonetheless, patriarchy is not only a domestic ideology but a social ideology as well. It may have weakened its grip over the urban family, but it still permeates the society within which that family is imbedded, and it continues to dominate the countryside.[11] The rural family is not a barefooted replica of the urban family. Marrying a son in the countryside is a family affair with full involvement of the senior members of the family. Resistance to marriage and family reform has been strongest and most successful in the rural areas. The extent of that resistance was made apparent to the central government in 1953 when it attempted further implementation with massive rural campaigns. In many areas the very cadres who were expected to enforce them instead deflected ther impact. Young people and women who heard of the law and sought relief under it found themselves being harassed and criticized by the officials in charge of its enforcement. Women who heard radio broadcasts or came into contact with traveling Marriage Law exhibits discovered that they might apply for divorce and be free of a cruel husband only to find that the official to whom they must first apply was a local cadre and as such either a relative or friend of several generations to their husbands' families. The mechanisms for getting around such a roadblock were usually too complex for illiterate, inexperienced women who often had not left their husbands' villages since the day they were delivered there in the bridal chair. Those stalwarts who tried created a threat to the local political system by suggesting that it was not fulfilling its duties properly. Newspapers of the 1950's and early 1960's record tragedy after tragedy—young women beaten or tortured by their husbands' families for "loose behavior," women who found life so much worse after they tried to exercise their new rights that they chose suicide, women who were murdered by local ruffians as punishment and, quite obviously, as a warning to others.

Today if you raise the topic of divorce or forced marriage, you are told proudly that these things no longer happen because people choose their own spouses. Somehow this magic nod of yes or no—and it may amount to no more than that—transforms the old tradition of living peacefully with a man you loathe into a new principle of stable socialist partnership. Except for the urban elite, divorces are still hard to get in China, and nearly impossible in the countryside. I heard of only three in the families of the three hundred women I interviewed. I think, however, that there are a good many de facto divorces concealed behind the long-term separations that began as job assignments in different cities. In many cases, transfers had never been requested. I am almost positive from hints dropped that two women I talked with in different communes knew that their husbands, working in far-off cities, had formed second families there.

Every commune I interviewed in was careful to provide among my informants two people, one a woman who had defied her parents and rocked the community by insisting on marrying the man of her choice and the other a younger woman who had just married in a modern style. In no case were the preliminaries to these marriages as free as those in the urban areas, but that is hardly surprising in view of the social constraints in the rural areas. Indeed, it is only surprising that they occur at all. For example, all model collectives and probably others too have halls where people gather of an evening for study groups, planning meetings, Ping-Pong, and simple recreation of one sort or another. I asked repeatedly how often women, married or unmarried, went to these places and was assured that they went there to attend meetings, to turn in their daily workpoint reports, and so on, but I got a lot of hedging when I asked if they went there to "play"—that innocent-sounding word that in Chinese covers everything from visits among friends to sexual intercourse. Men said their wives were too busy in the evenings; mothers said their daughters' friends came to visit them at their homes. It was pretty clear that hanging around the team or brigade recreation room was not something women did too much.

I didn't realize how strong that restriction was until my thirty-year-old Beijing assistant told me of her experience in the recreation room of the brigade I studied in Shandong. She is an excellent Ping-Pong player and one evening she heard the familiar sound and traced it down, looking for some competition. She spent the evening beating, according to her report, every player in the room, and did some observing and interviewing as well. This, remember, was the brigade that was so "model" that it looked like a Hollywood stage set. Her fellow players told her that she was the first woman who had ever ventured into the Ping-Pong room. As far as the young farmers knew, women couldn't play Ping-Pong. I imagine after their experience with Comrade Zhao they intended to keep it that way. But that is not the end of the story. A few days later the (acting) senior Beijing cadre, also a woman, asked me if I had sent Zhao on this expedition. I said I had not. She said that it was considered unseemly behavior on her part and that she should not be walking about a village late at night alone or playing Ping-Pong with only members of the opposite sex at any time of the day or night. The cadre, a kindly woman, was merely passing on to me the complaints of local leaders, but it was clear from her manner that she too regarded Zhao's behavior as imprudent.

How, then, given this segregated social environment, do young people meet potential mates? A few meet them in work groups, but in many areas the senior generation still does not approve of mixed work groups. A few others marry classmates. But most are "introduced": that is, someone suggests a likely candidate to their parents, who decide on the suitability, make inquiries, and if it sounds reasonable, tell their daughters or sons about the prospect. The young people meet once or twice and signal their acceptance, and then the parents begin the complex negotiations over bride price, dowry, party costs, and so forth. That is the general outline. The details require as many qualifications as there are interviews, and even the general outline varies from province to province. The old saying in China that marriage customs change every ten *li* (three miles) remains true in the PRC. In order to spare the readers more than they may wish to know about some of these things and still give some sense of the variation, I will use my fieldwork in Shaanxi, in many ways the most socially conservative of the brigades I worked in, as the basis of discussion and show how the other areas differ from it.*

Fenghuo Brigade was originally three hamlets. When Old Village was undercut by the flooding Wei River, New Village was formed. Half a dozen families also lived on the other side of the river in what is now known as Great Leap Village. The men in all three hamlets were surnamed Wang and all worshipped in the same Wang lineage hall in Old Village. When I discovered a few women who also bore the surname Wang, I assumed that they had married within their father's lineage. Such was not the case. All came from families of unrelated Wangs in other villages. Not one of the women of any age in my Fenghuo sample was born in the brigade into which she married. This is staunch conservatism. In pre-Liberation days lineage exogamy served to ensure peace within the kinship group by avoiding even the possibility

---

*By way of a reminder: even though I frequently speak of my Shandong informants or the price of a dowry in Jiangsu, I use these provincial names as shorthand and do not mean to imply that my data are representative of the province in question.

of acrimonious in-law relations that might rupture the group's unity. Whether or not brigade exogamy continues for the same reason is hard to determine since in Fenghuo the brigade happens to be coterminous with the old lineage. The more interesting point here is that brigade exogamy would make it impossible for young people to marry the people they are most likely to know and choose for themselves.

The data in Table 15 suggest that there is a strong tendency toward brigade exogamy, but that in the most recently marrying cohort that tendency has weakened to the point that 23 percent of the women were born in the brigade in which they married. There are, it appears, some relatively minor changes in the number of women marrying within the commune and a decrease in the number of women marrying in from outside the commune. Parish and Whyte in their study of Guangdong emigrés also find that 23 percent of their most recently married women married into the same village. Another 42 percent of their sample married within the same commune but in a different village—a finding that also compares well with my 43 percent within the same commune. I found 34 percent of my sample marrying outside the commune of their birth; the Parish and Whyte study shows 35 percent marrying outside. The Guangdong study does, however, show a considerably lower rate of exogamous marriages in the pre-Liberation and early Liberation cohorts than my samples, and it therefore suggests a more decided trend toward geographically closer marriages than does mine.[12]

In sum, though the pattern is not entirely clear, there appears to be a recent tendency for rural marriages to be made closer to home. This pattern would have been frowned upon in pre-Liberation days, when young people were not supposed to know each other before marriage and in-laws were supposed to be kept decorously separated. I asked 45 women in Jiangsu and Shandong whether they thought it was better for women to marry nearby or farther away and only 10 of them said far was better. The pros and cons of the issue (discussed in later chapters) provide some interesting information about kin relations. One woman said her daughter married nearby and then had twins and now she wants

Table 15. Natal Residence of Marriage Partners in
Rural Field Sites, by Year of Marriage

Year of marriage	No. of marriages	Partner's natal residence		
		Same brigade	Same commune	Outside commune
Before 1970	160	16%	44%	41%
1970–81	53	23%	43%	34%

her to take care of them when she goes to work. She had enough to do with her son's children. A younger woman, clearly smarting from a recent spat, said it was better to live far from your natal family. "When you do get home, they really like you, and even your brother and sister-in-law welcome you." A mother-in-law of the old school voiced the opinion of several informants when she said, "If her family is nearby they will hear about every quarrel and come over to talk about it. That is trouble." But most women wanted their own daughters (or mothers) close by. "My mother is so close I can just go see her during breaks in work or else stop by on the way home. That is good. Some people have to lose a half-day's work and spend money on the bus." Another woman in her late thirties said, "They live fairly close so I can help them out with things they can't do for themselves." The most analytic of my informants laughed at my question and said, "If we are talking about my daughter, I want her close; if we are talking about my daughter-in-law, I want her from far enough away that her parents don't get involved every time I say a sharp word to her."

One of the advantages, I was told, of marrying your sons or daughters to partners who live nearby is that you can learn more about them before you make the final commitment of engagement. When I asked young women what things they looked for in a husband, their answers revealed their inexperience. Many of them seemed to focus on such superficial things as physical appearance, not necessarily requiring beauty but an "honest face," which to them meant an honest heart. Young men seemed to be even less prepared to make such a life-shaping decision. One woman told me, "Well, the girl was introduced to me but I let him [her son] make the choice. I sent him to take a look at her and when he came back he said, 'Chabuduo' [more or less]. I told him he had to decide, I wouldn't. So he said OK and that was that." A grandmother in Fujian spat with disgust and answered my question, "The boys don't care what kind of a job the girls have as long as they are pretty. Even if she works on the pig farm, they don't care." Fair skin and delicate features were the specific attributes desired, a long way from the poster girls of the Cultural Revolution who were sturdy sun-darkened types with their eyes always focused on the horizon. The girls, too, mentioned appearance, but they, or at least their parents for them, mentioned things like educational level, family conditions, temperament, and job. Family conditions means, I was told, how many brothers are in the family, whether they are married and will continue to live together, how old the parents are, what their economic future seems to hold. Having a skill, as we saw in Chapter 4, makes a big difference in income, but the biggest difference is in having an urban registration. This was not always mentioned, but if I raised it no one ever disagreed. For all but a very few it is a hopeless aspiration.

Given the difficulties of meeting and becoming acquainted with potential spouses, I wondered if people would admit that they had problems in fulfilling the requirements of the Marriage Law of 1950. I asked the straightforward question in two rural sites before giving it up: "Is it better for a girl to find her own husband or should she get help from her parents?" Of the 36 women in Fujian who answered, 75 percent said it was better for a girl to find her own spouse; Jiangsu, interestingly, was fairly evenly split, with 58 percent of the 40 answering saying self and 42 percent indicating a need for parental involvement. I gave up asking the question in other sites because it appeared to be no more than another measure of how quick the informant was at coming up with a politically correct answer. Using a potpourri of responses to different questions and volunteered comments, I was able to classify the marriages of a good many of my informants and their relatives in terms of who made the final decision about their marriage partners—their parents, themselves, or a combination of parental and personal participation. This index provides a fairly concrete evaluation of the success of the Marriage Law among this sample of women.

The data in Table 16 are subjective in that often the informants would say in response to one question that they chose their own husbands and to another that they met them once before they were engaged, in a formal situation after which they agreed to the engagement. I interpreted those to be marriages arranged by the parents. When they said that the parents had arranged an introduction (or a series of them) and the young people had met several times in situations of increasing privacy before they agreed to the match, I took that (if there was no information to the contrary) as constituting a marriage decided by the principals.

Fenghuo in Shaanxi is clearly the most conservative of the four sites. Of the 47 marriages for which I have information, not one was formed on the initiative of the young people themselves, nor, as Table 16 shows, was a single marriage decided jointly by parents and children. Eleven of these marriages had been made within the past nine years. No marriages in the Shaanxi brigade were between members of the brigade, but 83 percent of the women in the youngest cohort had married in from villages less than ten li away. The finding is curious because all the children within that radius were eligible to attend the primary school and the middle school located in the caves above Fenghuo Brigade, which meant that many of the young people in the area were classmates and had some basis for getting together after school days were over. The fact that these acquaintanceships did not produce a single self-arranged marriage among my informants says something about the independence of Shaanxi's youths.

Among the other three collectives studied, the findings are less startling. For both the youngest and the next-to-youngest cohorts, just under half of the marriages were decided by parents, with around a third said to be the decision of the couple themselves. When one compares these figures with the first cohort to marry during the decade after Liberation (age 40–49) when the Marriage Law campaign was under way, the results are almost

Table 16. "Who Chose Your Husband?"

Age of respondent in 1981	No. of respondents	Chooser of husband		
		Self	Parents	Both
20–29				
Fujian	10	30%	70%	0%
Jiangsu	19	32	53	16
Shandong	20	35	30	35
Shaanxi	11	0	100	0
TOTAL	60	27%	55%	17%
30–39				
Fujian	4	50%	50%	0%
Jiangsu	16	31	69	0
Shandong	13	38	23	38
Shaanxi	15	0	100	0
TOTAL	48	26%	65%	10%
40–49				
Fujian	5	20%	80%	0%
Jiangsu	7	43	43	14
Shandong	8	38	50	13
Shaanxi	9	0	100	0
TOTAL	29	25%	68%	7%
50–59				
Fujian	5	0%	100%	0%
Jiangsu	5	20	80	0
Shandong	3	0	100	0
Shaanxi	7	0	100	0
TOTAL	20	5%	95%	0%
60+				
Fujian	6	33%	67%	0%
Jiangsu	5	0	100	0
Shandong	5	0	100	0
Shaanxi	5	0	100	0
TOTAL	21	9%	90%	0%

NOTE: These data are reported in terms of the age of the women in 1981 because they include data about the children of my informants. Although I knew their birthdates, I did not always know the year they married.

identical: 35 percent decided by the young people, 55 percent by the parents. Shaanxi, as indicated, showed no change at all among my sample of women. If these data are the accurate indicators I think they are, it would appear that for half the women in China, the Marriage Law has not had much effect; for another

10 to 20 percent it has given them a say in their futures; and for only a third has it given freedom of choice about whom they will spend the rest of their lives with. This lack of change over time is a very discouraging finding. Again and again in China I was reminded by cadres that women were coming from a position of great backwardness, illiteracy, and social deprivation. I was assured that every year they made great strides. Autonomy in choice of marriage partners does not seem to be one of those strides.

There are good things to be said for arranged marriages. (Nobody calls them arranged marriages anymore because arranged marriages are illegal, but the circumlocution is too tedious to use here.) A twenty-eight-year-old woman whose marriage had been arranged by her father said, "It really is better for parents to help with this. They have more experience with people and can tell whether a man is good or bad." A mother in Shandong who had recently married off the last of her children and was overjoyed to be rid of that burden said, "Generally girls obey their parents when it comes to marriage. A few bad girls insist on having their own way, but not the well-behaved girls." But a mother in Fujian made an observation I heard fairly frequently: "Oh, I would rather have them find their own mates. If it doesn't work out then they can't come back and blame me." Another Fujian mother whose oldest son was reaching marriageable age answered my first questions with the usual formula that children should find their own spouses, but when I asked if her son would live with her after he married she said he would. "But what if he goes out and finds someone who will be difficult for you to live with? Shouldn't you have some say in it?" I asked. She responded without hesitation, "Of course. I don't even consider girls I know are hard to get along with." When one considers how painfully shy most young women and men are and how little opportunity they have to discover the qualities and defects of potential mates, the statistics in Table 16 may imply less oppression than our ethnocentric view of human relations at first suggests.

In the villages of northern Taiwan, it seemed to me that one of the harshest of the many cruelties visited upon women was that of taking young women so timid they can hardly *talk* to strangers and marrying them to total strangers. Many of the young brides I knew in Taiwan spent the first few weeks of their married life in ashen-faced shock. Naturally I wanted to know to what extent this ordeal, even with the high incidence of arranged marriages, was avoided in the new society. This was not always easy to do with my limited opportunities for observation and casual conversation, but I believe that strangers are less likely to be wed now than in the old days, and I have a few statistics to support this. Again, starting with Shaanxi, our most extreme case, there was only one woman among the 43 for whom I have information who had actually met her husband before they were engaged. However, 10 of these 43 women said that between their engagements and marriage they saw their intendeds fairly often or at least a few times. In Jiangsu, 25 of the 31 women under the age of forty knew their husbands before they married them, but of these 25, 6 met them only after they were irrevocably engaged. In Shandong there was only one woman under the age of forty who had not met her husband before her wedding day, but only 10 out of the 33 for whom I have full information met their husbands before they were committed to marry them. My Fujian data are less complete, but it may be indicative that the daughter of a high level cadre in the brigade was married the year before our visit to a man she had not met until the day of the wedding.

In general, marriage practices today do seem more humane than in the past, though not quite as free as the government reports have led us to believe. The period between engagement and marriage can extend anywhere from a month to several years. In rural society, an engagement is as binding as a marriage, but the time between the two events is now used in many cases for getting to know each other, for the kind of interaction the average American teenager thinks of as dating. I heard gossip in Beijing about young women who fell in and out of engagements like American girls going steady, but such behavior in the countryside is inconceivable. It is inconceivable because even though a third of the young said they had chosen their own spouses, once that decision was made their concerns were no longer central. Indeed, that decision might have to be set aside if the go-between and the two families could not reach an agreement in the negotiations over bride price and dowry. I was told of a few strong-minded young people who insisted on simple weddings without the gifts and feasts that mark the formation of a new couple, but they were always brought up with such excitement that it was clear that they were most unusual.

I do not mean to imply that rural young people take no interest in the economic negotiations that go on prior to their marriages. As the woman quoted on page 160 said, for a country girl this may be the only time in her life that she will have new clothes and such fine things as a watch or a bicycle. Of course she is concerned and interested. Her fiancé is interested for the same reasons, but also because he knows that the costs are straining his family's domestic budget to its outer limits. To make a "good" marriage one must spend a lot of money. For a woman the quality of her marriage still defines the quality of her adult life. A young man whose family tries to skimp on gifts or suggests a token feast will find himself looking far for a bride or settling for one with defects. During the Cultural Revolution and the interregnum period that followed, the cadres were in painful conflict with regard to their children and their political status. As village leaders they were expected to marry off their children in fine style; as political leaders they were expected to set an example by practicing simple living and abstaining from feudal displays. The compromises they reached were often very human, with dowries being delivered at night, bride prices paid surreptitiously, and feasts held indoors and in relays. For thoughtful young people, the conflict is undoubtedly greater, because they know that the high cost of marriage increases their dependence on their parents. A young urban worker can shrug and say, "Less money, less wedding," and if he has found a girl who wants him for himself and the future they might build, they can marry (assuming that the state has no objection). A young farmer cannot possibly provide himself with housing, let alone the furniture to put into it, because his earnings are not separate from those of his parents and siblings. And though a young woman might come without a dowry or finery, she is not likely to be very welcome in the house of her mother-in-law. She will be by definition a troublemaker.

Are the costs as great in the countryside as in the city? Turning again to Fenghuo, our most extreme case on other issues, the range for marrying a son is between ¥300 and ¥1,000, for a daughter considerably less—from ¥100 to ¥300. Both are well below the urban figures given me. In our Shaanxi site there were two gift presentations before marriage, one at the time of the engagement and another in the months just before the marriage. Since engagements are still much earlier in Fenghuo than in any of the other sites studied, the family has a little recovery time. Some of the young women did not even know when they were engaged, let alone how much was given to their parents. This first gift, the *caili*, is a conventional sum: a base amount of ¥120, which may be multiplied by two or by three, depending on the negotiations. Anything under ¥240 is sniffed at in this day of prosperity. The caili binds the engagement and must be returned if the bride dies or backs out, but otherwise it is the property of the bride's family. In the months just before the wedding another gift is given to the bride's family which may include clothing or lengths of cloth, jewelry in the old days, and a highly variable amount of money. The determining factor now seems to be whether the groom's family intends to provide all the furniture or only part of it. This second gift of money, *houchengli*, is earmarked for the bride to use for her dowry, and it is considered very bad form for her family to pocket it. There is a pithy saying that translates loosely, "All the mother-in-law's money comes back to her." The groom's family is also expected to provide housing for the new couple, usually in the form of a freshly papered and/or plastered room, accompanied in some brigades by a promise to help build a separate house for the young couple at some later date—unless the son is the youngest and therefore expected to care for the aging parents and inherit their house. The furniture is usually considered the responsibility of the groom's side, but a few items may come in the dowry. And often the most expensive single item is the wedding feast, which may include as many as twenty tables of guests.

Several Fenghuo informants said that if you subtracted the price of the feast and the cost of preparing a room for the young couple, the woman's family had to spend as much or more as the man's on preparing her dowry. I doubt that it is more, but the costs are not negligible. The basic items are a minimum of two but often four or five of the big puffy quilts seen neatly rolled on the kang of every household, kang mats, sheetlike covers for the quilts and for warmer weather, fancy door curtains, boxes in which all these things are stored, and the local essential dowry item, lamps symbolizing longevity. The things people look for to evaluate the quality of a dowry are such items as a sewing machine, watches, clocks, mirrors, a radio, thermoses (several), and a bicycle—the real sign of a big dowry.

To return to the question of whether wedding costs are as high in the countryside as in the city, it would appear that in the Shaanxi site they exceed those in Beijing and Shaoxing, but not by a great deal. However, in Fenghuo a man's average yearly earnings from collective labor are ¥420, so it takes somewhat more than two years' income for the highest figure mentioned on the men's side and something less than a year's income for the highest figure mentioned on the women's side, some of which would be offset by the houchengli. Without the help of family, neither a man nor a woman in Fenghuo could hope to marry in this way.

In Fujian the current bride price tended to be cheaper, ranging from ¥40 to ¥120, but the gifts were more elaborate. A second round of gift giving on the day of the wedding did not include money but did require big outlays for mooncakes and candy to announce the marriage to the bride's relatives and friends, pieces of pork, lengths of cloth, watches, and so on. Ten to twenty tables of guests at about ¥25 per table added another ¥250 to ¥500 to the cost. Excluding housing costs, ¥1,000 was considered average and ¥2,000 fancy. Dowries were equally large and costly. Though they were said to average between ¥200 and ¥500, some families were certainly spending more. Eldest children apparently can expect even more elaborate weddings in the country.

I was invited to view the dowry of a young woman who had married a few days before my arrival in Fujian. The display was overwhelming. There were 110 pieces of gift cloth hung on wires strung around the room, a huge new transistor radio was blaring, mirrors, clocks, and thermoses (I counted six of them) were displayed on the ancestral altar, and the kang was so covered with comforters that it was hard to seat people on it. Above the altar was a list of donors and what they gave. The bride was careful to tell me that fifty of the lengths of cloth were gifts, but sixty came in her dowry, of which about one-fourth were bought with the bride price, the latter separately arranged in one of the chests that are part of the traditional dowry. All the women in the household had pretty red hair ornaments—gifts from the bride— and the house was sprinkled with tiny metal disks symbolizing harmony. (The bride on this her sixth day looked exhausted and pasty-faced.) This was an impressive—even reckless—display in a part of China where the average yearly wage from collective labor for a farmer is only ¥276. A ¥2,000 wedding in Fujian was the equivalent of more than seven years' labor for a male farmer. One should remember, however, that Fujian had the second-highest income from sideline activities of my sites, averaging ¥638 per family. I suspect that a family with several marriages in its near future raises more pigs and expends more effort on all its sideline activities than others. The fact that women are responsible for these activities lays a heavier burden on their shoulders but at the same time increases the debt of gratitude borne by their sons or daughters, a topic we will explore further in a later chapter.

In my Jiangsu site, where the average yearly wage of a farmer was somewhat higher, ¥327, the costs of marrying a son were said to range from ¥2,000 to ¥3,000 and of a daughter from ¥300 to ¥1,000—very close to those we were given in the cities though income was not nearly as high. It would take from six to nine years of collective labor to pay for these weddings. The bride price would take from one to three years of collective labor. As in

Fujian, several women commented that the cost of weddings was going up each year and had doubled in the last decade.

Knowing the political climate of Shandong, I was doubtful at first that I would get any information at all on this touchy subject. Traditionally, there was no bride price in Shijiazhuang, so I was surprised to turn up a twenty-six-year-old woman who told me that her family received ¥60 when she became engaged and that she was given ¥300 by her husband's family a few months before the wedding "to buy whatever I wanted." The general estimates ranged from ¥500 to ¥600 to marry a son and from ¥100 to ¥300 to marry a daughter. Men's families are expected to provide housing and the feast; women's dowries include clothes, quilts, wardrobes, and a set of five chests. One of the fancier weddings I heard of had ten tables of guests, at ¥20 per table. All in all, Shandong weddings were the cheapest, staying near or under a year's income for a man from collective labor. Since this was so obviously a desirable place to marry into, it may well have been that the expenses given me were accurate, that it was not necessary for this brigade to compete in an increasingly expensive marriage market. They could maintain a more modest set of marriage practices (albeit considerably more than the tea-and-speeches marriages of the Cultural Revolution) without losing out in the quest for superior brides.

Parish and Whyte in their study of emigrés from Guangdong Province found that dowry had nearly disappeared, but bride price as well as other wedding expenses for the man's family had increased. They also had some estimates of women's involvement in collective labor that are very different from those I have presented in Chapter 4: "Though we have no precise estimates of the extent of women's participation in farm work in our data, our impression agrees with that just cited. In our villages virtually all women below the age of forty-five work regularly in the fields, and may contribute up to 40 percent or so of the total labor effort in agriculture."[13] My interviews in Fujian, the province closest to Guangdong, and elsewhere show a very different pattern. This difference may be due to cultural divergencies or to policy changes that have occurred since Parish and Whyte's informants left the

PRC, but it was clear to me that many, many women dropped out of the collective labor force at the first opportunity and others worked only during the busy seasons of planting and harvest.

Parish and Whyte go on to sum up their argument:

> We argue, then, that in Kwangtung as elsewhere women are now producing a larger share of agricultural work than they used to. Since family income now depends overwhelmingly not on landholdings but on the number of laborers and their level of earnings, women's labor should be more important to the family economy than formerly. Insofar as bride price payments represent, in part, the acquiring of rights to the fruit of a woman's labor, those rights should also be more valuable today. In short, we argue that bride prices remain substantial because the rights whose transfer they bring about continue to be important, and probably have even gained in value. A woman's parents now depend heavily on her earnings, and will not want to part with her without substantial compensation. A man's family, on the other hand, may be willing to pay such sums without seeking a commensurate dowry in return, since they know that a new bride's earnings will, over time, more than compensate them for their initial expenditure.[14]

Again, my informants disagree. In the four areas in which I interviewed, bride price and dowry are both present and, according to the complaints I heard, have increased at an equal rate. I have no doubts about the uses to which the bride price was put: it was plowed back into the dowry, and parents claimed much more was added besides. The only exception would be those areas that had double payments, such as Shaanxi. The gift given at engagement, which often occurred when the girls were quite young, did not necessarily show up in the dowry, but the second gift given just before marriage most certainly did.

I do not mean to suggest that Chinese women have not increased their participation in the rural labor force markedly since Liberation. I think the evidence is clear that they have. But I have no evidence that this increased "value" for women has been expressed in bride prices. What would be needed to test Parish and Whyte's hypothesis is a ratio of the value of dowries to bride prices for contemporary marriages and a similar set of figures for pre-Liberation marriages. My own data are not as precise as they might be, but the pre-Liberation data are even less satisfactory.

The only data of any substance are those collected by John Lossing Buck in the 1930's, and they do not isolate the measure we need. Buck's data give a figure for dowry, but the figures used for the other side are "marriage costs," which include bride price but are not confined to that.[15] Since my informants said that the other costs of marriage, such as feasts and gifts to the bride herself, have risen most sharply, we could hardly use "marriage costs" as an indication of money given by the groom's family to compensate the bride's family, or a comparison of the ratios as an indication of the changing value of women.

Why do these extravagantly expensive marriages persist? There are a number of reasons, but in the countryside they all come back to one fundamental truth. Marriages are a celebration and a reaffirmation of the continuation of the family, and in rural China the family remains the canvas on which all else is painted. It was this reality that the proponents of the Marriage Law ran up against in 1953, and it is this reality that causes the resurgence of elaborate marriage festivities whenever prosperity and politics will allow. For the senior generations in a family, a properly managed wedding demonstrates that they have fulfilled their most important duty to their children, that of arranging their marriages; it also allows them to demonstrate to the community as a whole their ability to spend lavishly. The young people are not likely to object, for, as the city informant said, this is the only time they will have new clothes and a watch. They may be aware that they are still being exploited by the senior generations and they may see this as an opportunity to take some of their share out of the family budget to which they have thus far only contributed. Certainly for a young woman, it is her last chance to have access to the proceeds of her labor in her natal family.

There was a time when all young people, urban and rural, depended upon their parents and grandparents for their living, their marriages, and their status. Many a reformer expected that a time would come when the young people would find their own jobs, make their own marriages, establish their own status. In the last three decades there have been many changes in China, particularly in the cities, but the reformer who anticipated individual autonomy must be disappointed, at least in the area of marriage. Young men and women in the villages still must seek their parents' permission to marry, their help in finding a mate or at least in negotiating the match after one is found, and their cooperation in accumulating the money and goods to have a proper wedding. Without parents, as many a sent-down youth discovered, one cannot borrow money on which to marry and one cannot alone accumulate enough to marry in the conventional rural fashion. A young man or woman who wishes to marry without his or her parents' permission is in dire straits. A girl's income is not separated from the family's until after marriage (and not even then for the man), so there is no chance of accumulating money for a bride price or dowry. A young man who defies his parents in this way will have no home to bring his bride to, and his production team is all too likely to be on the side of the older generation, hence unwilling to assist. There is no opportunity in China of moving away and starting fresh. A young woman who defies her parents and relatives will come empty-handed, a decided disadvantage in starting life in a new village. The state speaks of the freedom that comes to women with employment outside the home, but in the countryside that freedom has thus far been in the abstract. The fundamental decisions that determine lives are still very much in the hands of the parents.

Things are different in the cities. Parents do not control jobs, the state does. The state also grants permission to marry, allots coupons to buy rationed items of furniture and clothing, and decides whether the young couple will live in the same city or not. In other words, the state has, in the area of marriage at least, taken unto itself those sanctions and indulgences that once were the family seniors' exclusive rights to dispense. The change in the city has not led to increased freedom for young people but to a transfer of authority from the family to the state—the creation of public patriarchy, to use Judith Stacey's terminology.[16]

SEVEN

The Setting of Chinese Women's Lives: Family Organization

Even a worthless son can give his mother three hot meals a day, but a filial daughter can only give her one that has cooled while shaking along the road.   —*Rural folk saying*

For the majority of Chinese women, rural and urban, it is still within the context of the family and in their performance of familial roles that they are judged. A fine worker who neglects her husband and beats her children is a bad woman. A fine worker who neglects his wife and beats his children is a fine worker. Most women sense this distinction, and as we saw in Chapter 1, government policy statements recently have encouraged it. It is time we took a closer look at the organization of the contemporary family in rural and urban China before going on in the next two chapters to look at the social and emotional environment of the domestic unit.

Although currently it is not fashionable in anthropological circles to define the family in terms of its functions, the Chinese, practical as always, think the family *is* what the family does. (By family, here I mean *jia*, or domestic unit.) Farm families in Taiwan told me that the family was the group of close relatives who shared a stove, that is, ate together and shared a common budget. A longer answer might add that they tilled the fields together and shared their produce.[1] In another terminology, the family in China functioned in the city and the country as a unit of consumption and a unit of production. It produced food and organized its consumption; it generated future members of the jia and looked to their upbringing; it cared for the aged and the ill; it served as a buffer between the individual and the state. And beyond this it was the setting in which women lived out their lives. They did not go, like their fathers, husbands, and brothers, to the fields, the marketplace, or the teahouse for another perspective. These experiences of men did not make the family less central to their lives in traditional China, but the lack of these experiences did make the family both central and delimiting for women's lives.

As we have seen, there have been major changes in the family in urban China. It is most certainly not the buffer (or barrier) it once was between women and the state, but it remains the unit of consumption, the primary caring unit for the weak, ill, or elderly, and its proper functioning is still seen as women's responsibility. Here again, the rural family reflects the vast differences in China between city and countryside. Although it is no longer the only unit of production, that function in 1981 being shared with the production team, it still provides much of the family's resources, and much of that production is women's responsibility. More importantly, even though the rural family is now a setting from which women of certain ages go out for varying periods of time to interact with the work world of men, it is still the natural habitat of women. How does family organization reflect these changes in function, such as they are?

The data in Table 17 describe the form of family that resulted from the marriage of each of my informants. Looking first at urban women, we see a steady rise in the frequency of elementary families to a peak of 53 percent among the couples marrying in the 1950's and then a more gradual decline to a low of 33 percent among the couples marrying in the most recent decade.* My interview data suggest that many of my informants came into the cities singly or with their new husbands to find work and a better way of life (see pages 157–58). Parents and parents-in-law were left behind in the villages. If this accounts for some large part of the elementary families formed in the optimistic decade following Liberation, it is not difficult to see why the harsh antimigration laws were imposed.

---

*An elementary family is one in which there is only one married couple or remnant of a married couple in the household; a stem family has a married couple or remnants of a married couple in two generations but no more than one per generation; a grand family is one in which there is a minimum of two married couples in one generation.

Table 17. Form of Family Resulting from Marriage, by Year of
Marriage and Urban/Rural Location

Family form resulting from marriage	Year of marriage				
	Before 1939	1940–49	1950–59	1960–69	1970–81
Urban					
Elementary	24%	31%	53%	46%	33%
Stem	62	62	27	31	54
Grand	14	8	20	23	13
N	21	13	15	26	24
Rural					
Elementary	12%	12%	6%	4%	8%
Stem	55	67	65	65	74
Grand	33	21	29	30	19
N	42	43	34	46	53

My rural informants show a strikingly different pattern and one that reflects the demography of a society still influenced by traditional values enjoying a period of comparative prosperity. If an increase in the formation of elementary families at marriage were to be taken as an indicator of modernization, rural China appears not to be modernizing. There is a decrease in the frequency of elementary families formed by the marriages of my rural informants and an increase in the incidence of stem families, the latter accounting for fully 74 percent of all new families formed in the decade just before my research. The next largest group of couples (19 percent) also went to live with parents (nearly always those of the husband) who already had another married child in residence, thus forming a grand family.

These diverging patterns reflect both the failures and the successes of the state in its struggle to balance material progress and ideological transformation. The decline in newly married nuclear units in the countryside can be considered a tribute to the economic stability that socialism has produced in the rural areas. In the old days, poverty shattered families, sending brothers away from home to search for work, causing parents to die of disease or malnutrition before their children were old enough to marry, or delaying marriages beyond the point of practicality. Now farm families can afford to marry their children in the manner to which their parents and grandparents aspired with the goal of founding a large family of many generations. Though the goal is not likely to be realized, it is still in the minds of farmers when they think of a proper marriage for their sons. This is not, I think, a goal the state supports in its desire to destroy the feudal thinking of its populace, but it is one of the ways in which farmers choose to express their newfound prosperity.[2] More agreeable to the state would be an increase in number of newlyweds forming their own nuclear units. Here, it is the state's economic failings that keep this statistic in the cities as low as it is. If sufficient housing were available, I have no doubt that more urban young people would choose apartments of their own for their first experience of married life.

The data in Table 18 give us another perspective on the composition of the family in contemporary China. The summary column ("All Women") shows that only 10 percent more of the urban women in my samples are living in elementary families than are the rural women, but that the number of women living in grand families is the same whether in the city or the countryside. The other columns in this table imply that though rural and urban are different in many ways, women's lives as indexed by their domestic settings are not that different. Both rural and urban women seem to spend the various phases of their lives in similar family arrangements. We know from Table 17 that urban women are more likely to live in elementary families after they marry, so it is not surprising that there are more women living in elementary families who had been married for nine years or less in 1980–81. Perhaps more surprising is the fact that there are so many rural women living in elementary families in this early period of their marriages, since we know that they are very unlikely to begin married life in such families. However, this is also the age group in which most of the family divisions are occurring. Except for Fujian, where spacious housing aroused the envy of the Beijing cadres traveling with me, few of the new homes in the countryside can accommodate more than two married

Table 18. Family Form in 1981 by Number of Years after
Marriage and Urban/Rural Location

Family form in 1981	All women	No. of years after marriage				
		0–9	10–19	20–29	30–39	40+
Urban						
Elementary	60%	52%	83%	83%	36%	39%
Stem	34	38	17	17	57	48
Grand	6	10	0	0	7	13
N	99	21	23	18	14	23
Rural						
Elementary	50%	42%	78%	74%	44%	20%
Stem	44	46	18	26	49	76
Grand	6	13	5	0	7	4
N	216	48	40	38	41	49

couples comfortably. In the past, an expanding family might add on a wing or room to house a newly married couple, but the new row house styles are not expandable. The biggest units I saw had two kang rooms, a cooking and eating room, and an upstairs loft that in some areas would be nearly unusable in winter because it could not be heated. Since married couples are expected to have a room of their own, this places a decided curb on family complexity. In some areas a man and his wife are expected to move out to another house when the man's younger brother becomes engaged so that he can begin preparing the extra room for his marriage. Other families make the switch shortly after marriage, using the loft or other makeshift arrangements as long as possible. In Fujian, where people were still building houses to their own design, expansion was possible, though not common. In one family I interviewed the father had helped two of his three sons build a large separate house which they and their wives and children shared; the youngest brother was still at home with the parents. Not all family divisions, as we shall see in the next two chapters, result from simple pressure on housing, but in the country a young couple during this early period in their marriage are more likely to be living with their parents than are young couples in the city.

Residence in stem families drops dramatically among rural women who have been married for ten to nineteen years but starts to rise again among women who have been married for twenty to twenty-nine years. At this stage in the family cycle, the elderly parents-in-law of women who have been married for ten to nineteen years begin to die off, and in the next decade of marriage stem families increase again as these women's own children begin to marry. In the urban sample this increase does not occur until the next cohort because the later age at marriage of both parents and their children delays the whole cycle.

The last two cohorts of rural women, those married thirty years or more, continue the cycle associated with traditional society, that is, parents who are no longer able to work living with married children. Not surprisingly, the urban women in the oldest cohort are somewhat less likely to be living with their children than are the rural women. As their children marry and produce children of their own, it becomes difficult to find housing large enough for everyone, so the family divides. Urban old people are also likely to have pensions that will allow them to take care of themselves. Moreover, the old values on a united family under one roof are no longer as strong in the city. In this instance the state has come to regret the success of its attack on feudal traditions. The recently revised Marriage Law contains a new provision that extends the obligation of children to care for their aged parents to the generation of grandparents. I asked an official of the Beijing Women's Federation the reason for this change and was told that young people learned bad habits from the Gang of Four and were neglecting or even mistreating the elderly members of their families. Another more disgruntled cadre told me these "bad habits" had started long before then. It seems that the state has run into another conflict between social policy and economic reality. There are those who would happily define the economic burden of aged pensionless grandparents as feudal ties; the state cannot afford to carry the cost.

The low frequency of grand families in both rural and urban samples is surprising when compared with the distribution Arthur Wolf found in his study of Chinese farm families in rural Taiwan in the early part of this century. In Table 19 these figures are arrayed alongside those reported by Whyte and Parish, who found an even lower incidence of grand families (only 2 percent) among their Guangdong urban families in 1972–78. In 1906, nearly half (49 percent) of all married couples in the Taiwan sample were living in grand families, whereas only 6 percent of those in both my rural and urban samples were in such families in 1981. Even Fujian, the area culturally most similar to Taiwan, does not approach this high frequency, having only 13 percent in grand families. Whyte and Parish report statistics from studies made in the 1930's that indicate higher frequencies of grand families in urban areas, up to 19 percent among upper class Shanghai residents and 18 percent among Peking residents.[3] Clearly there has been a decline in the frequency of grand families since Liberation, although my data and Whyte and Parish's show minor disagreements on the extent of the decline. The explanation seems fairly straightforward: intense propaganda opposing the old patriarchal family system, a decline in parental authority, and less and less living space allotted to more and more people have combined to make grand families relics of the past.

A common misconception of those who are opposed to China's revolutionary government is that it has an antifamily policy. This is not true. The state wants to weaken the power of the old family *system*, but it wants to do so without destroying the economically and socially necessary functions of the small domestic unit. On the surface, the goals are reasonable. Although not all areas of traditional China had strong lineage organizations, all Chinese did practice patrilineal descent, venerate their elders, and subordinate their women. Whether or not a village had a lineage hall or other corporate property, there was an ideological family of males that transcended the domestic unit and legitimated the authority of men. The importance of line and genealogy contributed to the need to control the reproductive capacities of women, requiring restraints on their activities and causing their economic dependency. The standard Marxist analysis relates this back to property, and for this reason Mao and his revolutionaries were convinced that the old family system was

Table 19. Family Form: Other Distributions

Place and date	No. of families	Elemen-tary	Stem	Grand	Single,[a] other
1. Taiwan, 1906	1,024	24%	26%	49%	—
2. Jiangsu, 1935–37 (rural)	30	40	53	7	—
3. Fujian, 1935–37 (rural)	40	38	35	28	—
4. Tianjin & Wusih, 1935–37 (urban)	64	55	38	8	—
5. Guangdong, 1973 (rural)	131	50	37	2	12%
6. Lingnan, 1972–78 (urban)	451	68	22	2	8
7. China, 1981					
Urban	99	60	34	6	—
Rural	216	50	44	6	—

SOURCES: Row 1, Arthur Wolf and Chieh-shan Huang, *Marriage and Adoption in China, 1845–1945* (Stanford, Calif., 1980), p. 69; rows 2, 3, and 4, Olga Lang, *Chinese Family and Society* (New Haven, Conn., 1946), p. 350, table II; row 5, William L. Parish and Martin King Whyte, *Village and Family in Contemporary China* (Chicago, 1978), p. 134, table 19; row 6, Martin King Whyte and William L. Parish, *Urban Life in Contemporary China* (Chicago, 1984), p. 154, table 13; row 7, table 18 above (p. 186).

[a] The absence of any women living alone in my samples is probably more relevant to the way officials chose my informants than to the incidence of single-member households in Chinese society, particularly in the urban groups. Whyte and Parish do not indicate what "other" might include.

the source of women's oppression. Only when private property ceased to exist, household tasks were socialized, and women were fully engaged in social production would the problem of women be solved. Social planners in China, alas, have ignored the fact that patriarchal thinking, the ideology of the men's family system, pervades every aspect of Chinese society and continues to inhibit women's full participation in political as well as economic life. Although there were brief spurts of ideological retraining in 1953 during the Marriage Law campaign, and again in 1974–75 during the Anti-Confucius campaign, the restructuring of the Chinese family has been left to the natural erosion expected to result from other societal changes. Of more concern to the CCP was the destruction of the power of the lineages and of the landlord class controlling that power. The ideological base of male supremacy on which the power rested has largely been ignored, or at least discounted as of no further threat to the state.

As a result, depressingly little has changed in rural domestic organization. Though there are fewer grand families now, most young people still spend some part of their married lives under the domination of an older married couple. The youngest son and his wife, or the only son and his wife, will live jointly with the parents until their deaths. No farm woman would consider living with her daughter and her daughter's husband if she has a son. The patrilineal principle requires that an old couple live with their sons if they have any, no matter how incompatible the two couples may be. A woman in Fujian told me, "Of course you live with your son. How could you live with your daughter? She has married out. You can't eat other people's food. You live with your son and eat your own food." Another woman, from Jiangsu, told me, "Old people live with their sons. Daughters don't take our property and don't feed us. If I stayed more than a couple of days with my daughter, people would begin to talk."

The head of the family is still the senior male, but he turns over more and more of his authority to his sons as his production capacity diminishes. Sheer strength of character, bolstered by a tradition of filial piety, is no longer sufficient to maintain control over family decisions when status within the production team begins to drop. I neglected to ask at what point the team leaders register the family's workpoints in the name of the son rather than the father, but until that time, as indicated in earlier chapters, the pay-out at the end of the year goes to the head of the family, no matter how scrupulously separated the individual records have been kept until that point. Adult sons and daughters do not receive their own earnings at the pay-out—it is handed over to the head of the family. When a woman marries, her workpoints are added to her father-in-law's pay-out as are her husband's. The team will decide for a woman newly married into their collective what her job will be. Her husband's family, however, will decide the extent of her participation in collective labor. Many women retire as soon as they have a daughter-in-law (or mature daughter) to take their place in collective work, but I have also heard of younger women who were returned to the domestic sector long before they had replacements because cooking for a large family was too much for the older woman in the household to manage or because of her illness or death. The rural family, as we have seen, is still a producing unit, raising pigs for sale and vegetables for family consumption. In some areas, up to half the family income comes from these sideline enterprises, so it is to the family's collective advantage to put women to work at home once enough workpoints have been earned to secure the family's grain rations. Who does what in the rural family is not a contractual matter as it is in urban families, but first a sexual division of labor and second a generational one.

Although women may be consulted about how they will participate in the household economy, younger women are unlikely to have much voice in that decision. A woman in her late thirties told me a long sad tale about her early married years. She had been recruited in her natal village by a provincial revolutionary opera troupe and spent several years, chaperoned by her musician brother, touring the area giving performances with the troupe. She loved her work and was apparently good at it. Before she married, her fiancé's family agreed that she would be allowed to continue performing, returning home several times a month. Not long after the marriage, however, her mother-in-law and husband began to put pressure on her to stay at home, and finally refused to allow her to leave. Her brother came and got her twice, but inevitably she was forced to stay at home. She is still bitter, some fifteen years later, about their treatment of her. Even now, when she is an old woman as she puts it, local groups come and ask her to do guest performances with them, but her husband's family looks sour-faced and asks her who will do the cooking and feed the pig.

Another woman, in telling me of the great good fortune of her daughter who had managed to get a city registration and to marry in the city, also unwittingly commented on the economic position of women in the rural family. "She sends me money quite often. If she had married here, she would have to beg for money from her mother-in-law and half the time wouldn't get it."

Women in the country work hard, but even if it is collective labor it is still considered to some extent an extension of their domestic chores. Young women who work regularly either in the fields or in some village enterprise occupy a slightly different status in the eyes of their mothers-in-law, but in general women are indoors and men are outdoors. Men attend the important team and/or brigade meetings. Men represent the family to the outside world. Perhaps one of the most amusing examples of this came to me by chance in Shandong. We met a usually jolly cadre on the path one afternoon looking quite downcast. My assistant asked him what the trouble was, and I think to the surprise of us all, he blurted out the fact that he had just come from a meeting at the commune headquarters at which he had been severely reprimanded and ordered to write a self-criticism. What was the offense? His daughter-in-law had recently borne one child beyond the number allowed under the birth limitation program. The reprimand did not in any way suggest that he had fathered the child, only that he had not managed his family's affairs properly, that is, in the manner expected of a good cadre.

I have made the point several times now that what I call the men's family and its ideology remain dominant forces in the countryside. I hope I have also made it clear that the family writ small, the domestic unit, also remains the basic and most important social grouping in the countryside, no matter how much is said about the economic and social functions of the team in writings both within China and abroad. The young people sent to the countryside from the cities learned this in a very painful way. In his excellent book on this difficult period in China's recent past, Bernstein describes the plight of the young people who, bereft of family, had no one to take care of them when they fell ill.[4] Without a wife and children they could not do the sideline activities that supply the other half of most farmers' incomes, so no matter how much they labored for the collective, they were always poor. And they had little chance of getting a "good" wife even if they were resigned to spending their lives in villages, because without a family it would be impossible to save enough money to marry properly. Many of these young men received remittances from their urban parents, a bitter reversal of the Chinese tradition. All the sent-down youth learned a lesson that the state was trying *not* to teach: in times of crisis, one must turn to the family, not the state.

But what changes have occurred in the social and economic organization of the urban family? And how is this related to the struggle between the ideologies of the family and of the state for the loyalty of the individual?

As we observed in Chapter 3, for both women and men the urban workplace absorbs a major share of their energy and, less confidently, their interest. A young Beijing woman told me, "Now we spend most of our time at our workplace and only go home to eat and sleep, so work is a bigger part of our lives." I asked, "But what happens after you retire from work?" "Retired people focus all their attention on the family." The answer is a little too pat, but it illustrates, I think, what the state has in mind. For women, of course, it is an impossible scenario. I asked a thirty-four-year-old Beijing woman which was more important, her job or her family. She did not find it an easy question to answer, but finally said, "Generally work comes first, but if the children are sick, you have to take time off work, don't you?" I was not given the opportunity to interview individual men in Beijing, but I doubt very much that they would have answered in this way.

The economic organization of urban families is very different from that of rural families. The father of unmarried adult children is still the head of the family and controls some form of joint budget. Senior women may handle the day-to-day cash outlays, but none of them said they would make major purchases without permission from the head of the household. Unmarried daughters turn over their entire pay packets to their mothers, receiving spending money back from them. Sons may or may not do the same, but are somewhat more likely to keep at least part of what they earn. Certainly both sons and daughters now feel that the disposition of their earnings is negotiable, not, as in the old days, entirely a matter for their parents to decide. After marriage, the family economic arrangements I was told about sound very un-Chinese indeed. The most common agreement is for the young people to contribute a set amount toward food, retaining the rest of their wages for their own use. With the birth of children, they add on to their contribution, the amount depending on whether or not the senior generation provides child care. I also ran across a few urban couples who do not contribute at all to the family budget, essentially living off their parents, using their own incomes to buy special treats (to be shared with the family), clothes, and so forth. In each of these cases the couples had not been married very long. In general, the financial arrangements between urban parents and their married children can be characterized as contractual, not foreordained. There seems to be no sense that they "owed" their earnings to their parents. They might join together to make a major purchase, like a television or, among the really well paid who also have access to special stores, a tiny washing machine, but the shared budget assumed among rural families does not seem to exist in the cities. One old lady in Beijing sniffed at my questions about the disposal of a daughter-in-law's earnings and said, "Most of them give it to their mothers. They certainly don't give any to their mothers-in-law."

A good many of the families of the women I interviewed in the cities shared even less than a common budget. Sometimes one member of a couple works so far from home that he or she lives in a factory dormitory and returns home only on weekends. Others live in distant cities and return home only once a year. In a good many families the children are farmed out, either because there are no old people in residence to take care of them, the old people are too infirm, they have too many other grandchildren to care for, or they are still themselves members of the labor force. In one family I met, the eldest child, a son, spent the first of his ten years living with his mother's parents, seeing his own parents only on Sundays. A middle child spent her first eight years in a live-in nursery school, also coming home on Sundays, and the youngest child, now six, is in day care, coming home each evening. Other families have even stranger combinations, such as the woman who has her daughter's two children living with her during the week, feeds her son-in-law lunch every day, and shares her house with her son and his wife whose one child is in the factory nursery days but home nights. The son and his wife usually eat lunch and dinner at the factory where they are both employed. Any patriarch who tried to maintain autocratic control over such families as these would have hard going.

Before Liberation, urban fathers, like rural fathers, were instrumental in finding employment for sons. Some took them into their own shops or workplaces if they could; others introduced them into the employ of friends or relatives; those who could afford it set them up in business for themselves on whatever level they could manage. There have been a number of editorials and reports in the Chinese press in recent years criticizing the use of the "back door" to obtain jobs for children, but usually only fairly well placed officials have access to these routes. A legal ploy made use of by some families is to have one parent or the other who is near retirement step down early to be replaced by their child, but not all workplaces are willing or able to make this switch. For the average factory worker whose twenty-year-old child comes on the job market while she or he is still in midlife, this technique does not work. Although the exceptions are many and sometimes scandalous, the general assumption in China's cities is that parents are no longer the primary source of one's job.*

Nor is the family or the father as its nominal head any longer the mediary between other family members and the outside world. Except for the young who have not yet been assigned jobs, each adult deals with the world beyond the family through his or her workplace. Those who have never worked outside their homes or have worked only in neighborhood collective workshops take the Residents' Committee as their *danwei* (unit). It is there that they are told about new government regulations, given inoculations against epidemics, provided with welfare if needed and so forth. For some, the Residents' Committee *is* the state, for others it is the intermediary between the state and the individual, a distinction that I suspect arises as much from the personality of the particular Residents' Committee member one encounters as from anything else. But whatever the relationship,

*Under the new economic policies that permit some workers to apply directly to employers for work, parental influence may again become a significant factor. See p. 263.

it is not a matter of the male head of a household going out and representing it in the world beyond its gates.

What do these changes in the family, urban and rural, mean for women? In the old China every woman knew that the quality of her life, both at the hands of her mother-in-law and in her old age, depended upon having a son. The tragedy her life would become if she did not have a son or if she were widowed young caused many a suicide and was the theme of many a melancholy folk song. Although these are still delicate topics in China and brought me to grief on several occasions with my research assistants, I felt them so important to my understanding of the position of women in the family in new China that I persisted in interviewing about them. My two basic questions were "What happens to people who have no sons?" and "Should a widow remarry?" but I had to devise many variations in order to elicit answers, and sometimes even the variations were not successful. I think the difficulty my informants had in answering was less one of politics, although certainly that entered in, and more one of discovering for themselves what they thought.

With the simple question "What happens to people who have no sons?" I did not expect any problems. It should have been an easy question for the rural women to answer. The birth limitation campaign was in full swing and as a result the *wubao* (five guarantees) system of old age insurance was being given a lot of publicity. Every collective member, according to the publicity, was guaranteed five benefits in old age: food, clothing, housing, medicine, and burial expenses. Those who had only female children or had no children at all need not worry: the collective would take care of them. I never interviewed anyone who was enjoying the five guarantees, and most of my informants were pretty uncertain about whether there was anyone in their collective who was receiving the benefits. Far more interesting were the answers given by women who did not think first of the five guarantees. A thirty-year-old woman said, "No sons is bad. There is nobody to take care of them when they are sick. Nobody to bring them food or boil water for them. That is a bad thing." Another woman, also young, just shook her head and muttered,

"Nobody to see them to the mountain," a euphemism for a proper funeral. But the most common answer (other than that the collective will take care of them) was that they would call in a son-in-law, that is, marry a daughter uxorilocally. Very, very few rural women said they would depend on their daughters. Daughters belong to their husbands' families, unless you "call in" a husband for one, and then he as well as she belongs to you. Uxorilocal marriages were never considered desirable in old China, and it is quite clear that they are still a measure of last resort. A political activist may get a lot of credit among the cadre for making an uxorilocal marriage, but the rest of the village will just look knowing. I asked an old lady in Shaoxing who had only one child, a married daughter, and made a precarious living for herself selling buns on the street why she had not arranged an uxorilocal marriage for her only daughter. "I like my daughter very much. She helps me all she can." The implication was clear: she liked her daughter too much to force her into an inferior marriage.

I had expected the politically more sophisticated urban women to respond to this question with allusions to the new responsibility of the state, and Shaoxing women did not disappoint me. Eighty percent of them said the government would take care of the elderly who had no sons. Interestingly enough, they did not say they would live on their pensions, but that the government would take responsibility. The real surprise came from the Beijing women: 30 percent said they would get by on their pensions and another 19 percent said the government would take care of them, but 41 percent said that as long as they had daughters they would not worry. Many of my Beijing informants told me what they thought their government wanted me to hear, but in this instance their unexpected answers fit in well with other information gleaned from their interviews. For centuries the relations between mothers and daughters in China have been ambiguous, with the older knowing full well that it will end with the daughter's marriage and both of them knowing there was little either could do to ease the bitterness of the other's life. What the Beijing women were saying openly was that the conflict in that relationship was no longer there, that they could afford to invest in it emotionally. Most women commented on the material aspects of the relationship, which makes them sound somewhat more mercenary than in fact they are. A lively seventy-year-old with tiny bound feet told me: "Most women are closer to their daughters now than their sons. In the old days they loved their sons best because it was their sons who supported them in their old age, but now women can do that too so they are all close to their daughters. If the son treats the mother kindly, live with the son; if the son treats the mother badly, live with the daughter." A middle-aged intellectual gave a more sensitive analysis when she explained that at least in her social class sons and daughters seem to be equally valued now with perhaps the edge going to daughters: "Sons are as likely to be assigned a job in another city and move away as are daughters, but the girls have stronger emotional ties to their parents and are more likely to put the effort into maintaining the relationship and the responsibilities it entails." A third woman who was listing for me in detail the contributions of her daughters to her income said when she came to her son, "That one. He belongs to his wife."

My very strong feeling is that in the cities sons are no longer as important as they once were to their mothers. If given a choice, most women, I suspect, would still prefer to have the single child the birth limitation program allots them be male rather than female, but they are also less likely to be devastated (or beaten) if it turns out to be a girl. This is not the case in the countryside. The woman above who said so casually that sons are as likely as daughters to move to a distant city would strike terror into the hearts of rural mothers with such a statement. The automatic answer rural women gave when I asked which was more important, sons or husbands, was sons, although they often quickly revised it to add that husbands were more important when the children were young. A woman who in response to one question told me smugly that the five guarantees took care of the childless, in another pointed out to me a woebegone-looking woman who the month before had given birth to her third daughter and had been beaten senseless by her husband for so doing.

Daughters have financial obligations to parents in cities, but in the rural areas they do not. A rural man's workpoints will be garnisheed if he refuses to support his parents, but not a married daughter's. She belongs to someone else's family. Even a cadre told me frankly that people were shamed if they had to live off the five guarantees, and that moreover the living was not very good. Their personal property became the property of the brigade after they died, and, in several cases I heard of, even before their deaths they were moved out of their homes into a room in some-one else's house to make their old homes available to others. Nonetheless, uxorilocal marriages are still rare and unpopular. In the old days in south China (and still in the New Territories of Hong Kong), a man contemplating an uxorilocal marriage for a daughter had to get formal permission from his brothers and from his lineage, and both were prone to say no.[5] They did not wish lineage property to pass into the hands of "outsiders." I asked if it was now necessary to get this permission and was told that a man would of course discuss it with his brothers. An exemplary woman cadre who had made such a marriage told me that her family also had to go before a meeting of the production team who granted permission only after looking into the background of her husband.

Probably the most telling evidence in the rural areas for the continued importance to a woman of male progeny is in the con-tinued tension between a woman and her daughter-in-law. This topic will be discussed in detail in the next chapter, but the fact that campaigns are still necessary to mute this disruptive rela-tionship and that even uncooperative informants admit to its po-tential for family disruption is indicative of the contribution a son's undivided loyalty makes to a woman's peace of mind. And yet the anxiety seems less acute—perhaps because it is perfectly clear to even the simplest rural woman that the best interests of the production team are served if sons continue to support their aged parents. With that authority behind them, there is less panic about old age and starvation than there used to be. A wretched daughter-in-law might make old age less peaceful, but the team guarantees that she will not physically neglect her elderly mother-in-law.

What has not changed, however, is the basic notion that from a woman's perspective marriage is an economic arrangement. After listening to women day after day, city and country, tell me what a drain on them raising children was, I began to ask them why in heaven's name people had children. Some of the answers were disarming, but many were blunt profit-and-loss statements: that was the way you provided for your old age. When I asked whether widows or divorcees should remarry, in the final analysis the answers again turned on the level of financial need. In the country, if such a woman had small children and no in-laws to support them, she should. Otherwise most thought not. If her sons were nearly old enough to support her, she should not. When I asked if this were the only reason a widow might re-marry, uncomprehending faces said yes. I used as an example my favorite aunt who in her late sixties married a fine man with whom she has had many years of good companionship. Didn't Chinese widows or divorcees ever marry just because they were lonely? Everyone in the room looked scandalized and then embarrassed for me and my outrageous aunt. Subsequent interviews made it abundantly clear that it would be disgusting for a woman past childbearing age to marry again. Marriage is not for companion-ship but for the serious business of production and reproduction.

Interviewing about widows brought to light many attitudes to-ward women that I could discover in no other way. The data in Table 20 summarize the answers I was given to the general ques-tion of whether a widow should remarry. The second column in-cludes all yes answers that were not qualified, ranging from a firm "yes" to a lukewarm "It is allowed"; answers in the third column are essentially "no" answers, but informants chose to evade the necessity of saying so by saying that people would gossip; the fourth column combines those who said simply no with those who said it was a foolish question because no widow would con-sider such a thing; and the last column includes all the answers in which a "no" was qualified by such comments as, unless the man was very old or mentally incompetent, or unless the woman had many small children and no one to help her raise them. Al-though I expected the question to lead to some interesting con-

Table 20. "Should a Widow Remarry?"

Site	No. of respondents	"Yes," or "It is allowed"	"There would be gossip"	"No," or "It wouldn't happen"	OK in special cases
Beijing	20	60%	0%	40%	0%
Shaoxing	18	44	50	6	0
URBAN	38	53%	24%	24%	0%
Fujian	12	17%	25%	0%	58%
Jiangsu	27	22	30	33	15
Shandong	22	36	0	32	32
Shaanxi	44	50	0	18	32
RURAL	105	36%	10%	23%	30%

versations, I was surprised to find so many women who gave negative responses. The remarriage of widows has been one of the few issues concerning women about which there has been persistent propaganda, ranging from an occasional article in the newspaper to the excellent filming of one of Lu Xun's short stories. There is a certain irony in the fact that in the model brigade in Shandong that very kindly arranged a private showing of this film for us, only 36 percent of the women unqualifiedly said widows should remarry. A public screening would have been more appropriate, it would seem. But the Shandong site was not especially unusual. Only 53 percent of the urban informants felt that widows should remarry, and a considerably smaller proportion of my rural informants, ranging from 17 percent in Fujian to 50 percent in the Shaanxi site. This Shaanxi figure was unexpected in view of Fenghuo's conservative bent on other issues associated with women. A closer look at the interviews indicates that 68 percent of the women who said widows should remarry were under the age of forty. Whether this indicates a new awareness among younger women in this area or recent participation in a study group on widowhood is impossible for me to say. If the Shaanxi statistics are set aside, however, the positive response for rural women drops to a low of 26 percent.

Trying to discover what the Chinese have against widows is a research project in itself, but what contemporary women say is wrong with widows is that it will reflect badly on the young man who marries one. People will ask what is wrong with him. An old man or a cripple or a mentally defective person might marry a widow because he could not find a willing virgin, but not a young man who had never married, unless there was some secret flaw. And there must be real and pathetic need on the part of the widow or she would not consider remarriage. Why would she want to remarry if she had children to support her or in-laws to help her out until the children were old enough to support her? Certainly in the model brigades no one would prevent a widow from remarrying, but I suspect that in the less spotlighted collectives a young man who fell in love with a young widow would have trouble on his hands. It is, incidentally, quite acceptable for a widower—even one with several children—to marry a young virgin.

It was only toward the end of my interviewing that I recognized the significance of a question that I had asked occasionally in the rural areas: "What happens to the children of widows who decide to marry again?" Of the 57 women asked (from Jiangsu, Shandong, and Shaanxi), only 9 (16 percent) said that decision was up to the widow. The rest said that either the mother-in-law would decide who should keep them or simply that they belonged to the parents of their dead father. No matter what the Marriage Law has said for thirty years, in rural China women still have no rights to the children they have borne. They belong, as they have for centuries, to the men's family. It is useful to recall at this point the comment of a weary old charwoman in Beijing who told me that the children now all belong to the government. Only, it would seem, in the cities.

⌒

EIGHT

Sharing a Stove:
Urban Domestic Relations

I had a neighbor whose wife and mother quarreled all the time. If the mother was wrong, the son wouldn't say a word, but if the wife was wrong, he lectured her. Our Chinese tradition is to respect our parents, so even if the old people are wrong, we keep silent.
— *Woman doctor in Beijing, age 43*

It is almost impossible to learn the intimate details of behavior within families in another country without living among them, or better yet, within one. I lived with families in various rural places in Taiwan; other people have done the same in rural places in pre-Liberation China. But for a glimpse of the inner dynamics of pre-Liberation urban families we have had to depend upon novels that all too often depict the lives of the elite (Pa Chin's *The Family*, for example, or Cao Xuequin's *The Story of the Stone*), and a few gems such as Ida Pruitt's biography of a working-class woman, *A Daughter of Han*. Since the revolution we have had even less information to base our hypotheses upon. Until recently even novels and short stories were so didactic as to be useless as sources of insights into actual behavior.[1] It is therefore with a good deal of apprehension that I attempt in this chapter to put the responses of my urban informants in some context. Because of my own past experience (primarily rural) with the Chinese family, I am in danger of glibly making comparisons with a past that may never have existed in urban China. Nonetheless, there are a few basic generalizations that seem valid. Urban family organization in the prerevolutionary period bore about the same relationship to rural family organization that it does in contemporary society. That is to say, elementary family units were more common in the cities than in the countryside whereas stem and grand family units were less common but by no means absent.* And all domestic units were and, again to a lesser extent, still are embedded in the complex field of kinship. The realm of the family is, as Maurice Freedman puts it, "that of domestic life, a realm of co-residence and the constant involvement in the affairs of the hearth, children, and marriage. Kinship is something different."[2] Kinship in China is the set of relationships that is traced exclusively through males and bounds the behavior of a man by reason of his rights and duties to other men. In pre-Liberation China many of these rights and duties were considered even by the state to take precedence over all other obligations, including those to the state. In the PRC that precedence no longer obtains; nonetheless, even in the cities, the ideology of this kinship, what I often refer to as the men's family, persists and continues to color men's relations with men and women's relations with society. Moreover, it is the medium in which the family must live.

Since I was not allowed even to visit the homes of my Beijing informants, let alone live with a family, and spent only two to three hours in the homes of my Shaoxing interviewees, I had very few opportunities to observe the interaction of family members. Thus my understanding of family dynamics in the PRC necessarily comes from the descriptions of interested parties. Conversations that began in response to questions about how a good wife, husband, or son might be expected to behave often described specific family situations. Other details came as bonuses in the responses to questions totally unrelated to family interactions. There seems to be a cross-cultural inclination for women to discuss apparently abstract concepts with reference to particular relations and relationships between people. My interview notebooks are filled with statements like "I don't know how other workers felt about that, but my husband and his cousins always . . ." and "We didn't think it was a good idea, but my father's older brother told us . . ." The three relationships most often mentioned were, not surprisingly, the three that are most basic to the Chinese domestic unit: parent and child, husband

*See Table 19, p. 189.

and wife, and mother-in-law and daughter-in-law. Rather than trying to stretch my data further than it can reasonably extend, I will in this and the next chapter on domestic relations focus primarily on these three relationships.

In traditional China filial piety was the fundamental principle of society. Some little boys (and a few girls) learned to read from the Twenty-four Tales of Filial Piety, a collection of outrageous stories about the incredible sacrifices made by filial sons to provide for the comfort and well-being of their parents. No sacrifice was too great for a son or daughter who had a parent in need. (Daughters, of course, were expected at marriage to transfer this devotion to their husbands' parents.) Wives and/or children could be sold or killed if rations were insufficient to feed everyone, since in theory they were replaceable and one's parents were not. Many of these social priorities were in fact codified into law; but without an emotional force behind it, no law could account for the potency of the concept of filial piety to the average Chinese citizen.

How did one inculcate this level of devotion? Anyone who has observed the coddling of Chinese male children has reason to wonder. Until they could "understand," little boys were permitted to break nearly every rule of proper behavior with only light reprimands. Needless to say, this was not the case with girls, although even they were given considerably more leeway than older children. But at the age of reason (around six years in northern Taiwan in the 1960's), all the rules changed and last week's tyrant found a father casting a cold disapproving eye on this week's mischief. Chinese parents had few qualms about physical punishment, and their techniques were both ingenious and painful. Mothers were considered by children to be the protector from the implacable punishment of the father, but grandmothers were superprotectors from both mother and father. Both mothers and grandmothers used this role to produce the behavior they desired and the gratitude they required in socializing the next generation. Shaming by peers, older children—caretakers, and neighbors gradually tamed the naughty new member of society and taught her or him the basic rules of society, one of the most important being to honor one's parents. By the time the child was ready for school she had learned to respect the strength of a parent's arm as well as the fact that hitting a parent back was either infantile or a serious crime. Those who had a school experience learned that this was true in the world outside home as well.

Death did not entirely release the junior generation from their obligations to the senior, for they would also be considered remiss by society if they did not provide a slightly more extravagant funeral for their deceased parents than they could afford. They would, of course, continue to make offerings and burn incense to their spirit tablets until they too took up residence on the family's ancestral altar. The next generation—the procreation of which was a critical filial duty to one's parents—would then carry on the line and the sacrifices of those who had gone before.

One of the ways in which a mother in the old society protected herself from the unquestioned power and authority of the men's family was through subversion, transforming the filial loyalties of the family's sons into emotional bonds with their mother. Several women in Beijing and in Shaoxing said things to me that were familiar from my days in Taiwan, where I first came across what I call uterine families: "Mothers are more important than fathers because fathers only contribute money"; "Children like their mothers best. There are many things they don't want their fathers to know and mothers keep their secrets"; "Fathers raise children with money. The children know the difference"; "Mothers love and comfort their children, but the children are afraid of their fathers"; "Mothers show more concern for their children, always asking about their studies and what they want to eat and checking on their clothes. Fathers don't pay any attention. Now when my children come home from work they always come looking for me first." The majority of the women who said these things were in their fifties and sixties, mothers who would have been struggling to form their uterine families at or slightly before Liberation. Nothing in my interviews with younger urban women led me to think that they were anxious to form special, unyielding ties with their children that excluded their husbands.

Because of China's birth limitation program, forming a uterine family in contemporary China would be even more of a challenge than it was in the farmhouses of rural Taiwan. When there is only one child in a stem family, that child becomes the pampered darling of all the adults in the family. Moreover, in urban China today, mothers are doing considerably less of the caretaking than mothers did in previous generations. As we have seen, children are in day care, or in the home of a relative, or even in boarding homes from a very young age. And many of the situations described to me by working mothers imply that their double burden of work at home and at their paid jobs may have a strong qualitative effect on the nature of their relations with their children. A Beijing factory worker in her late thirties told me, "Both my children prefer their father to me. He has more time to play with them and help them with their studies. He even reads the paper to them. By the time I get home from work, cook dinner, and do some chores, my temper is too short. I'm too tired to help them." Another mother, also complaining of chores, said, "The children like their father best. He brings them good things to eat; I hit them."

My best guess is that the uterine family has disappeared because the need for it has disappeared. Urban women do not express the same degree of anxiety about their old age that they used to. Young women work and expect pensions; older women who do not have pensions are assured by the government that they will be cared for. Moreover, the male family is no longer the threat in contemporary urban China that it was in rural China. I do not mean to say that the ideology of patriarchy does not make the lives of contemporary Chinese women difficult, but male privilege is rarely identified by these women as the source of their problem. Without a threat, without an identifiable enemy to circumvent, women apparently see little need to turn their children away from their fathers. As we shall see further on, the nature of the husband-wife relationship has also changed considerably, and that necessarily has an effect on mothers' attitudes toward the fathers of their children.

If the uterine family has disappeared because it no longer fills a need, what does this say about the present status of filial piety? The uterine family was in a sense a feminine response to the patriarchal excesses of filial piety, excesses that worked against women's security even though they were, by extension, presumed to foster it. In modern China one does not hear much about filial piety, at least not in so many words, but as the epigraph to this chapter suggests, the idea of obligation from child to parent is still very much present. That may seem contradictory in view of some of the horror stories of the Cultural Revolution. Beyond a doubt, some children and young adults spied on their parents and denounced them to their radical peers with occasionally fatal consequences. But far more young people simply dropped out of school and sat out the Cultural Revolution at home. Even those who were participants did not necessarily relate this to their relationship with their parents. A long but casual conversation with a thirty-year-old male worker revealed to me how complex the values were at that time. This young man had taken off on a round-the-country trip as did so many others, but he admitted that he had had to delay the trip for a year because his parents would not let him go until he was sixteen. He told me that he felt guilty about his older brother who had had to stay at home and help their parents while he spent the year seeing the sights. "It is not easy to be the oldest son" was his conclusion. But he did not question the obligation. The ceremonious expression of filial piety is gone, but most young people still seem to have a strong sense of being in their parents' debt for the simple act of bearing or begetting them.

The recently revised marriage law reflects the state's attempt to reaffirm some of the pre-Liberation values in interpersonal relations. The 1950 Marriage Law stated that parents had the duty to raise and educate their children, and children had the duty to support and assist their parents. The new 1980 law is explicit about the rights of children to the support of their parents *and* grandparents (both paternal and maternal) and is equally explicit about the rights of parents *and* grandparents (again both paternal and maternal) to the support of their adult children and grandchildren. Undoubtedly these changes are in reaction to the social disruptions witnessed during the Cultural Revolution, but they also reflect economic hardheadedness as the state recognizes that it cannot possibly provide welfare supports for what will soon be a very old population.

The revised marriage law is not only a reflection of traditional values in the relations between parents and children, however. The wording of the law and interpretations made in the study papers about it on the radio and in editorials, and also in comments made casually by my informants, all suggest a strong new emphasis on the direction of obligation from parents to children. Naturally, I was particularly struck by the effect the law had on the relations between women. Older women are now under strong pressure to take responsibility for the day care of their sons' and/or daughters' children. I met one young woman who had come home to Beijing to have her first baby and then returned to the frontier region where she had been assigned some years before, leaving the child for her mother to raise. When I met her she was pregnant with a second child but hoped to be transferred permanently back to Beijing after it was born. If a transfer was not possible, she thought she would leave this child with her mother too. Other women said they were happy to leave their children with their mothers or mothers-in-law since "she knows about raising children and I don't." If this sort of thing is carried to an extreme, the cities of China could end up with a generation of women who never learned how to care for children, but in 1980 the state seemed far more concerned about obtaining babysitters so that mothers could work than it was about the social problems this might create. In the old society it was assumed that grandmothers doted on their grandchildren, but that stereotype also included a grand family form with daughters-in-law around to take over when grandmother got bored or tired. Grandmothers now are urged to provide full-time care to their children's children, and many of them, particularly those who have been workers and have their own pensions, are not willing to do it. Those without pensions often need the money and so have little choice in the matter.

Besides the new emphasis on two-way obligations in the parent-child relationship, there seems to be a decided shift among women in the matter of emotional attachments. In the old days, only a foolish woman failed to recognize that her future lay with her son; but as I reported in the preceding chapter, a good many urban women now look upon their daughters as being quite as reliable, sometimes more reliable, than their sons. Shaoxing women seemed particularly close to their daughters. Among the children who were still living at home, I noted time and again that the daughters turned over all their paychecks to their mothers, receiving back whatever they needed: "She asks me for whatever she wants." Sons were far less likely to hand over their pay packets. After marriage, the ties between mother and daughter are not severed as they were (ideally) in the old society. A Beijing woman told me flatly, "Married daughters are closer to their mothers than married sons are." And in both Shaoxing and Beijing I was surprised at how often women were taking care of their daughter's children, not their son's children. When I expressed surprise about this to a cadre, she said curtly, "It prevents trouble." This can only mean one kind of trouble—that between mother-in-law and daughter-in-law. Transferring children from one household to another twice a day causes a lot of another kind of trouble, which obviously is less threatening.

In Shaoxing I asked 26 women whom they thought women were closer to, their sons or their daughters, and all but 4 said daughters. However, of the 28 women I asked if they would prefer to live with their married sons or their married daughters, only 8 said they would prefer to live with their married daughters. I think these answers suggest that there are changes occurring in women's lives that are in fundamental conflict with the ideology of the patriarchal family system. "Society" still regards it as less than respectable for elderly parents to live with their married daughters, but the state wants to encourage this shift to uxorilocal residence whenever possible to accommodate the one-child program. It appears that women also would prefer it. And yet, virilocal residence remains the norm—a rather telling example of the strength of ideology.

I regret that I was not able to interview men on these two

questions in Beijing, for it would have been interesting to see whether or not they were as completely divided on the subject as were the Shaoxing men. Of the five Shaoxing men, two said men were closer to their sons, one said men were closer to their daughters, one said fathers were closer to sons and mothers to daughters, and one said fathers were closer to daughters and mothers were closer to sons. A more random assortment of answers one could not ask for. But when I asked them whom elderly people would prefer to live with, two said married daughters, two said married sons, and one said fathers would prefer to live with their daughters and mothers with their sons! I really do not know what to make of that other than there does not seem to be a consensus.

As I have noted in many places in this book, even though a fair amount of propaganda has been directed at the low contribution of men to domestic chores, the amount of time men put in seems to have changed only slightly. Involvement of men with their children, however, seems to have increased over the old days. Even mothers say that the men help the children, particularly the older ones, with homework. Two women said they had made a deal with their husbands: they would take charge of the child until she or he reached middle school and then the father was to take over—rather strong evidence that these two women were not concerned about uterine families. No mother told me that her husband actually was in charge of her middle school-aged children, however. Certainly from the mothers' perspective, the physical care of younger children, which means feeding them, washing them and their clothes, cutting their hair, sewing on their buttons, and so on, was the mother's job. Fathers were more likely to be held responsible for education, work habits, and providing a larger share of the income. One Beijing mother said, "Well, he is in charge of the big things, not the little things like bad manners and dirty hands. If the children quarrel with a neighbor child and hurt her, my husband is the one to handle it." Whenever I asked a mother why fathers did less, they nearly always answered, "Men aren't patient. They can't handle small children."

Finally, though it would have been more appropriate to ask men, I asked 27 urban women whom they thought a man would side with in a quarrel between his mother and his wife. It was a rather blunt frontal attack on a delicate question, that is, has the new society succeeded in weakening the feudalistic filial bonds in favor of the marital bond? This has, of course, been the goal of every daughter-in-law since time immemorial. Fourteen of the women avoided the question completely by insisting that such quarrels never happened or saying that the son would side with "whoever was right"; the other 13 were almost evenly split, with 6 siding with the wife and 7 siding with the mother. The younger women tended to say that the man would side with the wife and the older women tended to say that he would side with the mother. Again, though the numbers are few and the results murky, the fact that there was no consensus seems to indicate that there are some basic changes going on in the expected be-havior between parents and children. One can no longer assume that the parent-child relationship is the most potent one in the Chinese household. A twenty-eight-year-old nurse in a neigh-borhood clinic told me, "Quarrels between a woman and her mother-in-law are very hard on her husband. In his heart he may side with his wife, but he doesn't dare express it. Instead he urges them to make peace." A fifty-three-year-old mother-in-law said gruffly, "In quarrels between wives and mothers-in-law the sons now side with the wives. That is why women don't want to live with their daughters-in-law anymore." And then a woman in her middle forties gave me one of those hard-to-interpret answers: "Most men side with their wives in an argument with their mothers. A few well-behaved sons will side with their mothers."

If the parent-child relationship was the most potent in the old society, the infamous relationship between mother-in-law and daughter-in-law was the most tense. The great majority of Chi-nese women at some time or another in their lives will live with a mother-in-law or a daughter-in-law or both, and it is assumed that they will quarrel. There are nearly as many explanations for this stressful relationship as there are sinologists. They range from the belief (common in China) that women are naturally quarrelsome to the only slightly more sophisticated one that mothers-in-law mistreat their daughters-in-law because they themselves were mistreated—a sort of hydraulic balance theory. Another theory holds that two women in one kitchen produces competition, a hypothesis more appropriate to sisters-in-law, I would think. In my work with women in Taiwan, it seemed to me that the friction of close daily living usually sparked into flame over some problem with the son and husband.[3] The older woman feared that her uterine family was endangered by the young woman she herself had introduced into her son's bed. She had watched other families pulled apart by young wives who saw it to their advantage to separate the household, and if she was the worrying type, every sign of intimacy between the young couple turned the screws on her anxiety.

The uterine family is no longer the sole resource it once was for women. Moreover, sons are as likely to be transferred to another city by the state as they are by a conniving daughter-in-law. Mothers are reassured by the state through promises of pensions or state aid, so a thoroughly loyal son is no longer the only alternative to a cold and hungry old age. For the older women this should take some of the tension out of their relations with their daughters-in-law. For the younger women the knowledge that they will not have to live with their mothers-in-law forever, that it is socially acceptable (even desirable) for them to live separately, should reduce some of the wife's hostility toward a less than diplomatic mother-in-law.

Looking over my interviews after I had finished work in Beijing, I realized that many women had volunteered comments about tense mother-in-law/daughter-in-law relationships. A woman who had been married about ten years told me that many of the quarrels between husbands and wives start out as quarrels between the daughter-in-law and mother-in-law. A thirty-year-old shop clerk told me smugly, "My mother-in-law and I never quarrel. In other families they do and the son ought to make peace. The younger generation must show respect for old people. My mother-in-law knows our habits well: she always has dinner ready when we get home, so there is no quarreling." In Shaoxing

I decided to ask directly about the frequency of mother-in-law/ daughter-in-law quarrels. Of the 14 women who were willing to respond, 13 told me that mothers-in-law and daughters-in-law were far more likely to quarrel than husbands and wives.

I was able to talk 43 urban women into telling me what they thought caused quarrels between mothers-in-law and daughters-in-law. Disagreements over disciplining children caused 21 percent of the quarrels. Nearly always the disagreement arose because the mother wanted to spank the child and the grandmother disapproved. About the same number of quarrels grew out of disputes over how to spend the family's money. These ranged from disputes over how much of the budget was to be spent on food (old people were far more interested in eating well than in saving for television sets) to who was contributing the most and the implications of that for decision making. Another 9 percent of the discord between mother-in-law and daughter-in-law was clearly friction between women with different ways of doing things, ways not unrelated to their different generations.

But the most frequent of the mother-in-law/daughter-in-law troubles (49 percent) are those I have labeled power struggles. Younger women told me that the quarrels resulted from mothers-in-law who were too bossy or nagged too much; or, as one put it, "They think the younger generation should listen to them, so if the son sides with his wife, there is a quarrel." Older women said the quarrels resulted from the same conflict, but they were more likely to phrase it to their advantage: "The mothers-in-law try to establish some rules and the daughters-in-law don't like it." A very astute seventy-year-old woman in Zhejiang said, "The older women resent the younger's independence. They try to keep it in their hearts but then one day it just all comes out and there is a big quarrel." Jealousy was also frequently mentioned. The young women think the older woman shows favoritism to another daughter-in-law, the older woman's daughter, or even to her own son (and the younger woman's husband). The older women are jealous of their sons: they are angry when they side with their wives, angry if they don't scold their wives, and hurt when they give their wives more money or attention than they do their mothers.

Few of these explanations would seem odd to the women in the traditional society or women I interviewed in the 1950's. Yet most of them had a different tone. In the old days young women resented the mother-in-law's authority and as they became more confident occasionally expressed this resentment. Now, even new wives are likely to disappoint a mother-in-law's expectations of obedience if she does not give her orders in polite terms. In the old days older women frequently were angered and anxious if their sons paid too much attention to their wives, but now the older women seem to vary between resignation and suppressed hostility. There has not been a resolution of this age-old conflict, as the answers to my questions clearly indicate, but neither does it seem to be the same conflict. Young women are still aware of and even motivated by the old system. Two women in Beijing told me proudly that their sons' fiancées came to their houses several times a week to help them with their chores. (One of them was the woman mentioned earlier who said her son had selected a girl who lived nearby so that she could conveniently help his mother.) But the older women are also impressed with their juniors' status in the world outside the home, with the fact that they bring home a wage and that that wage is earned independently of the family. They may be even more impressed than are the younger women, who rather take it for granted since that is the way it has always been in their lifetimes.

Nonetheless, although the new economic system has altered the power relations between mother-in-law and daughter-in-law, it has not severed their dependency relations. Child care facilities in Chinese cities are totally inadequate, and without the help of mothers and mothers-in-law, working women would be at their wit's end. Also, among the women who are now in their fifties and sixties, there is still much economic dependency. Most of these women worked in neighborhood workshops, if they worked at all, and got no pensions or other benefits. When their husbands die, they are totally dependent on their sons and daughters. They trade off their labor at domestic tasks and child care in exchange for rice as long as they can, and then they must depend, as did their mothers before them, on their ties with their sons. The difference now is that mothers-in-law do not have to contend with daughters-in-law who are frantically trying to develop the same kind of security for their own old age that their mothers-in-law are concurrently trying to defend. They either already live separately or they have decided for themselves that it is more convenient to live with the senior generation and benefit from their services.

A forty-eight-year-old textile worker in Shaoxing described the situation this way:

There aren't as many mother-in-law/daughter-in-law quarrels now because the young people often live separately. My mother-in-law is very kind to me and treats me like a daughter. Not many are like that. She came all the way from Shanghai to help out when my husband was sick, doing all the chores and so on. Generally people say the mother-in-law and daughter-in-law cannot be on good terms because the older woman treats her daughter better than she does her daughter-in-law. One thing is certain. A woman quarrels with her daughter and the next day they forget about it. But once a woman quarrels with her daughter-in-law, they hold their anger forever.

This last comment, that a daughter and her mother make peace easily and a mother-in-law and her son's wife rarely do, is an ironic twist on the ideal of the kinship system. The daughter, who according to the men's patrilineal patriarchal ideology is an outsider who really belongs to another family, that of her husband, is infinitely forgivable in the eyes of her mother. A daughter-in-law, who by the same ideology is a member of the mother-in-law's family, is treated with the suspicion and lack of forgiveness that is the lot of all outsiders. One sometimes wonders if in fact women and men in China operate in the same ideological system.

The relationship between husband and wife has probably received more attention from policy makers than any other. As we saw in Chapter 6, the initial propaganda at the time of the proclamation of the first Marriage Law and subsequent editorials, study papers, and handbooks have made an effort to help young people choose their mates and after marriage to alter the content of the marital relationship. In the old days the marital relationship was not an end in itself but only the means to the real end, that of continuing the family. Very little thought was put into matching personalities or interests: it was assumed that the fact of marriage would bind the two sufficiently. Indeed, if they showed too much interest in each other it was considered slightly indecent and, as we have just seen, a threat to the mother of the man. Women were assumed to be both pliable and devoted. For them there should never be any other man in their life but the one to whom their parents gave them at an early age. They were expected to invest their emotional life in their husbands, to be distraught when they died, and certainly never to remarry. Widowers, of course, were expected to remarry: their primary obligation was to their parents and to the line, so they indeed *had* to remarry to provide additional descendants and a daughter-in-law who could be a comfort in their parents' old age. A woman's primary obligation was diffused between her husband and his parents.

Now, the relationship between husband and wife is expected to be focal in the domestic unit—not superior to that of the group but focal. Marriage is supposed to be based on love, and love, according to the manuals, is expressed in shared labor, mutual support in studying, mutual criticism, and comradely solidarity.[4] Choosing a husband or wife is a task for which China's young people are ill prepared, as we saw in Chapter 6, and for many the first years of marriage are years of disappointment. Many of the women I talked with indicated that during those first years they were still closer to their mothers than to their husbands. A woman in Beijing said, "You gradually get closer to your husband, but it takes a few years. At first you just talk to your mother."

The redefinition of the role of wife and of husband is clearly still in process, particularly for the woman. When I asked women to tell me what a good husband was, they quickly came up with a stereotype: good husbands are good-tempered, kind-hearted, and hard-working. Some added that they helped with chores or were capable of contributing to the country. In Shaoxing, where for variety I asked a number of women to describe a bad husband, I was surprised to find that "bad behavior," a common euphemism for sexual transgressions, was frequently mentioned. (I was even more surprised to overhear women gossiping with my assistants about two of my married informants who were reputed to have boyfriends.) Even those women I felt to be "good informants," that is, people who volunteered information and were open to most questions, had little to add to this rather colorless list of attributes.

When asked to describe a good wife, the women's responses were more revealing. The most frequent requirement was that the woman be a hard worker and not quarrelsome. I was struck by the difference in terms: a man was supposed to be good-tempered but a woman not quarrelsome. More importantly, when describing a husband, the characteristics mentioned did not involve relationships, but when describing a wife I often heard, "She takes good care of her husband," or "She obeys her mother-in-law," or "She treats her parents-in-law and her husband's siblings like they were her natal family." A few women added characteristics that were part of their supposedly new role, such as studying hard and working hard both at home and on the job, but even young women included the same list their mothers and grandmothers gave. One earnest old lady, after saying that a good wife should obey her mother-in-law and take good care of the children, thought a minute and then said she should be a good needlewoman also. (None of the younger women mentioned needlework.) I finally pointed out this peculiar list to one of the cadre watching over me. She gave me a steely look and said, "Tradition and the Party both say a woman should obey her parents-in-law and take care of her husband."

Simply because she works all day a woman's relationship with her family has not changed. She is still expected to be the nurturing agent and the caretaker. A very guarded woman technician in a lens factory (age 39) answered my question about the qualities of a good wife this way: "She helps her husband to do his work well. Both must do chores, but she tries to do most of them to relieve her husband's burden. She takes care of the children and takes charge of their education so her husband will have more time to work." Once again I could not restrain myself from asking, "What about the wife's work?" She looked nonplussed for a minute and then said, "His job matters more." What she meant, I think, was that doing her job well meant doing her job in the household well, not her job in the factory. She was first of all an "inside person" and only secondly a factory worker, nurse, or whatever. I think that this ordering is still much the same for younger women also. Women have always been judged by their accomplishments in the home, and for some time to come, I fear, their self-image and that held by their kin and friends will continue to be tied to their domestic roles.

Although women should not be quarrelsome and men should be good-tempered, my informants admitted that husbands and wives often quarreled. They did not quarrel as often as mothers-in-law and daughters-in-law, but nonetheless it was normal for them to quarrel. The causes of the quarrels mentioned in Beijing differed from those described by my Shaoxing informants. Shaoxing women frequently said that people did not quarrel over money problems nearly as much now as they used to in the bad old days, but money was still mentioned as a source of friction by 71 percent of the women. Twenty percent said it was the only cause; 38 percent said the two main causes were money and children. Husbands and wives quarreled over how money was to be spent, who was wasting it, who was holding out their share. Quarrels over children (mentioned by 56 percent of the women) almost always arose over one wanting to discipline more than the other. Miscellaneous reasons ranged from the wife's having a short temper to the man's being lazy and refusing to help with chores.

In Beijing, the quarrels between husband and wife were over the same things but in different proportions. Only 39 percent had to do with money; 57 percent were started by problems with children's affairs. More than a quarter (29 percent) said the causes were varied—such as arguing over who should do the chores, or because people were tired and rushed, or because they had different temperaments. I was amused by a woman in her mid-sixties who had never worked outside her home (she had eight children) but told me that a lot of quarreling that went on now in the family was the result of "this law" that said men had to help with the chores. "They don't want to."

These data present only one measure of life's satisfaction and quite a negative one at that. Nowhere in these figures do we find any indication of the comfort people find in one another's company or the laughter shared when a child's antics delight her parents. One cannot interview about such topics in China, and unfortunately it was not possible for me to participate in or even observe the simple pleasures of family life. I think most Chinese still assume that happiness originates in the warmth of the family, but I suspect that they are still, men and women alike, uncertain whether or not they can expect it to come from their relations with their marital partners. A friend wrote me recently from a city in China about a conversation she had had with a Chinese colleague concerning his impending marriage. She asked him if he were excited about the event. He said, "Excited? No, I'm not excited. I know my fiancée is a good person, and will be a good wife because she is quiet, obedient, and patient. But I do not know whether married life will be happy or not." He had found himself a wife, but happiness might have to come from some other source.

NINE

Sharing a Stove:
Rural Domestic Relations

In the old days the daughter-in-law didn't dare say anything, but now the chair and the table are on the same level.—*Jiangsu farm woman, age 68*

No, the daughter-in-law isn't the boss now, but she dares to complain.
—*Jiangsu farm woman, age 47*

Women are inside organizing the family; men are outside earning a living.
—*Fujian farm woman, age 29*

Life is easier for rural women in China now than it was before Liberation, but the difference is one of degree, not of kind. Whereas young urban women now have separate identities in their workplaces and at least a promise of independence in their old age, rural women are still the daughter or wife of so-and-so in their workplace, and know that their material welfare is dependent upon their husbands and sons. Although it was impossible to do the kind of observation and casual interviewing necessary to confirm it, I think women in Fujian, Shaanxi, and perhaps Jiangsu still weave ties to their sons designed to subvert the sons' loyalties from the families of their fathers. However, the women do so with less single-mindedness than formerly (and as a result may be less effective) because now there are (or appear to be) other alternatives, other places to turn.

Nor is the male family the same impenetrable opposing force it once was. The patriarchal ideology is still dominant, but the old patriarchal structures have been badly mauled by the state. Even though teams and brigades may still be single-surname groups under another label, the next level in the bureaucracy is less likely to be peopled by relatives. Beyond a doubt, the state is less amenable to manipulation by groups of kinsmen than it once was. For women, this means that no longer are all their interactions with authority also interactions with their husbands' relatives. This may be more true in model communes than in the hinterlands, but even there women are probably not quite as defenseless as they once were against the men's system.

The state says that women, too, are part of the collectives, not untrustworthy outsiders linked to male members of the collective. In Chapter 2 I cited numerous examples and gave references to sources for many others that indicate how tenuous state support can be for a woman who acts contrary to the wishes of her family, but women can also see for themselves that some of the pre-Liberation abuses by men are now subject to punishment. Women are not yet the equals of their male peers, but being subordinate is less painful than it once was.

Nonetheless, my interviews with rural women provide much evidence that suggests that women continue to interact with their sons in a traditional way, whether or not their goal is the formation of uterine families. Children are not just encouraged to study for their own benefit, but, in the words of a twenty-nine-year-old mother, "If he doesn't want to do his homework, I explain to him how much I have sacrificed and how hard I work so he can have an education." Mothers also use punishment judiciously. A Shaanxi mother told me, "I don't hit them much. I let their father hit them and then use that as a threat." A thirty-six-year-old Fujian mother told me, "Boys and girls are both closer to their mothers than to their fathers because the fathers work outside and the mothers are at home. Besides, fathers never have anything to say to them." Taiwanese women used the same techniques and attitudes in order to build loyal uterine families who would look to their mother's interests in time of trouble and defend her when she came into conflict with the men's family.

State propaganda through the medium of the radio and of traveling exhibits has produced among country women some very peculiar notions about urban life. Many rural women confuse the colorful posters and boring documents telling how one *should* behave toward one's mother-in-law or keep one's courtyard with how things *are* done in the cities. Not a few women told me that though they knew all city women lived with their daughters, or most city children took their mother's surname, in the country it wasn't done that way. In the city, as we have seen, it wasn't done that way either, but a very basic difference was being expressed by these women, however naïvely exaggerated. In the countryside sons still are more important than daughters. Sons are your own; daughters belong to other people.

I asked a few people why they bothered to keep their daughters if they were of so little value. Some women gave me very practical answers: "You need a daughter to help around the house—a son won't do that. Of course a son will bring in a daughter-in-law to help after your daughter marries out, but when they are small, you need a daughter." When I asked women in Shandong if mothers were closer (emotionally) to their sons or to their daughters, 10 out of the 11 asked said mothers were closer to their sons because that is whom they lived with. Out of the 93 rural women asked whom people preferred to live with, sons or daughters, only 4 (5 percent) said daughters. (One of these women had a daughter living in the city and made no bones about why she wanted to live there with her. The other 3 women quickly added to their answers that of course they *couldn't* live with a daughter if they had a son.) As Chapter 8 showed, 29 percent of the urban women reported that people would rather live with their daughters.

The reasons rural women prefer to live with their sons are quite simple. Only women who have failed to produce sons live with their daughters, and they are considered to be living on charity (unless, as only rarely happens, their daughter married-in a husband). Even a woman who despises her daughter-in-law and has little affection for her son will still live with them rather than with a beloved daughter. A daughter's house is someone else's house and a daughter belongs to someone else's family. Although land is not individually owned in China now, various other kinds of property (including houses) are carefully divided up among brothers after the parents die or vacate the leadership of the family. Of old China it was said that a father maintained control over his adult sons by retaining control over the land (or shop or business) that provided the family's living; in new China the

father no longer has this means of control, but the state requires that a man support his aged parents, and the old ideology
concurs. Aside from the loss of face involved in living with a
daughter, culturally the ties of obligation between parents and
daughter are ambiguous, based almost completely on psychological factors. There is a fear that the daughter's husband, who is
not under any social obligation to her parents, may at a time of
crisis simply throw them out. As one woman put it, you must
always be watching his face.

Ideally, in the old days a man's married sons did not divide the
family until after the death of the patriarch, and if the family
were truly virtuous not even then. Few families managed such
unity and most divided long before the grandchildren were ready
to marry. For a family with even a small amount of property, formal division was a trying event. I suspect it still is in non-model
collectives, but in the teams and brigades I visited, division was
described to me as being virtually automatic. Each site did it a
little differently, but the end result was pretty much the same. In
some places a son left immediately after marriage; others remained a part of the family until the next younger son was about
to marry or had married. The youngest son or the last to marry
usually stayed on with the parents and the original house. In
most cases a careful agreement among the brothers was worked
out so that the economic burden of supporting the parents when
they were no longer able to contribute was fairly evenly spread,
unless one brother was considerably better off than the others.
Farmers say that one son can only earn enough to support one
parent. A son who rejects his financial obligations to his parents
will find their share of his grain rations and/or end of the year
pay-out turned over to them rather than to him. The brigade or
team will not search out a married daughter, however, since she
belongs not only to another family but also, in most cases, to another team or brigade.

As with many of my interview topics, I received both an official position on family division and a fleeting glimpse of what
actually was occurring. When I finally asked women what *caused*
family division, their answers described a process considerably

less automatic than I had been led to believe. In fact, many of the responses were traditional: quarrels between brothers and their wives over allocation of goods, quarrels between mothers-in-law and daughters-in-law, lack of domestic harmony. A lively old lady of seventy-four years who lived in Jiangsu assured me that "many" divisions now were instigated by the father: "If he has sons who want to eat but not to work and are always wanting fine clothes to wear, the father may just say move out and supply yourself." This may or may not have been a veiled reference to the serious problem of motivation among young members of the collective who were raised in a different social milieu and have different attitudes toward hard labor. Perhaps the most frequent answer I was given by women of all ages was that the older couple found the large family too difficult to manage and the work too hard to do. A forty-two-year-old woman in Shaanxi whom I asked if parents would rather live with their sons all in one house or with only one son, answered, "Sure, they would like to keep them all together, but it makes too many people to feed. It isn't just the young people who want to divide but also the old people who have to do all the cooking and housework."

This last response was not confined to Shaanxi. I heard complaints in the other three rural sites as well. Older women are of less value to the collective than younger women. They are taken out of the fields and returned to the house where they are expected to do all the cooking, cleaning, and child care so that the younger, stronger women will be free to work in the fields. Even though the younger women, as we saw in Chapter 4, receive so little for their labor that they are willing enough to take time or even whole seasons off, that is not always possible, and the burden of running the household falls primarily on the older women. In times past, a mother-in-law's burden was alleviated by the corps of daughters-in-law who were expected to cook her meals, bring her tea, and do her bidding, but now with their new role in agriculture, she must have *their* meals ready on their return from work as well as those of the menfolk. Anyone who has seen a Chinese rural kitchen knows how arduous this task can be, particularly if the cook has several small children demanding attention as well. For many an older woman the golden years of watching her daughter-in-law work, playing with her grandchildren, and gossiping with her neighbors are replaced by the drudgery that also marred her younger years. Small wonder if the older woman is as willing as the younger to set up separate households in the new society.

But to be without a son completely is still to be desperate. A young Fujian woman said, "Not to have a son? That is a bad thing. There will be no one to take care of you when you are sick or boil water for you or bring you food or help you. The 'five guarantees' come from the hand of a stranger." A striking example of this desperation was related to me by one of my informants in Jiangsu. In 1974, when she was forty-five, the woman's only son was killed when a tractor tipped over on him. Although she had three daughters, she was allowed to have her IUD removed in order to try for a son. Incredible though it may seem, she became pregnant shortly thereafter and bore a son (whom I can attest to being bright, healthy, and extraordinarily spoiled).

I asked a number of women in Fujian the indelicate question of whether sons or husbands were more important. It was not a popular question with officials, but the women had little hesitation about answering it. The older women said sons, the younger women said husbands, and the more thoughtful answered like this fifty-two-year-old: "When you are young, your husband is more important. If your son dies, you can bear another, but when you get old, the son is most important, because it is on him you will depend in your old age."

Most of the questions I asked of rural women were open-ended and many led them to talk about phases in their or other women's lives, but women rarely answered questions in terms of "before I got married" or "after I got married." Instead, they said "before I had children" or "after my third child was born." I was also struck with how rarely women mentioned their husbands in interviews and how often they mentioned their sons when searching for an example or a telling anecdote. In part this can be attributed to the general reticence in the old society to talking about one's sexual partner, but I think both these examples attest to how salient the role of mother is for women in China. Being a mother, especially the mother of a son, still outranks just about any other status a rural woman might realistically aspire to.

What kind of response do they get from their children? In the country many daughters' relations with their mothers are essentially severed by marriage. It would not be seemly for the older woman to visit too often, and the younger woman is too busy and perhaps too rarely receives permission to visit her mother. That they would like to do otherwise was clear (see Chapter 6). In referring to their natal families, women nearly always said "in my mother's house" rather than "in my father's house" and always spoke of going home to see their mothers, not their fathers or the natal family in general. But, as they themselves say, in time the close relations between mother and daughter give way to other demands on their emotions, usually from their own children.

Since I did not interview many men, my data are less full, but I find them nonetheless convincing. Rural sons are concerned about their mothers and value their relationship with them. I asked a twenty-eight-year-old Fujian mother whom her husband turned to when he needed advice. She said, "In my family my husband gets advice from his mother. Sometimes I don't even know he needs it." I asked a number of people whom a man should side with if his mother and wife quarreled. Some hedged, but all but one of the men who were asked said they should side with their mothers and "teach" their wives. The one exception, a young Youth League officer, said a man should judge who was right or wrong and then talk privately to the one who was wrong. Women were more forthcoming. A thirty-eight-year-old Shaanxi woman told me, "A son should side with his mother. Sons are closer to their mothers. If they sided with the wife, there would be bad trouble. They scold the wife whether the mother is right or wrong. A son must not scold his mother." A sixty-year-old Fujian mother of two married sons said, "My sons know the hardships I had in raising them so they always side with me. Once my eldest son made his wife walk all the way over here to apologize to me." Arthur Wolf asked some of the older women he was interviewing why they had stopped collective labor and several of them told him it was because their sons asked them to. Many of the women I talked with proudly told me their sons ordered their wives to help mother with this or that. How much of this was show and how much genuine concern is hard to determine without direct observation, but I heard far fewer stories about bad sons than about bad husbands (although those were usually other people's). All in all, the relations between mothers and sons in rural China are close and rewarding.

The test of the quality of mother-son relations comes with marriage and the contestants are, as in the city, the mother-in-law and the daughter-in-law. Although the Party has been generally obtuse in dealing with the effect of ideology on social relations among women, it has recognized the cost both to individuals and to society of the domestic discord centered on these two roles. Unfortunately their analysis of the problem is not very subtle, focusing first on the evil mother-in-law who bullies the younger generation, and only in recent years speaking with sympathy of the older woman's many duties. It is significant that after thirty years of Liberation a "be kind to your mother-in-law" campaign was deemed necessary.

From the perspective of the brigade or team, the ideal division of labor between mother-in-law and daughter-in-law is very efficient. The daughter-in-law should work full time in the fields and the mother-in-law should do the domestic chores. After work the younger woman should pitch in and help with what the mother-in-law could not complete during the day, but a *good* mother-in-law tries to get it all done so that the daughter-in-law can just rest when she gets home. A *good* daughter-in-law gets up earlier than everyone else to grind the grain or do the laundry and relieve her mother-in-law of the heaviest chores. A Fujian mother-in-law in her fifties gave me an idealized picture along these lines, after which I asked her about some items in a brief checklist of chores I had been using to find out who did what. I asked who did the laundry. "She does [meaning the daughter-in-law]." Would her husband help her? "Certainly not. No man would wash clothes." Do you sometimes help? "A mother-in-law wouldn't wash her daughter-in-law's clothes even during the month [i.e. the month following childbirth]." Another woman told me spiritedly, "The mother-in-law is busy all day with the grandchildren and the housework and when the daughter-in-law comes home she wants to eat at once and gets angry if the food isn't all ready for her. A mother-in-law is just a servant now and can't do anything about it because she needs her son."

The real division of labor and of power in the family is difficult to sort out, but I expect it is no more the ideal view given by the collective cadre than it is the version supplied by the two women quoted above. Young women put in long hours in the fields, particularly during harvest and planting seasons, but this is not the same as the regular day-in and day-out employment of urban women. It does, however, impress the older women who may never have worked outside their homes. But not that much. In every site I interviewed in, older women did most of the sideline work, such as raising pigs or chickens, and in many of these villages this work produced a sizable income (see Chapter 4). Moreover, this income came in cash often, but alas not always, into the hand of the producer. A mother-in-law in her prime will usually earn more than her daughter-in-law working for the collective. The daughter-in-law may have more face, because she "works" and the mother-in-law stays at home, but the older woman will nonetheless let the younger know how she measures up in the important world, that of the family.

Nor is the daughter-in-law likely to try to make her mother-in-law into a servant. Certainly young women know that they no longer have to put up with the hardships borne by their own mothers. They have witnessed the endless series of campaigns and may even know a man or a mother-in-law who has been made a target of criticism for mistreating a young wife. However, they are still strangers in their husbands' villages; they cannot divorce without ruining their lives; they have no control over their earnings; and their behavior is still judged to a considerable degree by the old standards. I asked a young woman in Jiangsu if a woman would complain if her mother-in-law didn't have dinner ready on time. "No, she wouldn't dare. She would just help her."

A twenty-seven-year-old mother of two in Fujian told me that if there was a disagreement between mother-in-law and daughter-in-law, "the daughter-in-law must give way. She is the younger." What either of these women actually did is another matter, but the rules seem not to have changed much.

In the last chapter I reported that all but one of the fourteen Shaoxing women asked said that there were more quarrels between mothers-in-law and daughters-in-law than between husbands and wives. Table 21 shows a similar set of answers for my Fujian and Jiangsu samples, but a dissimilar pattern for Shandong and Shaanxi. I am at a loss to explain this difference. The two "aberrant" sites, model communes in Shandong and Shaanxi, are both in the north and both in areas that I have for other reasons labeled more conservative (see Chapter 6). It is conceivable that the women answered as they did because they felt that it was somehow more respectable to admit to quarrels between husbands and wives than to admit to quarrels between generations. Indeed, a number of women explained their answers in that way. But others, particularly some in Shaanxi, pointed out that mothers-in-law and daughters-in-law did not live together as long as husbands and wives and so of course there were fewer quarrels over the years. Another possibility is that these two model communes are undergoing a more dramatic transformation of their domestic relations than my other worksites and this is reflected in reduced tensions between women and increased tensions between spouses.

I obtained the most useful information about the content of the mother-in-law/daughter-in-law relationship when I asked the question "What causes mother-in-law/daughter-in-law quarrels?" The cause most often mentioned had to do with power struggles. Some 61 percent of the quarrels described by my women informants involved a battle of wills over objects, chores, or status markers. Specifically, in all the villages studied, the situation most often mentioned was that of the daughter-in-law who would not help the mother-in-law with chores (or who argued about who should do the chores). Many of the other causes mentioned for quarrels between the two women were also traditional—disagreements over money (10 percent), nagging, the

Table 21. "Who Quarrels Most?"

Site	No. of respondents	Mother-in-law and daughter-in-law	Husband and wife
Fujian	20	90%	10%
Jiangsu	39	95	5
Shandong	30	53	47
Shaanxi	34	35	65

younger woman gossiping in the village about family affairs—but some reflected the new society. Several women (8 percent) who said mothers-in-law and daughters-in-law come from different eras and have basic disagreements showed real insight into the new set of conflicts within the family. And the women who complained about the mother-in-law's refusal to provide child care were clearly discussing quarrels that would not have occurred in pre-Liberation days.

Disciplining of children was, in fact, the second most frequently reported cause of trouble between mother-in-law and daughter-in-law. Twenty percent of the quarrels were over children; furthermore, 24 percent of the quarrels between husbands and wives were attributed to the same cause. The disagreement was nearly always between a daughter-in-law (or wife) who wanted to (or did) strike or beat up a misbehaving child and a grandmother (or husband) who objected. Half of the equation seems reasonable enough: Chinese grandmothers are infamous for spoiling their grandchildren and protecting them from the wrath of their mothers, and tired frustrated mothers are likely to slap a whiney demanding child, thus setting off a quarrel between mother and grandmother. However, the other half of the data are less obvious. Mothers, also by tradition, are supposed to intercede for children whom fathers are about to punish, not the other way around. When I seemed puzzled by this in an interview an older woman cited for me a proverb that I had heard in Taiwan as well. "Beat the chicken to teach the monkey." A woman who cannot express her anger with her higher-status husband or mother-in-law will grab the nearest child on the first provocation and punish it unduly, verbally or physically, in the presence of the adult they would *really* like to punish. Both adults usually know what is going on, and depending on the circumstances a quarrel ensues between adults. The "cause" of the quarrel is children.

Most Chinese dismiss troubles between mother-in-law and daughter-in-law as inevitable. A thirty-one-year-old Fujian farm woman put it succinctly: "Mothers-in-law and daughters-in-law are born to quarrel. Everyone knows this. If the mother-in-law says certain words to her daughter, there is no problem; but if she uses the exact same words to her daughter-in-law, she will get angry." Or as a Jiangsu woman said, "It is always one thing or another. The mother-in-law takes the side of her grandchildren or else the daughter-in-law quarrels with her husband's sister and the mother-in-law sides with her own daughter." When I asked whom the son-husband would side with in such conflicts, she said, "He should side with his mother. She raised him." In the cities such ideas may be considered part of the old feudal society, but in the country they are still part of contemporary reality. Although urban women may expect their husbands to side with them or at least be diplomatically neutral, rural women believe men pretty much belong to their mothers.

The most significant fact about relations between husband and wife is how little expression they receive in the culture and how colorless they appear from a reading of my interviews. When I asked what caused quarrels between mothers-in-law and daughters-in-law, I was given a rich collection of anecdotes. The same question about the husband-wife relationship produced categorical answers with much less elaboration even after many probes. The most frequent answer concerned chores—who should do them, why someone had not done them, and so on. This accounted for 28 percent of all the responses. It was the most commonly reported cause in Shandong and Shaanxi, tied in Jiangsu, but was not mentioned once in Fujian. The reason household chores are not a problem in Fujian is not difficult to discover: men are not expected to do them, so there is nothing to quarrel over. When I asked in Fujian if men helped with the cooking, cleaning, or laundry, the women laughed at my absurdity or, in the case of a couple of old ladies, were outraged at the very idea.

The second most common cause of quarrels between husbands and wives is children (24 percent). In a few cases, women described genuine differences of opinion over how children should be trained or disciplined, but more often it was a matter of "one hits and the other says she shouldn't." I imagine these are "Beat the chicken to teach the monkey" quarrels. Both parents are tired at the end of the day's work, and the mother still faces dirty laundry, crying hungry children, and the task of cooking dinner. She scolds the children because she cannot scold the husband. He knows the real object of her fury but scolds her for over-punishing the children (who undoubtedly are relieved to have the hostility deflected to its true object).

Money problems come a distant third (15 percent) in the cause of marital quarrels, but they achieve that frequency almost entirely from two samples, Fujian (29 percent) and Jiangsu (25 percent). Essentially, the problem was over how money was to be spent—men waste it on nonessential personal luxuries, according to the women, and women want to save it for children's clothes, family needs, and so on. Why Shandong (4 percent) and Shaanxi (5 percent) have so few of these kinds of disagreements is hard to say, but it may have a historical basis. The Shandong and Shaanxi brigades I studied were both extremely poor prior to Liberation, whereas the brigades I studied in Fujian and Jiangsu, although not wealthy, had apparently not suffered the same degree of hardship. The comparative prosperity the two northern field sites now enjoy makes it almost sinful for residents to quarrel over money. Another explanation might be that they are geographically so far away from the material temptations that urban centers can provide that there is little to quarrel over.

Fujian and Jiangsu also differ from the other two sites in the frequency with which personality differences or character defects are mentioned as sources of conflict: "Neither will give in." "Both have hot tempers." "Women are tired and short-tempered and men won't tolerate it." "They both want to be boss." (I asked this last woman who should be boss, and she said, "The man," looking at me curiously.) Other women said, "They don't discuss things, they just fight."

Another pair of questions I asked most women in all four field sites was designed to get at ideal types: "What is a good husband?" and "What is a good wife?" Occasionally I asked about bad husbands and bad wives, but women usually found this more difficult to answer. Certainly the good husband/good wife answers are formulaic and were recognized as such by the women giving them. Their answers form a clear pattern. A good wife works hard (33 percent), obeys her husband (22 percent), and is good-tempered (18 percent), in that order of frequency. A good husband is kind-hearted and good-tempered (31 percent), helps with the chores (24 percent), and works hard (15 percent), again in that order of frequency. It is interesting that there is a reverse order between good tempers and hard workers in the two gender categories. Women see hard work in wives as more important than in husbands, but if frequency of mention can be used as an index, a good-hearted man is more important than a hard-working one. In the handful of male interviews I was allowed to do, the same pattern exists: good husbands "show concern" for their wives and talk things over with them; good wives work hard, put their husbands first in everything, and are obedient.

The women's responses within each field site are slightly different in emphasis. In three provinces, a good wife works hard and is obedient to her husband, but in Fujian a good wife is most frequently described as family-oriented and a hard worker. Her husband is frugal and good-tempered. As with other questions, the Fujian women were far more open in their responses. A woman in her late thirties volunteered:

It is easier to tell a bad wife than a bad husband, but there is a bad husband in our team. He won't give his wife any money. He "plays" with other women and if his wife says anything about it he hits her. He hits her whenever he feels like it. People talk about him but few dare to say anything to him. I once got up the courage to tell him that his wife would commit suicide if he went on this way, but it didn't do any good. He is very friendly with a widow who lives in this village. They often go to the movies together. Someone saw him coming out of her house at dawn one morning. The widow's husband was a good friend of his. Nobody has ever caught them in the act, but then nothing would happen if they did. The relatives would see to that. Anyway, he is getting older now and he won't be able to do it much longer.

He will, no doubt, still be able to beat his wife for some time to come. There is ample evidence that wife-beating is still a common problem in China. Small wonder that 10 percent of the women describe a good husband as one who doesn't beat his wife.

The most important attribute of a good husband in Fujian is that he be frugal, that is, not waste the family money on gambling or women. Jiangsu women also prize a frugal husband, but they value an even-tempered one more. As one woman expressed it, "A good husband helps his wife with chores, but if he has a good temper it doesn't matter whether he does chores or not." Doing chores matters a lot in Shaanxi, however, where 56 percent of the women mentioned it. The Shandong women, like the Jiangsu women, most of all wanted a good-tempered man who was considerate of his wife. I think, but cannot be sure, that these women are not just talking about a man with a sunny disposition, but in fact are talking about a man who does not fly into rages and beat them or their children. I gave up trying to interview on wife-beating, however; it was obviously a topic that made cadres nervous, which in itself suggests that the problem remains a serious one even on so-called model communes.

In rural China marriage is still very much a contractual matter. A woman exchanges her reproductive and labor potential for a man's economic commitment. As a Shandong pig raiser explained, "I earn money for her, she cooks for me." City women may expect some sort of emotional fulfillment or even companionship from their marriages, but the most rural women hope for is an even-tempered man who might help a bit with the heavier chores. A Jiangsu woman told me half-jokingly, "A good husband is one who comes home once a year but sends his wages every month." Rural women get a lot of pleasure out of their relationships with their children. One cannot help wondering where, if anywhere, men find such solace. At least once in each of the provinces I visited I had occasion to note in my journal how peripheral men seem to be to the lives of women and how often they were treated almost as intruders in the household. In fact, good fathers-in-law were described to me by some women as men who didn't interfere in family affairs. A Shandong woman said, "A good father-in-law just comes home to eat and then goes out again. He doesn't get involved in family arrangements." A Shaanxi woman remarked, "Fathers-in-law are always out somewhere. When they come home, they are treated like a guest and everyone is a little uncomfortable. They mainly come home for meals." In the evenings men seem to gather in informal groups at the team headquarters or recreation room if there is one, places where women are not welcome.

For a Chinese woman, marriage is supposed to be forever. As we saw in Chapter 7, widows are expected to stay widowed if they possibly can, and if they have children they are thought to be almost immoral if they consider marrying again. Only real financial distress can justify it. Being lonely or falling in love only makes the match more disgraceful, and the woman less respectable. True, there are exceptions and there is much propaganda by the government to alter this attitude. I interviewed a woman in Shandong who with much embarrassment admitted that a few years earlier at the age of fifty-two she had been married to a widower with four children. She herself had no living children. I could discover no prior acquaintance between them and I think there was none. I suspect it was a matter of a brigade with an aging widow on its hands matching her with a man who had four youngish boys on his hands. In this instance the collective could do something no family could respectably manage. And, if she can tolerate the gossip, the woman in question will probably have a more satisfying old age than she would have as a propertyless, childless widow living on the "five guarantees."

Not being allowed to wander in the villages of China or to accept invitations to visit in homes cut me off from that aspect of Chinese society that is so valuable and that rural people find so difficult to express in words. I know from past experience that there are happy families and devoted husbands and wives in rural areas. My interviews have little to say on this subject. One can ask if a woman's husband is the sort she has described as a "good husband" in a general question, and she will just shrug her shoulders and mutter something like, "He'll do." A cadre may insist that he is a model husband who does more cooking than does the informant, who may or may not grudgingly agree. I, like my informants, have learned to be skeptical of *ganbu hua* (cadre talk). Occasionally one runs across someone like the slightly wacky young woman in Fujian who even after bearing her husband two children is still singing his praises like an American teenager speaking of her boyfriend. (The cadre and her neighbors were disgusted; I was charmed.) On the whole, I fear that rural marriages, at least in their early years, are less satisfying than the relations between mothers and their children.

The quality of domestic life in rural China has certainly improved since Liberation, and much of that improvement results from a dramatically raised standard of living. How many of these improvements go beyond the model communes is something I cannot judge. State pressure to alleviate some of the worst abuses of women has been successful, and even though wives are still beaten, they are not sold into prostitution or slavery. But I was not very surprised by what I was allowed to see of family life in the villages. Mothers-in-law have lost a lot of power but are not yet out of the running. Daughters-in-law have a new respect but are not yet managing the household. Mothers seem less frantic in their need to tie their sons to them, but their sons still seem to place them first in their affections. No matter how well the family limitation program works, I think that in twenty years there will still be mothers-in-law and daughters-in-law sharing a stove and quarreling over the man who is significant to the lives of both.

TEN

The Birth Limitation Program: Family vs. State

It is best to have three or four children. Most important is to have two boys. My husband wants four boys. He says if one boy can earn 40 yuan a month, four can earn 160 yuan. If it takes one all day to weed your private plot, it will take the four of them two hours. — *Farm woman, age 37*

In the old society we felt the more children the better. The old people wanted them so someone would take care of them in their old age. Now, everyone has a job and can get a pension to take care of their old age. Besides, the daughters can help if you have no sons. On the other side, if we all depend on the government, the burden will be too heavy. If there are no children to help, the government will have to take care of all the old people. Also if there are no children in the house, there is nothing to do when you come home from work in the evening.

— *Beijing teacher, age 38*

The birth limitation program in contemporary China has aroused much international interest, both because of its remarkable success in controlling population growth and because of the enormous problem that China must overcome. Although the Chinese government is not generous in making data available even to its own statisticians, no one doubts the enormity of the population problem. Past experiences with China's "remarkable successes" have made foreign observers cautious about the optimistic reports first released by the government. And it may well be that the national government itself is not very confident of the extent of its apparent achievements. Central government pressure has in the past caused provincial governments to provide optimistic reports based on little more than hope for a brighter future, and the same is true in increasing magnitude as one moves down the bureaucratic hierarchy. We were told, for example, in Shijiazhuang of the very successful birth limitation record their commune held: in 1980 out of 556 births, only *three* were reported as being of the disapproved second-order type, that is, the mother's second child; in 1979 the commune registered 604 births of which only six were second-order. Yet among the few women I interviewed or met under other circumstances in just one brigade of that commune, there were two second-order births in 1980 and five in 1979. It seems unlikely that most of the deviants would be in this one (model) brigade. For reasons of their own, the birth limitation committee chose to give us and our Beijing cadres false statistics. Nonetheless, such eminent demographers as Ansley J. Coale and John S. Aird now are convinced that dramatic changes have occurred in China's population structure,[1] and the recently released Chinese Fertility Survey with its sample of one million women provides very convincing evidence. Data drawn from the Fertility Survey (see Table 22) show a dramatic drop in both urban and rural fertility since the inception of the birth limitation program. From a high in 1963 of 7.78 children in the rural areas and 6.21 children in the urban areas, the total fertility rate fell by 1980 to a low of 2.48 in the countryside and 1.15 in the cities. The reader with an eye for statistics will find in this table some remarkable evidence of the hardships suffered by women during the Great Leap and the terrible years of famine that followed when the total fertility rate, untrammeled at that time by a birth limitation program, nonetheless fell to a low in the rural areas matched again only after the imposition of government rewards and punishments.

In the thirty years since Liberation, the CCP has been cautious about interfering in family matters in rural China. This policy, as Judith Stacey, Kay Ann Johnson, and others have pointed out, has by and large been to the detriment of women and women's issues. In the matter of birth planning, however, the state has shown no hesitation about involving itself in the most intimate of family matters, and in so doing it has caught rural women in the middle of a fundamental struggle between family and state. In this chapter I will look at the birth planning program in China first from the perspective of the state, then from that of the family, and finally from that of my women informants. Readers interested in the demography of China are advised to look

Table 22. Rural and Urban Total Fertility Rates by Year, 1950–1981,
According to Chinese Fertility Survey

Year	Rural rate	Urban rate	Year	Rural rate	Urban rate
1950	5.96	5.00	1966	6.96	3.10
1951	5.90	4.72	1967	5.85	2.91
1952	6.67	5.52	1968	7.03	3.87
1953	6.18	5.40	1969	6.26	3.30
1954	6.39	5.72	1970	6.38	3.27
1955	6.39	5.67	1971	6.01	2.88
1956	5.97	5.33	1972	5.50	2.64
1957	6.50	5.94	1973	5.01	2.39
1958	5.78	5.25	1974	4.64	1.98
1959	4.32	4.17	1975	3.95	1.78
1960	4.00	4.06	1976	3.58	1.61
1961	3.35	2.98	1977	3.12	1.57
1962	6.30	4.79	1978	2.97	1.55
1963	7.78	6.21	1979	3.05	1.37
1964	6.57	4.40	1980	2.48	1.15
1965	6.60	3.75	1981	2.91	1.39

elsewhere, for I will be concerned here primarily with the impact of the program on the citizenry rather than with the details of its successes and failures.[2]

Mao's great faith in Marxist theory made it difficult for him to accept the need to control the runaway growth of China's population in the relatively calm years following Liberation. When the census of 1953 and some sample surveys revealed a natural increase rate of 2 percent per thousand, even Mao had to recognize the seriousness of the problem and reverse his policy. A first birth planning campaign began in 1956, but it was abruptly terminated in 1958 when Mao launched the Great Leap Forward, China's first major economic disaster. A second campaign began in 1962 as the nation began to recover from the Great Leap Forward, only to be terminated again in 1968 when the activities of the Cultural Revolution disrupted production and distribution of, among other things, contraceptives. By 1972 when society was again functioning, the "later, longer, fewer" campaign was announced, urging later marriages, longer intervals between births, and fewer children born. In practical terms this meant no marriages in the cities for women under twenty-five years of age and in the country for women under twenty-three. The corresponding ages for men were twenty-eight and twenty-five. In the rural areas couples were told to wait at least three years before having a second child and in the cities at least four years. Until 1977 the "fewer" part of the slogan was translated into three children in the countryside and two children in the cities. After 1977 rural couples were also limited to two children each. Late in the 1970's as the postwar babies began to reach marriageable age, it became all too clear that another giant upsurge in the population would occur unless even more drastic measures were taken. The one-child campaign was announced in 1979, and even this is considered a compromise with the central government's goal of zero growth by the turn of the century. To accomplish that, some large number of the population would have to agree to have no children at all, a highly unlikely prospect in China.[3]

China's demographers have made various population projections in attempting to convince the people and the government of the urgency of the problem. In order to implement the current one-child campaign, the government has used these projections to set a desired growth rate for the year and then set specific growth rates for each province. The provincial governments in conjunction with Party leaders and birth planning committees then set what amounts to quotas for each of the units (counties and/or municipalities) directly under it. This quota is then further reallocated down the line until, theoretically, each team or urban unit knows exactly how many babies it may have for the year. It is a very efficient system in that it allows for flexibility at each level as well as responsibility at each level, but at the same time it is vulnerable to serious abuses that may occur among local less sophisticated cadres who focus more on the target to be met than on the methods necessary to achieve it.

The system essentially owes its success to three main features: (1) the quality of the contraceptive devices available and the excellent distribution system for them; (2) a very inviting set of incentives for having one child, matched by a very worrying set of penalties for ignoring the government's "call"; and (3) a massive bureaucratic control system that does not allow the individual much room to maneuver. Pi-chao Chen and Adrienne Kols give an excellent summary of the contraceptives currently available to rural and urban women in China.[4] IUD's are the most common method, followed closely by female sterilization. The pill is an urban technique and not the most popular method even in the cities, but there is also considerable experimentation going on with other types of steroid contraceptives. The "visiting pill" is available for couples who see each other infrequently owing to job assignments in different cities. The government is also producing and experimenting with further refinements in a once-a-month contraceptive (both oral and by injection). Condoms are available although they are not very popular because of their poor quality and design. Abortion is available and free, but it is not encouraged as anything but a means of correcting contraceptive failures. The Chinese have used the vacuum aspiration technique since the late 1950's. Working in conjunction with China's impressive health care delivery system, the birth limitation program literally delivers contraception to every fertile married woman in rural and urban China. Each woman is in the charge of a birth limitation worker who checks with her regularly to make sure she is using the contraceptive provided and to discover early if she has begun an unauthorized pregnancy.

In order to overcome resistance to a program that is in conflict with several of China's most cherished traditions, the state offers a set of economic and social incentives for those who agree to limit their families. As with all things in China, there are differences between rural and urban incentives, but there are also many differences between provinces and even between communes within the same county. In cities, a husband and wife who agree to limit themselves to one child are given a hefty cash incentive (as much as 8 percent of an average monthly income) until the child is fourteen, priority on housing lists, extra maternity leave, free education through senior middle school, free health care for the child, preference in job placement when the child has completed school, and an increment to their pension when they retire. Not all urban workers are employed by state-run factories, of course, and lower level collectives often cannot afford to be so generous. Furthermore, many people have been quick to realize that if most young couples sign the pledge, the offer of high-priority status on job lists for their child at school-leaving will be meaningless, just as in some urban clinics an express line for the single child has already become as long or longer than the regular line. Rural rewards for pledging one child are less extensive and show even greater variation. Even among my model communes the increment ranged from twenty or thirty workpoints per month to a flat rate (impressive by rural standards) of 50 yuan a year. Some couples were promised housing allotments suitable for a two-child family, adult grain rations for the child from birth, extra-large private plots, reduced or forgiven school fees, and free medical care. I was told of places where the couples were given sewing machines, and of others where rewards were only a thermos bottle or a tin wash basin.

The young woman in charge of the birth limitation clinic in the neighborhood in which I interviewed in Shaoxing described for me how the system worked in her unit:

The bonus here is 50 yuan a year and free medical care and schooling for the child. There is also a speedy care section in the hospital for them. The only exceptions for people who want more than one child are (1) the firstborn has an accident; (2) one of the pair has been married before and brings a child to the marriage; (3) they have adopted a child and then are cured of infertility. If they cannot meet these qualifications, they will be told they cannot have another child and will be encouraged to have an abortion. If they don't agree, we talk to the mother-in-law and husband because they are usually the ones who object.

She went on to say that some women never make the one-child pledge at all: "They just wait and see if the government will change its mind." When I asked, "What happens if a woman hides her pregnancy until the fifth or sixth month?" she replied, "We call a meeting and discuss it. If the committee sympathizes, she will be allowed to have the baby. Otherwise there will be an abortion. Actually, it is impossible to hide a pregnancy for that long because people will discover it. Those who are known to want another child are watched more carefully."

The degree of control the central government has over its citizens is impressive and has served the state well in this incursion into the family domain. Late marriage in the cities, as we have seen, is nearly universal in no small part because it is almost impossible to get the necessary forms to marry before the "recommended" age. The later marriage rule in the country is more often circumvented because as far as most country people are concerned, the real wedding is the social event that can be registered at a more "convenient" date. So long as there are no public quotas that might embarrass the collective's leaders, they are inclined to ignore such minor infractions as the early marriage of the son of their father's brother.

But having a third (now, with the latest directive, a second) child is another matter, a matter of great interest to the authorities at all levels. Penalties vary widely from province to province, but their shared characteristic is to treat that second or third child as if it did not exist. Housing is assigned for a one-child family, grain rations for the child must be purchased on the open market, medical care must be paid for, and the child is not eligible for any of the cooperative plans offered by the parents' work units. If they have signed a one-child pledge, the parents must return all cash subsidies paid out to them. Emergency loans or subsidies are not available to families who have broken their pledges. In some urban units, a couple who has the temerity to produce a third child will suffer a 10 percent wage reduction and will be passed over for all future increments and bonuses until the child is fourteen.

Persuasion remains the preferred enforcement technique, and the signboards and airwaves of China are laden with discussions of what was once an unacceptable topic in polite conversation. In a land where menstruation was (and in the country still is) the symbol of women's degradation, some factories now have the menstrual cycles of their women workers posted on a bulletin board to be checked off each month. Newspaper editors and radio commentators find an amazing number of ways to encourage and exhort the population to practice contraception for the good of the country. On an individual level, women who are known to be pregnant with an illegal child are visited both at home and at work by officials, colleagues, and friends until they acquiesce to an abortion. One of the methods of persuasion used with recalcitrant pregnant women in urban factories is to halt payment of the one-child benefits to all members of her work unit for a month, or until she agrees to an abortion. A much-quoted comment by a local level birth planning cadre gives some insight into the fine line between persuasion and coercion: "Mobilization is different from persuasion. We persuade people to do this or that. But we mobilize people to do this or that when we fail to persuade them in spite of our efforts. We hope they will understand later."[5]

Perhaps because they have been more resistant to persuasion, rural women have been more subject to "mobilization." After the birth of their first child, they are mobilized to have IUD's inserted, and after the birth of their second child (still allowed in some rural areas in 1981) they were in many places mobilized for sterilization. During the mass sterilization drives of 1979, nearly all women in some villages who had borne three or more children were sterilized. The issue of forced abortion, a subject burdened with moral questions in the West, cannot be ignored. In interviewing about contraceptive techniques in one rural commune, I was told that their commune had performed 587 abortions in 1980: of these 587 abortions, 252 were "big month" abortions. "Big month" abortions are those performed on women *past* their fifth month of pregnancy. When I asked why there were so many of these late abortions, I was told that it was a far greater number than usual, but when the new government regulations were announced disallowing third-order births, these women were already far into their pregnancies. They were nonetheless considered illegal pregnancies. I have no way of knowing whether or not these women were willing to have abortions. Abortions are, beyond a doubt, performed with unknown frequency on women who do not want them, and they may sometimes be done under cruel and degrading circumstances.[6] Whenever abuses of this sort burst forth into the newspapers, central government and provincial authorities make strong and sincere statements condemning the local cadres who are held responsible. They may even take more punitive actions, but the pressure on local cadres to meet their quota remains.

In March 1982 an editorial appeared in *Renmin ribao* giving a semiofficial version of a new, more militant directive on the birth limitation program. According to the editorial, there will be no exceptions to the ban on third births, and "emphasis on implementing the population policy must therefore be placed in the rural areas."[7] That emphasis will include a new drive to enforce the one-child rule in the countryside. Second births will be approved only with prior review by local authorities. More worrisome was the promise that the government would begin formulating eugenic regulations to prevent the birth of "congenitally retarded and dull-witted people" and to forbid those "with hereditary deformity" from giving birth. The CCP has apparently decided to push forward with its goal of a radically reduced population by the turn of the century.[8]

As the data in Table 22 indicate, many urban couples have responded to the government's call. In urban areas the state has more direct control over the futures of young people now than does the family, and this may well be the clue to the rural-urban difference in the response to birth planning. The generation of people whose children have been reaching marriageable age in the last few years were raised in a China that had no respect for its own government and little hope for a future that they did not provide for themselves in the form of progeny. In the last thirty years they have seen their lives restructured by a government that took responsibility, perhaps at times too much responsibility, for their well-being. They have been promised retirement pensions and now see some of their neighbors living on those pensions. They have also seen their children shipped off to the farthest corners of China, some of them never to return, others to return infrequently, and many of them unable to take on the social and economic duties once considered essential to being a proper son. One of these duties, the continuation of the ancestral rites, has not only been made illegal but has been ridiculed to the point that few urban parents openly perform the rites themselves and certainly would not ask their sons to do them. And however much the old people might like to have a house full of grandchildren, the traditional sign of a family with good fortune, that house is now too small for the people already in it, let alone for the several sons of the several sons they themselves bore. The state's success in controlling urban fertility comes from its success in usurping the authority of the family over the reproductive decisions of its youngest generation. Not doing things the old way has become far more attractive than doing things the old way. This is not to say that the state has failed in its efforts to convince people that they should for their own sakes limit births. It has done that too, but it has also effectively deflected the counterforce that might have, and I think still could, convince the average couple that having three or four children as additional insurance is desirable.[9]

Thus far, rural China is still dominated by the family. (I am here using that difficult word to mean both the domestic group and the ideological family of male relatives who live in the same village or collective.) A rich and prosperous family is still one with many grandsons (and few granddaughters). Ancestor worship is no longer carried on in the lineage halls, for they have been converted into granaries or stables, and the domestic ancestral tablets were burned during the Cultural Revolution. But many of the homes I interviewed in had pictures of deceased relatives, incense sticks, and makeshift bits of religious paraphernalia. Funerals, even in model collectives, are again becoming elaborate, with mourning clothes and Daoist rituals to help the deceased through the various stages of postlife existence. Qing Ming, the traditional day for cleaning the graves of the ancestors and making offerings to them, is now a national memorial day, but after the children get home from school trips to the graves of martyrs, the family still treks off to the mountains (usually no more than a hill) to visit the family graves. The children may joke about ghosts and act superior to it all (they also did in conservative Taiwan some twenty-five years ago), but they learn their place in the long line of relatives who were there before they were born and who depend on them to continue on in the years ahead.

In times past, many grandsons was not only a sign of a prosperous family, it often was the cause of that family's prosperity. Aside from being a support to their parents in their old age, sons were a father's legacy to the future of the family they had inherited from their fathers. In very practical terms, as the man quoted in one of the epigraphs to this chapter said, four sons earn four times as much as one son. Even if in the end his sons fell short, the father would still be cited as one who did his duty to the family insofar as he was able. That his grandsons failed to add to the family coffers or nurseries was beyond his power to control, but his sons owed him respect and support in his old age as a man who had fulfilled his filial obligations. The ideology of this great male-linked chain of ancestors may have lost some of its saliency in recent years, but the obligation of sons to support their parents has not. And it is here, in the need for old-age support, that the farmers dare to speak out about the dangers as they see them in the birth planning program.

Pension plans do not exist in the countryside. A few experimental systems have been tried out, and the brigade I worked in in Shaanxi has plans for one "next year," but even the plans would cover only a few old (male) people. For the common farmer, sons are their retirement policies. Daughters belong to someone else and cannot be forced to support them, so a couple with no sons is in serious trouble. The oft-mentioned five guarantees are welfare of the last resort and not something on which hard-working self-respecting farmers want to end out their days. A daughter might be able to bring in a son-in-law, but this has always been a low-prestige form of marriage, a sign of a family's failure, and in the better-off collectives is not actively encouraged by the cadre, who, like the lineage members of the past, are disinclined to share the local wealth with an outsider. Two sons are the only solution, the second for insurance in case the first proves unfilial or sickly, or happens to die young. And even that is bare-bones support, for the usual rule of thumb is that one can support one—that is, one son can support one of the old people and the second son provides for the basic needs of the other. The state promises that elderly parents will not be abandoned, putting their rights into the new constitution and even, rather illogically, making it a criminal offense with up to five years' imprisonment for failure to support parents or grandparents.[10] I have yet to see a convincing answer to the farmers' question: how can one married couple support four elderly parents? The official answer is that there will be pensions, but collectivization has educated farmers in the economics of farming. They ask how, in twenty years' time when the supply of able-bodied laborers will be far below the present level and the number of elderly nonproducers will be far above, will the team pay for something it cannot afford now?

As if the left hand did not know what the right was up to, the government has also begun a major economic reorganization of the commune system. Instead of the land being farmed by a production team under the direction of team leaders, families are working the land as individual units. The right to work a particular piece of land is more or less auctioned off, with the individual family allowed to keep as its profit whatever it makes over the bid. If the family does not meet the bid, it is in debt to the collective. Even some of the small brigade factories are being leased out, usually to a group of men who join together for that purpose only.

The farmers grasp the situation and draw their own conclusion. They see that they are once again in economic control over their own destinies, and that the larger their family work force, the more prosperous that destiny will be. The consequence of their thinking is that the birth rate in some communes has already begun to climb precipitously.[11] In recent months (1983) attempts have been made to prevent farmers from ignoring the economic sanctions against having several children by tying their contract with the collective to a family limitation agreement.[12]

Some provincial newspaper reports have implied a blatant disregard for the birth quotas in certain areas, but this appears to be an exception rather than the rule, except for notoriously bad

Guangdong Province.[13] More common than outright rebellion, I suspect, are the collectives in which the cadres are showing "understanding" for more would-be parents than their quota will allow and are doctoring their statistics in order to avoid outside interference. The government has changed its policy just often enough that many families reject sterilization but allow their womenfolk to be fitted with IUD's, leaving themselves the option of another child should the government change its mind again before the wife is past childbearing. The recent announcement that women (or men) must be sterilized after the birth of a second child would seem to foreclose that option, however, and it appears that the government is going to be tougher in the future about enforcing the family limitation program.[14] If it is committed to enforcing the one-child limit in rural areas, it may have to invoke real coercion, for from the point of view of the farmer, the very basis of the family is being threatened.

    The birth planning program puts women in the unenviable position of meeting either the demands of the state or the needs of the family, but not both. An analysis of the current reproduction histories of the women I interviewed would lead one to believe that they had elected to obey the state. I no more believe that these women made that decision themselves than I believe that a purely voluntary program of birth planning would work in China. Nonetheless, the reproductive histories of my women informants from model collectives are exemplary. Of the 14 married women under forty years of age in my Beijing sample, only one had a child that did not meet the spacing and/or single-child limitation. She not only had two children but had them within a year of each other. Her explanation was that she was in Beijing only to bear her child and that her work assignment was in Inner Mongolia where there was no limitation on births. Three other Beijing women in this age category had borne two children, but all three had borne their last child before the single-child ruling went into effect (1979) and they were spaced according to the four-year waiting period. None of the women was married before the minimum age of twenty-three (twenty-five for those married after 1972). Shaoxing was a slightly different story. Of the 22 married women under the age of forty, 3 had had children out-side the rules. The youngest, an illiterate woman in her mid-twenties, had married when she was eighteen and had borne two children just two years apart. Her husband was also illiterate, sur-prising for his age and urban residence, and I think there may have been a bad class background, for my companions clearly viewed them with some distaste. Certainly their living condi-tions were pathetic. The other two women who were not quite in line with the policy had borne in one case an extra child and in the other an improperly spaced child, but all three women had completed their childbearing in 1974, which was fairly early in the third birth planning campaign.

The fine record of compliance with the birth planning rules of the women I interviewed in the rural collectives occasionally made me wonder if this was the criterion for their selection. In Jiangsu, compliance among my sample was perfect. All children were born three or more years apart, except for those born before the campaign began, and all marriages made after 1971 were with women who were twenty-three years old or older. The Shandong women in my sample were not quite so law-abiding. Two errors had been made early in the campaign, and there was another more recent error—two children borne within the last three years by the daughter-in-law of a cadre. I also came across several of the disapproved second-order births by women who were not among my informants. The Shaanxi site had four cases of too many children and two cases of improperly spaced chil-dren, and all but one of the marriages in my sample had occurred *before* the women reached the age of twenty-three. Fujian women did little better in observing the age rule: only two of the twenty women who had married since the campaign began had married within the age limit. There were also four cases of extra children having been born (one, a daughter, to a woman who already had five living daughters), and one woman had borne two children between 1977 and 1979. Clearly, early marriages have not been stopped, but birth limitation among these particular women was fairly successful.

My own sample of three hundred women is too small to compute fertility rates of any accuracy, but Arthur Wolf has kindly provided me with these rates for our combined informants, plus three other rural collectives in which I did not work. These rates are presented in Table 23. A comparison of Tables 22 and 23 makes it clear that, as I suspected, model collectives are exemplary in their adherence to the birth limitation rules, at least when compared to the national picture. Although in 1950 Arthur's total fertility rates are quite close to the rural total fertility rates in the Chinese Fertility Survey, by 1979 the rates for our rural paragons are much closer to those of the urbanites in the national sample than they are to those of the rural dwellers. Beyond a doubt, there are reasons for this disparity that go beyond the model status of the collectives we studied, but that is a topic I leave to Arthur and the demographers.

Women in China are not embarrassed about discussing their methods of contraception. I realized this only after I had finished my Beijing interviews and most of those in Fujian, but I went on to pursue the questioning at all my subsequent field sites. The information obtained in the remaining field sites is presented in Table 24. In the Shaoxing site, the pill is as popular as IUD's are, but in the rural sites, IUD's and female sterilization are the most common techniques. In Shaanxi, where sterilizations exceeded IUD use, each of the women sterilized was over thirty and all had had at least three children. Only one young woman, from Fujian, said she used abortion as her only means of birth control. She had borne one female child and had had two abortions in the last three years because she was unable to retain an IUD, the pill was not available, and she was unwilling to be sterilized because "in one more year I can have a second child and it might be a boy." I was told that abortions were no longer an important means of birth control, but in the past in some areas they clearly were. In Jiangsu, for instance, of the 42 women I asked, 14 had had at least one abortion and 4 had had more than one. A woman in her forties with four living children had aborted four times and miscarried once. Shaoxing had nearly as many abortions: 11 of the 42 women I asked had had at least one abortion and 4 of them more than one.

Table 23. Rural Total Fertility Rate by Year, 1950–1979, According to Arthur Wolf's Fertility Survey

Year	Rural rate	Year	Rural rate	Year	Rural rate
1950	5.93	1960	4.76	1970	4.00
1951	5.86	1961	4.82	1971	3.62
1952	6.10	1962	5.01	1972	3.37
1953	6.04	1963	5.31	1973	2.92
1954	5.93	1964	5.35	1974	2.69
1955	5.91	1965	5.07	1975	2.41
1956	5.77	1966	5.03	1976	2.15
1957	5.26	1967	4.68	1977	1.91
1958	5.00	1968	4.48	1978	1.79
1959	4.74	1969	4.28	1979	1.70

Table 24. Means of Contraception

Site	No. of cases	IUD	Sterilization		Oral	Condoms	Nothing[a]	Husband away
			Male	Female				
Shaoxing	27	22%	19%	22%	22%	7%	0%	7%
Fujian	19	5	32	58	0	0	5	0
Jiangsu	27	63	0	26	0	0	7	4
Shandong	33	56	0	18	6	0	18	3
Shaanxi	34	32	0	62	0	0	6	0
TOTAL	140	38%	8%	36%	6%	1%	8%	3%

NOTE: Women who were nursing or pregnant are excluded.

[a]Includes one woman who used abortion as a contraceptive device (see text). Others were hoping for pregnancy.

My informants were generally not willing to reveal their attitudes toward the birth limitation program, but their response to another question gave some indication of how they felt about limiting their family size. I asked them what the ideal number of children would be if there were no population problem. If I got as an answer the number required by the government, I carefully explained that I already knew what the birth planning rules were, and I wanted them to tell me what they thought would be the best number if there was no need for such a plan. Sometimes it took a bit of coaxing, but a good many women were willing to say at least that they wanted more than they were allowed to have. More than three-fourths of the women in the one-child urban areas said that the ideal family would be two or more. The most common reason given was "one is so lonely." Jiangsu and Shandong had both been given the new one-child rule, but the majority of the women there still preferred two children. Shaanxi had not yet adopted the one-child rule and the women's answers reflected this. Many of them wanted more than two (see Table 25). The Fujian informants made no bones about thinking two was an inadequate family. Of the entire sample, 81 percent thought the ideal family size was three or more children.

I interpret the responses to my various questions to mean that the women did not feel the need to have as many children as they used to, but would prefer to have more than the government statisticians say is good for the country. The urban women seemed particularly convinced of the need to limit births, no doubt because they recognize the impossibility of fitting large families into their already inadequate housing and busy lives, and furthermore they do not have the anxieties about their old age that their mothers had. They also express a level of contentment with having only a female child that makes the chance one takes with a single birth less momentous. Nonetheless, 78 percent of them indicated they would prefer to have two or more children. The rural women in my samples are even less resigned to the government limits, preferring an extra boy for insurance and a girl to help around the house. I discount, as I so often have had to, the data from Shandong because I do not feel that any of the women were giving me their own opinions on this question. The Jiangsu sample puzzles me somewhat. Their living conditions and work were rural, but their responses to the questions related to birth planning sounded urban. Although patient inquiry of a number of officials produced no solid information, it may be that the commune was stressing birth planning just before or during my visit. Since we were not allowed to live on this collective, we had little chance to check on such statements. They did admit that they were under a lot of central government pressure owing to low economic productivity, so they may have been trying to

Table 25. "What Is the Ideal Number of Children?"

Site	No. of respondents	Ideal number of children				
		One	Two	Three	Four	Five or more
Beijing	42	21%	62%	14%	0%	2%
Shaoxing	45	22	62	16	0	0
URBAN	87	22%	62%	15%	0%	1%
Fujian	38	0%	18%	50%	32%	0%
Jiangsu	48	35	60	4	0	0
Shandong	46	17	72	9	2	0
Shaanxi	42	2	64	29	5	0
RURAL	174	15%	55%	21%	9%	0%

meet their other quotas more assiduously. Another factor may be that even though women's work and lives in Jiangsu were still primarily rural, their men were drawn more into an urban work pattern and may have been under some pressure to conform to urban fertility programs.

Abiding by the birth limitation rules is less painful for urban women than for rural women. The advantages of small families for city women outweigh the disadvantages. A forty-six-year-old saleswoman in a Beijing department store probably would find many urban women agreeing with her explanation of why she had been sterilized: "Too many children is too difficult if you have no old people to help you out. My mother-in-law helped me with my first two, but after work there was still a lot to do and I was always tired. I was sterilized after the third was born because my husband was working in the suburbs and couldn't help and his mother was too old to help anymore. Besides, once I had one of each I didn't need any more." A young woman in Shaoxing, also a salesperson, found in the birth limitation rules an escape: "When my son was born [1978], there was no one-child rule. I didn't want another one but my husband's parents wanted one of each. Two children are a lot of trouble and they make you look old. I was relieved when the one-child campaign began."

Even those whose only child is a girl are more sanguine if they are city dwellers. One Beijing grandmother, a bit more Pollyanna than most, nonetheless expressed opinions I heard fairly often in Shaoxing and Beijing:

Well, it is better to have two, one of each, but now they are only allowed one. At first my son was going to go ahead and have the second one no matter what, but then they talked it over with him and he signed the one-child contract. In the old days we all wanted to have sons and lots of them, but now that we can only have one, I think it is better to have a girl. Girls are a lot better at taking care of the old people and they earn as much as a boy. But that is just my opinion. I like girls because all I ever had was boys.

Rural women were rarely as cheerful as that about the restrictions now being placed upon their fertility. When I asked a young Jiangsu mother of a six-month-old daughter whether she would like to have another, she shook her head sadly and said, "What is the use of even thinking about it? It is impossible. They won't let me." Most country people would share her unhappiness. When I asked a woman in Shaanxi what she thought the best family size was, she said two. I asked, what if they were both girls? She looked surprised and then laughed. "Country people only *count* boys. City people say boys and girls are the same, but the country people want all sons or they are without descendants." I could cite a dozen interviews in which the same confusion occurred. The cadres who are in charge of running the birth limitation program in a community are in the main also members of the community, sharing the same values and often the same ancestors. Unless they are under strong pressure from above, they are likely to agree with the mother-in-law of the woman who had two daughters and no sons. Indeed, in a less formal situation, I asked a woman what the real quota was for the village I was in. She said, "Two is the goal, but if you have no son, nobody is going to say anything if you go for a third. After three there will be trouble."

The degree of open resistance to birth control is hard to ascertain. By all reports (many of which are usefully summarized in the essay cited earlier by Chen and Kols), Guangdong seems to be the most rebellious and to be suffering the most coercion. For another side of the picture, Victor Nee reports that in a village he visited in nearby Fujian there were remarkable drops in birth rates in 1979 because the penalties for having more than two children were economically too heavy to bear.[15] The new "economic responsibility system" was not yet operating at the time of Nee's study. Evidence from elsewhere, particularly Guangdong, suggests that successful farmers are now willing to pay the high cost of bearing extra children in order to reap the rewards of having extra labor.

The important question, for our purposes here, is whether women number largely among the program's supporters or detractors, and the answer is, as usual, not simple. Of course having fewer pregnancies has important benefits for women of all ages. Repeated childbirths and long nursings are an emotional and a physical drain on women living on marginal diets. Caring for four or five children is an exhausting job for a woman who works all day in the fields or for a grandmother whose health and energy have already been sapped by years of toil. Any woman who did not support a program that would allow her to limit the number of children she must bear would be a fool, other things being equal. Alas, other things are not equal in rural China, and a woman's only chance of equalizing the many strikes against her is still what she can produce from her own body. As we saw in the last chapter, motherhood remains women's primary role, and even women worn to skin and bones by many children still count them off with pride. A fifty-two-year-old mother of nine told me, "Nine children are the most anyone should have, but six is ideal—three boys and three girls. I had all these and my daughter has one little boy. The government says two is too hard to take care of and ordered her to have one. So she will help the government, right?" Without coming out and saying it, this woman implied that she pitied her daughter and thought she might be a mean-spirited thing to give in so easily.

Also, as I and my rural informants have said repeatedly, what happens to women without sons when they are old is not something the government is likely to pay much attention to. A woman with sons not only has an old-age pension, she also has a hold on her husband and his relatives through that son. Many things in China have changed, but women are still outsiders in their husband's communities until they are mothers in their son's communities.

It is, of course, on women that the burden of the birth limitation program falls most heavily and most painfully. In rural areas, women who bear girls are sometimes scorned and even beaten by their husbands and parents-in-law. Even those who should know better let the mothers take the blame. We see massive posters and miles of characters saying that girl babies are just as precious as boy babies, but little is said about how the sex of a child is determined. If that basic fact were well established in farmers' minds, it would save women a lot of grief.* But the major question, to comply or not to comply with the state's "call" for a single child, catches women in an impossible situation. If a woman's husband and his family decide that it is worth the economic risk, it is her body that must conceal the illegal pregnancy, her body that will be the target of the cadre's anger if his quota is exceeded, her body that will endure a forced abortion perhaps too late to be entirely safe. She will be treated as if *she* had made the decision to have this illegal child even though the same cadre who is condemning her may also have "guided" his own sons and daughters-in-law in their reproductive decisions.

In sum, the birth planning program that promises so much for women is also run at their expense. They must take responsibility for the contraceptive devices that they may or may not wish to make use of. An urban factory worker whom I asked what would happen if someone who had a one-child certificate got pregnant told me, "She would be encouraged to have an abortion." What if she refused? "She would lose her bonus and at the next wage increase she would be left out and lose her extra points. And her fellow workers would scorn her." The child is in her body so she must be to blame. I asked, to the point of being a nuisance, about male sterilization. The usual answer was that

---

*Recent visitors to China report seeing editorials and articles in urban papers explaining the contribution of both parents to a child's sex, so this information may soon be available in rural areas too.

men were not willing, but many said vasectomies "weakened" men, and since they must work for the family it was better to have the women sterilized. The weakening is nonsense, and although the failure rate is somewhat higher with vasectomies, the Chinese have made remarkable breakthroughs in other areas of contraception. Why not in vasectomies? They perfected the vacuum aspiration technique for abortions and have devised many safer and more effective IUD's, as well as a host of new, less dangerous oral contraceptives. One can only assume that the government agrees with the male farmer who told me that women were expendable, men were not, and that was why vasectomies were rarely performed.*

* In at least one area the prejudice against vasectomies seems to have been overcome. Arthur Wolf reports that in the commune he studied in Sichuan there were more male sterilizations than female sterilizations. Birth limitation workers said the male farmers agreed to sterilization when they saw that it caused no bleeding and left no scars, and that men who were sterilized got back to work sooner than women who were sterilized. So it can be done.

ELEVEN

The Other Revolution

Those who would make a revolution must first discover and enlist people of like mind to join with them. As many have discovered, a revolution imposed on a population is not a revolution but a change of masters. In acquiring his men and women of like minds, Mao Zedong found it necessary to change course a bit at each decision point along the way. Many of these decisions were made at the crossroads between, on the one hand, paths leading over rough terrain but toward new opportunities for women, and, on the other, smoother economic paths leading away from the largely unmapped lands of gender equality. In almost every case, Mao and his revolutionaries chose the smoother road, the one that led away from the revolution women thought they were making. It was always assumed (and is by some still assumed) that when the roads were repaired and life along them put in order, the revolution would return to this unexplored territory and women would have their revolution.

It is tempting to continue this metaphor of paths not taken, for it simplifies issues that are far from simple in reality and clarifies history that in fact is still being discovered. But in the end metaphor begins to shape, hence distort, the circumstances it attempts to portray. Patriarchy was the cultural lens through which Mao and his confederates viewed their work, and for this reason their decisions were time and again warped by the very perspective they decried. Judith Stacey's acute analysis of Chinese society, to which I have frequently referred in these pages, documents the influence of patriarchal thinking on the failure of the family and the feminist revolution in China.[1] Stacey and I disagree only on the extent to which China's revolutionaries *intended* to model their new society on the patriarchy of the old. Whereas Stacey believes and argues cogently that the CCP used the concepts of patriarchy to win a revolution and transform a society, I would argue, using the same evidence, that the leadership *did* hope to relieve women and young people of the patriarchal burden but were defeated because they did not recognize their own cultural blinders. Despite their good intentions, their patriarchal lenses ruled out alternatives that might have changed China's history and the future of international feminism. The economic policies laid out in the last few years lead me to fear, however, that their original vision may now have faded to the point that it could no longer motivate policy, even if the constricting lenses were removed.

Whatever the intention of those revolutionaries forty or more years ago, contemporary China proves beyond a doubt that socialism and patriarchy can exist in stable harmony. Some theorists may be tempted (as I am) to comfort themselves with the thought that Chinese socialism is a deformed brand of socialism at best. But thus far there has been no perfect socialism, and on the evidence now available we would be unwise to presume that a perfect socialism would necessarily create a feminist utopia. Political systems will always be flawed because they are dependent upon a very flawed species for their energy. In China a woman's life is still determined by her relationship to a man, be he father or husband, not by her own efforts or failures. The revolution promised women something more, but that promise has not been fulfilled. It may be exactly here that the problem lies. Revolutions are made, not delivered in a package; women must make their own revolution.

I would be glad in the last chapter of this none too cheerful book to report that China's women are stirring, that there are signs that they may be ready for concerted action. Alas, my interviews reveal no such signs, nor do the speeches made at the Fifth National Women's Congress in September 1983. Kang Keqing, chairperson of the Fourth Executive Committee of the All-China Women's Federation, reviewed women's achievements in the past five years and their problems. The achievements were essentially two: a 3.3 percent increase in women's participation in the labor force (sectors unspecified), and successes in athletic competitions. She also reported an increase in the number of senior women in the natural sciences, but since the numbers are absolute, I suspect this was not an increase in relation to the total number of natural scientists.

The problems are more basic, as we have seen. The *Beijing Review*, China's official publication for foreigners, reports on this section of Kang's speech as follows:

> The feudal idea of regarding men as superior to women has reappeared, along with other prejudices. For instance, in some places, open and subtle discriminatory demands have been put forward in order to impose restrictions on the involvement of women in study and work and on the selection and promotion of women cadres. In production, labour protection for women has been ignored. Arranged marriages have encroached upon women's freedom to choose their husbands. What is most intolerable is that some ugly things which had been eliminated since the founding of New China have recurred. Crimes such as female infanticide, abuse of women, maltreatment of mothers who give birth to girl babies and abduction and persecution of women and children have been reported from time to time.
>
> The cultural, scientific and technical education levels of most women are rather low. About 70 percent of the 200 million illiterates in the country are women.
>
> Heavy household chores still adversely affect the progress and health of women.[2]

I fear that under current policies this rather gloomy report will in the years ahead become longer and gloomier. Now that the early rhetoric of the Four Modernizations has been replaced with specific policies, it is becoming clear that the primary role women will be expected to play in the new New China is that of the helper—the good wife and devoted mother.

As usual, the scenarios for country and city appear to be so different that I must discuss them separately. Beginning about 1980, China turned sharply toward light industry, and in particular to the production of such modest luxuries as better-quality clothing and small appliances that will make life a little easier for the average citizen. This policy is in part a response to the generally low morale (and consequent low productivity) of China's factory workers since the excesses of the Cultural Revolution. China is also increasing its production of handicrafts for tourists and for export, both sources of foreign exchange. In order to achieve growth quickly in this new sector, the state has encouraged the formation of new urban collectives, many of them organized by city governments. Urban collectives showed a growth rate in 1982 twice that of the state-run factories.[3] The state has also moved to solve its unemployment problem, which worsened as sent-down youths streamed back from the countryside, by encouraging private enterprise. Young (and not so young) entrepreneurs have opened quick-food shops, street stands selling everything from vegetables to buttons, and innumerable service operations.

At a yet more basic level, the state is now insisting that state factories either operate at a profit or show why they cannot. They have, moreover, adopted a very different conception of workers and their relationship to work. In some factories workers now sign a contract with their employers indicating not only precisely what is expected of both parties, but in particular what is expected of the worker in terms of output. Should the worker consistently fall short, the contract will be terminated. As the editorials put it, the iron rice bowl is broken.

Another aspect of the change in employer-employee relations concerns the recruitment of workers. Such a concept did not exist until 1982, when factory operators were for the first time allowed to advertise for the skilled workers they needed, and workers were given permission to search for new jobs more appropriate to their skills or training. And material incentives are being tried experimentally in new forms, such as bonuses for higher personal output (as opposed to higher unit or shop production levels). Occasionally contracts specify the expected output for a basic wage, with a bonus paid on a piecework basis for output beyond the expected. Some factories are experimenting with a "floating wage," in which workers' pay is determined monthly or yearly by the degree to which they exceed or fall below the quota set for that particular job. Other innovations being discussed are part-time jobs, split shifts, short work weeks, early retirement, and "spurt" schedules for those jobs that fluctuate in workload from one day or week to the next.

At first glance, none of these changes seems particularly threatening to women workers, however threatening they may be to socialism as an economic system. Even a second glance might not be worrying were these economic changes not accompanied by a pronounced shift in official documents, speeches, and Women's Federation propaganda about women's place in society. Women are again being told that though they may be workers, their primary role is that of wife and mother. Sympathy may be expressed for their double burden, but patience and hard work are all that they are being offered.[4] As we have seen, this observation is now well documented.[5] Its implications in light of the new economic policies are what concern us here.

The new urban collectives, like the old neighborhood workshops, have few benefits, no pensions, and wages well below those of the state industries. They are also doing the kind of manufacturing and assembly work considered most appropriate for women's nimble fingers. Since this is currently *the* growth sector in China and women's labor force participation increased in 1982 by only 3.3 percent, it is not hard to guess where most young women are being assigned to work these days.[6] For the many other women who are employed in the new private-sector service enterprises, there are no benefits at all; indeed, for those working in family enterprises there are not even individual paychecks. Not only will women in the private sector who take time off to have a baby do so without pay, but a whole new generation of women will be, like their mothers, without pensions, and thus dependent on the goodwill of their children when they are too old to work.

The requirement that factories now be productive was already being used against women when I was in China in 1981. Because of their many other duties, women were not considered good workers. Moreover, they required maternity leave with pay, took more time off for family emergencies, and put pressure on management for child care centers. The factory head who is sent a list of new workers by the local official in charge of job assignments is going to be even more reluctant than before to accept women workers. Should the time come when the government resigns completely from its role as a placement office for new workers, women may well find that the only jobs open to them are the traditional low-paying female jobs requiring good eyesight, attention to detail, tolerance for monotony, and manual dexterity. An even greater increase in sex-segregated jobs seems likely. Sooner or later the emphasis will return to heavy industry, and one wonders what will happen then to the employees of these sex-segregated industries. But that is the long run. The short run is bad enough in that more and more women are being funneled into low-pay, low-status jobs.

It is hard to be critical of the "breaking of the iron rice bowl" in China, since the urban policy of guaranteed employment without respect to quality or quantity of output cost China dearly in terms of industrial productivity. Yet if factory managers see women as essentially low producers in the first place, they will do their best to avoid hiring new women workers and to replace as many of the women already on their payroll as they can manage. As we have seen, women do not work overtime as much as men and are more likely to take time off for family emergencies. In order to deal with the double burden, women in many work units have developed informal ways of coping, such as taking advantage of lulls in work to send someone out to do marketing or other domestic errands for the group. Will the double-day and the special arrangements it requires of women lead to accusations of poor work habits, or, more deviously, expressions of concern for their welfare that threaten their continued employment? Kang Keqing seems to think so. In the speech cited earlier, as quoted and summarized in the *Beijing Review*, she warned: "The idea that 'too many people are employed in China now, and as women shoulder a heavy burden in the families, they should return home and perform their household duties' is wrong because it is incompatible with the principle of equality between men and women and is bound to weaken the socialist modernization."[7] Nonetheless, she went on to support the CCP Central Committee's recently confirmed policy for work with women to continue "resolutely defending the legitimate rights and interests of women and children, ensuring the healthy growth of the young and giving full scope to the great role women perform in building socialist material and spiritual civilization."[8] Will women, in their own and their children's best interest, become the last hired and the first fired?

The new material incentive programs under study also have a sex bias to them. In an interesting essay on China's new economic policies, Marlyn Dalsimer and Laurie Nisonoff express several reservations about these programs.[9] They point out that both floating wages and piecework bonuses above a base wage are tied to women's original wage scale, which, as we have seen, is well below men's. As now constituted, these programs do nothing to decrease the disparity between male and female wage levels. Dalsimer and Nisonoff point out that simply calculating bonuses on the same basis for all employees rather than on an individual's base pay would be a major step toward a less discriminatory system. They also express fears that speed-ups may become a serious problem in the kind of industry women are being channeled into. Factory operators are under pressure to show high production rates; textile mills, machine embroidery shops, and detailed assembly lines are prone to a faster-paced, more intense work process; management speed-ups might well be matched by individual attempts to increase take-home pay and eventually become a threat to safety and health.

Between November 1980 and March 1981, two Chinese social scientists, Wang Yalin and Li Jinrong, interviewed 2,293 urban workers about their housework and spare-time activities. Although the fact that such a study was made is cheering, its content is not. Urban Chinese of both sexes assertedly spend more of their nonwork hours doing household chores than workers in any other country examined (including the Soviet Union and Czechoslovakia), and Chinese urban men spend far more time than other males doing housework (a finding contradicted by my observations, as well as those of Whyte and Parish). Wang and Li express concern about the plight of China's overworked urban women, but the suggestions they make to alleviate their problems are not encouraging:

Some people think that the only way to raise women's status is for all women to return to the home; others think that women should become exactly like men. Both of these views are mistaken. It is necessary to lengthen the time for maternity and childcare leave. Raising good children is also a contribution to society. Second, we must begin with the actual state of social production in China and provide more time for women to engage in housework. For example, we could move up the retirement age for women in certain occupations to let younger labor power participate in production. Work schedules could be changed to offer part-time employment, half-days or three-day workweeks, and so on. Some trades could let women work in spurts as the job calls for, such as the morning and evening markets which could employ women for two or three hours a day. Some businesses which only have a few rush hours each day could employ more people during the busy hours and retain only a few people for the rest of the day. In this way, women not only participate in social labor and add a certain amount to the family income, the tension on the homefront in terms of housework and childcare is also relieved. This system would enable women to combine their work capacity with their capacity as mothers, so they can do a better job of raising and educating the children.[10]

If the goal of involving women in social production is merely to increase the family income, these suggestions have merit. Women under less stress could do a better job of keeping house, marketing, educating their children, and providing for their husbands' comfort with part-time jobs, split shifts, and short work weeks. However, if the involvement of women in social production has other goals, such as economic and social autonomy and a heightened sense of personhood, these suggestions will do little to improve women's lot. Women who retire early to take care of their sons' children gain nothing in these terms. They and their daughters-in-law would be better off with more child care facilities.

Research in this country has shown that a professional woman who takes a few years off to raise a child or two will only rarely catch up with her male colleagues who work straight through the births and rearing of their children. The wage data presented in Chapter 3 suggest that even a six-month maternity leave is sufficient to drop women behind in the wage scales in China. Women who come in to work for a few hours during rush periods while the men stay all day will have about as much status in the work world as Christmas help in an American department store. However much such an arrangement may alleviate the double burden of China's urban women, it only serves to peripheralize them as workers. What is needed is radical steps to socialize housework and domesticate males.

Turning now to rural China, we find a different set of problems. For many years China's agricultural production has been running a breathtaking race with its population growth, sometimes falling behind but generally keeping barely even. However, without sharply increased production of food and sharply decreased production of children, the race will soon be over and the new economic policies in the cities will be of little use. Accordingly in 1980 the government began decollectivizing much of Chinese agricultural production. Although land and some of the more expensive tools, such as large tractors, are still held in common, much farming is now being done under the authority of heads of household rather than production team leaders. Even rural enterprises such as brick kilns and mushroom sheds have been let out to bidders who find their own workers rather than having them assigned by the team or brigade leaders.[11] Obviously these changes must be accompanied by major changes in rural social organization, with decreased power and funds available to teams and brigades for collective welfare and other social benefits.

Although any attempt to predict the long-term effect of these changes on rural women is necessarily tenuous, some of the short-term effects seem obvious. As we have seen, rural women, more than their urban sisters, have remained oriented toward family as opposed to workplace. Will the demise of collective agriculture produce any significant changes in their lives? I think it will, and I think the changes will easily be as far-reaching as those for urban women, for the new economic arrangements in the countryside are returning women to their pre-Liberation position in relation to the means of production. Now instead of reporting to the team leader for job assignments or informing the team leader when the pressure of domestic duties makes it impossible to spend the day working with the teams, a woman will be under the supervision of the male head of her household. He will decide when she works, what she does, and whether she can take time off. The rules that protected rural women from unsafe work, gave them maternity leave, or gave them time off to nurse babies or to mend winter clothing during daylight hours when the light is good (and kept their workpoint earnings low as well) carry little weight with a head of household who needs a field hoed and has an able-bodied daughter or daughter-in-law in the house. Liberation made it acceptable for women to work in the fields; before Liberation, social custom "protected" women from such duties in many areas. What daughter or daughter-in-law will report her father or father-in-law to team authorities if she feels overworked, and what authority would team or brigade leaders have to deal with such a complaint? Certainly laboring in the family fields will also decrease rather than increase the range of social contacts young women make, and is therefore likely to make parental involvement in marriage arrangements more rather than less common in the future. And for a young daughter-in-law such work is likely to extend the period of loneliness and powerlessness that follows her entry into her husband's village.

Nor will an older woman find much advantage in this new/old arrangement. She may have somewhat more control over the labor of her daughter-in-law, although the mother-in-law's former power is surely gone forever; but her real loss in economic autonomy will offset any such gains. While husbands were totally involved in the work and politics of the team, they left the management of sideline activities largely to senior women. Now that these activities are an integral part of the domestic economy, decisions about them will rest with the men rather than with women of whatever age. Certainly very few women thought of their earnings in eggs, pigs, or weaving as their own personal money, but most women saw the activities that produced these earnings as theirs to regulate. One wonders if they will be as productive in these activities under the direction of someone else.

The Party has decided that men are not, hence the new family responsibility policies. Why should women be?

The decollectivization of agriculture threatens other hard-won improvements in women's lives. For example, the production teams and brigades were important to the health care and welfare systems in the countryside since they were the source of much of the funding. Farmers who were willing to see funds from the collective go to provide medical care for other men's wives and children, or even (grumblingly) for a widow and her children, may be less amenable to handing over personal profits to support the same system. In pre-socialist days, when medical costs came directly out of the family budget, women and girls were the last to get medical treatment. In what promises to be a painful test of the strength of moral as against material incentives, the losers may well be the same.

Another painful contradiction between the new economic policies and the well-being of women derives from the conflict between those policies and the intensification of the birth limitation program. Men are again likely to become structural as well as ideological patriarchs. A man with a married son now forms a viable production team, and the women in his family will literally supply future manpower for the team's continuation. But a woman who produces only female children for her husband's production team brings disaster to the family. By the end of 1981 stories and finally editorials in China's newspapers were addressing a new problem, confirming rumors I had picked up earlier that year when interviewing in the countryside. Female infanticide was reappearing in rural China, in some areas with an alarming frequency. For example, the Anhui Provincial Women's Federation, which was sent to investigate persistent stories of female infanticide in Suixi and Huaiyuan counties, found that in Huaiyuan there were 16.4 percent more boys "born" than girls. A normal birth ratio would, of course, show 6 percent more boys than girls, so this leaves a startling 10 percent of the girls "missing." In some communes the discrepancy was even more dramatic, the highest being a 27 percent predominance of male births reported over female births reported. The investigators had no doubt about what had happened to the missing girls.[12]

Although many Chinese I am sure respond to this resurgence of an old problem with dismay, some have expressed their concern in bluntly sexist terms. For example, an editorial writer for *China Youth News*, an official publication for young people in China, made by implication a grim evaluation of women's worth in rural China when he observed, "If [female infanticide] is not stopped quickly, in twenty years a serious social problem may arise." Note that female infanticide is *not* the social problem. "In twenty years a large number of our men will not be able to find wives."[13] At least for this editor, women still seemed to be more important as potential wives than as fellow human beings.

The decision of young parents to kill their baby cannot be easy. Indeed, it may not even be theirs, but rather made for them by a senior generation for whom it may well be equally hard. The couple, together with their sorrowing parents, see before them a life of increasing poverty, for they have no sons to help them in the fields and no one to provide for them in their old age. Until now the only women who have succored their aging parents have been in propaganda films or newspaper editorials, or in some other village. The prospect of having a son later grows dimmer and dimmer as the birth limitation program becomes more strictly enforced. The threat of sterilization after the birth of a second child makes infanticide a serious option when that second child is another girl.

Nor is the resolution of this conflict between society's needs and the individual's needs a simple one. On the one hand, without draconian measures, overpopulation will destroy any hope of a better life for China's people. On the other, even if the family limitation program proves a total success from this day forward, there are still hard days ahead for the generation now being born. In another thirty years the dependency ratio in China will be totally different. It seems highly unlikely that the mechanization of agriculture will be sufficiently advanced and widespread to overcome the acute shortage of young able-bodied workers, or to compensate such workers sufficiently to enable them both to raise families and to care for their many aged and incapacitated dependents. Policy makers do not yet recognize how dependent China will then be on its young women. This may in fact be the last generation of women whose talents the nation can afford to stifle without serious economic consequences.

I am not speaking frivolously when I suggest that China's population problem is a case of the sins of the fathers being visited on the sons. Nor do I fault China's demographers, some of whom lost their profession and their freedom for trying to convince Mao Zedong that population control was not necessarily anti-socialist. But China's political leaders can be faulted, then and now, for their failure to carry through on their promises to women. Had that failure not occurred, women might now be valued members of the workforce, sharing leadership positions in the countryside, earning as much as their brothers, and being as much or more of a blessing to their parents in their old age. Family limitation would not pose such a threat to rural authority under these circumstances. A utopian dream? Perhaps, but then who would have believed that a tattered revolutionary band holed up in remote Shaanxi would one day unite and bring to modest prosperity one of the largest and poorest nations on earth?

Beyond a doubt, women participated in China's revolution and believed it to be as much their revolution as their male peers'. A few of them along the way saw the revolution narrowing to exclude those principles for which they thought they were fighting and protested. Whether Chinese women as a whole were not ready for their liberation, or whether, as many feminists now argue, it is impossible to carry out a socialist and a feminist revolution together, is now an academic question as far as Chinese women are concerned. Those few feminists who wished to enlist women in a revolution of their own were either silenced or convinced that their revolution must be postponed. But if that revolution is ever to happen, they must be allowed to do as Mao did, to gather together like-minded people who see the shortcomings of the present social order and want to change it. Everything I read and hear suggests that those people are out there, but thus far they are isolated souls only partially aware of their shared oppression. Until they join together, they are not a movement, let alone a revolution.

Reference Matter

Notes

CHAPTER I

1. Adele M. Fielde, *Pagoda Shadows: Studies from Life in China* (London: T. Ogilvie Smith, 1887), pp. 124–25.

2. Marius Hendrikus van der Valk, *Conservatism in Modern Chinese Family Law* (Leiden: Brill, 1956), p. 60.

3. Fielde, pp. 181–82.

4. Irma Highbaugh, *Family Life in West China* (New York: Agricultural Missions, Inc., 1948), p. 98.

5. See Margery Wolf, *Women and the Family in Rural Taiwan* (Stanford: Stanford University Press, 1972).

6. Martin C. Yang, *A Chinese Village, Taitou, Shantung Province* (New York: Columbia University Press, 1945), p. 153.

7. *Ibid.*, pp. 57–59.

8. Margery Wolf, "Women and Suicide in China," in Margery Wolf and Roxane Witke, eds., *Women in Chinese Society* (Stanford: Stanford University Press, 1975), esp. pp. 121–29.

9. In Ida Pruitt's *A Daughter of Han: The Autobiography of a Chinese Working Woman* (New Haven: Yale University Press, 1945), Ning Lao T'ai-t'ai expresses the enormity of the step, when because of her starving children she decides to "go out" and become a servant.

10. This topic is discussed in detail in Emily Honig's fine Ph.D. dissertation, "Women Cotton Mill Workers in Shanghai, 1919–1949" (Stanford University, 1982).

11. For background on this see Lucien Bianco, *Origins of the Chinese Revolution, 1915–1949*, trans. Muriel Bell (Stanford: Stanford University Press, 1971); Chow Tse-tung, *The May Fourth Movement: Intellectual Revolution in Modern China* (Cambridge, Mass.: Harvard University Press, 1960); Elisabeth Croll, *Feminism and Socialism in China* (London: Routledge & Kegan Paul, 1978); Kay Ann Johnson, "Feminism and Socialist Revolution in China: The Politics of Women's Rights and Family Reform" (Ph.D. dissertation, University of Wisconsin, 1977); Kay Ann Johnson, *Women, the Family, and Peasant Revolution in China* (Chicago: University of Chicago Press, 1983).

12. Honig.

13. Tseng Pao-swen, "The Chinese Women: Past and Present," in Sophia H. Chen, ed., *Symposium on Chinese Culture* (Shanghai, 1931), p. 344, quoted in Croll, p. 153.

14. Johnson, *Women*, p. 74.

15. For interesting accounts of Ding Ling's roller-coaster career see Jonathan

D. Spence, *The Gate of Heavenly Peace: The Chinese and Their Revolution, 1895–1980* (New York: Viking Press, 1981), and Yi-tsi Mei Feuerwerker, *Ding Ling's Ideology and Narrative in Modern Chinese Literature* (Cambridge, Mass.: Harvard University Press, 1982).

16. Johnson, *Women*, p. 70.

17. Johnson, "Feminism," p. 140.

18. See Vivienne Shue, *Peasant China in Transition: The Dynamics of Development Toward Socialism, 1949–1956* (Berkeley and Los Angeles: University of California Press, 1980), for an excellent account of CCP policy and practice. Chen Yuan-tsung's autobiographical novel, *The Dragon's Village* (New York: Pantheon Books, 1980),vividly describes the day-to-day problems of land reform cadres, many of whom were urban young people.

19. Johnson, *Women*, p. 112.

20. See Delia Davin, *Woman-Work: Women and the Party in Revolutionary China* (Oxford: Oxford University Press, 1976), for an interesting discussion of this difficult period.

21. Johnson, "Feminism," p. 95.   22. Croll, p. 235.

23. Johnson, *Women*, p. 146.   24. Croll, p. 257.

25. The Five Goods are listed in Phyllis Andors, "Social Revolution and Woman's Emancipation: China during the Great Leap Forward," *Bulletin of Concerned Asian Scholars*, 7 (January–March 1975), 33.

26. Judith Stacey, *Patriarchy and Socialist Revolution in China* (Berkeley and Los Angeles: University of California Press, 1983), pp. 207–8.

27. Andors, p. 40.

28. *Ibid.*

29. *Ibid.*, p. 39.

30. Kay Ann Johnson, "Women in the People's Republic of China," in Sylvia A. Chipp and Justin J. Green, eds., *Asian Women in Transition* (University Park: Pennsylvania State University Press, 1980), p. 93.

31. Stacey, pp. 155–57.

32. Phyllis Andors, "'The Four Modernizations' and Chinese Policy on Women," *Bulletin of Concerned Asian Scholars*, 13 (April–June 1981), 45.

33. Phyllis Andors, *The Unfinished Revolution of Chinese Women, 1949–80* (Bloomington: Indiana University Press, 1983), p. 168.

CHAPTER 2

1. See Norma Diamond, "Model Villages and Village Realities," *Modern China*, 9 (April 1983), 163.

2. Lucien Bianco, "Birth Control in China: Local Data and Their Reliability," *China Quarterly*, 85 (March 1981), 119.

3. William Kessen, ed., *Childhood in China* (New Haven: Yale University Press, 1975).

CHAPTER 3

1. See Emily Honig, "Women Cotton Mill Workers in Shanghai."

2. Martin King Whyte and William L. Parish, *Urban Life in Contemporary China* (Chicago: University of Chicago Press, 1984), p. 200.

3. *Ibid.*, p. 205.

4. *Ibid.*, pp. 204–6

5. In the 1981 *Statistical Yearbook of China* prepared by the State Statistical Bureau, Beijing, a table called "Employment by Sex and Occupation" includes only two categories that would suggest those being counted were in leadership positions. "Economic Management" is composed of 37.0 percent women, but the breakdown within that category shows women occupying classifications that are probably not managerial, e.g., statistical work 67.0 percent and accountants 60.7 percent. The other clear category is "Persons Engaged in Administration," which shows 27.2 percent women employees. See *Statistical Yearbook of China, 1981* (Hong Kong, 1982), p. 103.

6. Whyte and Parish, p. 204.

7. Wang Yalin and Li Jinrong, two Chinese researchers, confirm this observation. They also present data that says urban men do 43 percent of the housework, which seems unlikely to me. See Wang Yalin and Li Jinrong, "Urban Workers' Housework," *Social Sciences in China*, 3 (1982), 147–65.

8. Between 1968 and 1978 seventeen million young people were sent to the countryside after they completed their education in an idealistic attempt to bridge the ever-widening gulf between city and countryside and a realistic attempt to circumvent a massive unemployment problem. For a full and interesting account of this painful episode in contemporary China, see Thomas P. Bernstein, *Up to the Mountains and Down to the Villages: The Transfer of Youth from Urban to Rural China* (New Haven: Yale University Press, 1977).

CHAPTER 4

1. See Martin King Whyte and William L. Parish, *Urban Life in Contemporary China*, p. 200.

2. Marina Thorborg, "Chinese Employment Policy in 1949–78, with a Special Emphasis on Women in Rural Production," in *Chinese Economy Post-Mao*, Joint Economic Committee, Congress of the United States (Washington, D.C.: U.S. Government Printing Office, 1978).

3. William Parish, personal communication.

4. John Lossing Buck, *Land Utilization in China: A Study of 16,786 Farms in 168 Localities, and 38,256 Farm Families in Twenty-two Provinces in China, 1929–33* (New York: Council on Economic and Cultural Affairs, Inc., 1956), p. 118.

5. Norma Diamond, "Collectivization, Kinship, and the Status of Women in Rural China," *Bulletin of Concerned Asian Scholars*, 7 (January–March 1975), 25.

6. Phyllis Andors, "'The Four Modernizations' and Chinese Policy on Women," p. 55.

7. Thorborg, p. 550.

8. I thank Martin King Whyte for pointing out this fact to me in the 1982 Census, *Zhongguo Disanci Renkou Pucha di Zhuyao Shuzi*, State Council Census Office (Peking: Chinese Statistical Publishing, 1982), pp. 12–13.

9. Thorborg, p. 550.

10. *Ibid.*, p. 551.

11. *Ibid.*
12. *Ibid.*, p. 541.
13. *Ibid.*, p. 549.

CHAPTER 5

1. Margery Wolf, *Women and the Family*, pp. 74-78.
2. Marina Thorborg, "Chinese Employment Policy in 1949-78," pp. 596-600.
3. For example, Theodore Hsi-en Chen, *Chinese Education Since 1949* (New York: Pergamon, 1981); Suzanne Pepper, "Chinese Education after Mao," *China Quarterly*, 81 (March 1980); Suzanne Pepper, "Education and Revolution: The 'Chinese Model' Revised," *Asian Survey*, September 1978; Jonathan Unger, *Education under Mao: A Study of Canton Schools, 1960-1978* (New York: Columbia University Press, 1983).
4. Martin King Whyte and William L. Parish, *Urban Life in Contemporary China*, p. 60.
5. Thomas P. Bernstein, *Up to the Mountains and Down to the Villages*, p. 231.
6. *Statistical Yearbook of China, 1981*, p. 458.

CHAPTER 6

1. B. Michael Frolic, *Mao's People: Sixteen Portraits of Life in Revolutionary China* (Cambridge, Mass.: Harvard University Press, 1980).
2. See Arthur Wolf and Chieh-shan Huang, *Marriage and Adoption in China, 1845-1945* (Stanford: Stanford University Press, 1980), pp. 82-93.
3. *Ibid.*, pp. 143-201.
4. Judith Stacey would probably not agree with the latter half of this sentence in that her analysis of patriarchal socialism implies a more conscious intent than I am comfortable with. See her *Patriarchy and Socialist Revolution in China*, chap. 6.
5. Martin King Whyte and William L. Parish, *Urban Life in Contemporary China*, pp. 112-17.
6. Judith Stacey traces this new power of the state over personal matters, which she calls "public patriarchy," through various sectors of urban life, commenting on the fact that it "is less well-developed at the village level." See Stacey, pp. 227-35.
7. Thomas P. Bernstein, *Up to the Mountains and Down to the Villages*, pp. 161-66.
8. Whyte and Parish, p. 147.
9. Martin King Whyte, personal communication.
10. Elisabeth Croll, *The Politics of Marriage in Contemporary China* (Cambridge: Cambridge University Press, 1981), p. 57.
11. See Stacey, pp. 235-47, for a good discussion of the rural-urban difference.
12. William L. Parish and Martin King Whyte, *Village and Family in Contemporary China* (Chicago: University of Chicago Press, 1978), p. 171, table 30.
13. *Ibid.*, p. 187.
14. *Ibid.*

15. John Lossing Buck, *Land Utilization in China*, pp. 467–70.

16. Stacey, p. 193.

CHAPTER 7

1. Myron Cohen, *House United, House Divided: The Chinese Family in Taiwan* (New York: Columbia University Press, 1976), p. 57ff.

2. It is on this point, of course, that Judith Stacey and I disagree in our overall analysis of Chinese society. Whereas she suspects the state of consciously encouraging a patriarchal system, albeit socialist patriarchy, I am more inclined to see it as a not quite hapless victim of its own patriarchal biases. I return to this in Chapter 11.

3. Martin King Whyte and William L. Parish, *Urban Life in Contemporary China*, p. 154, table 13.

4. Thomas P. Bernstein, *Up to the Mountains and Down to the Villages*, pp. 129, 164.

5. James L. Watson, "Chinese Kinship Reconsidered: Anthropological Perspectives on Historical Research," *China Quarterly*, 92 (December 1982), 598–600.

CHAPTER 8

1. Helen F. Siu and Zelda Stern have put together a fine collection of new stories in their *Mao's Harvest: Voices from China's New Generation* (New York: Oxford University Press, 1983). See in particular the excerpts from a novella by Liu Xinwu called "Overpass," p. 29.

2. Maurice Freedman, "The Family in China, Past and Present," in *The Study of Chinese Society: Essays by Maurice Freedman* (Stanford: Stanford University Press, 1979), p. 241.

3. See Margery Wolf, *Women and the Family*.

4. See Margery Wolf, "Marriage, Family, and the State in Contemporary China," *Pacific Affairs*, 57 (Summer 1984).

CHAPTER 10

1. See John S. Aird, "Population Studies and Population Policy in China," *Population and Development Review*, 8 (June 1982), 268; Ansley J. Coale, "Population Trends, Population Policy, and Population Studies in China," *Population and Development Review*, 7 (March 1981), 86–87.

2. For discussions of the demography of China in general, I refer the reader to H. Y. Tien, *China's Population Struggle: Demographic Decisions of the People's Republic, 1948–1969* (Columbus: Ohio State University Press, 1973), and the pages of the journal *Population and Development Review*. Judith Bannister also deals with the subject in her forthcoming book from the Stanford University Press.

3. For this overview of China's population policy I am deeply indebted to a very informative essay by Pi-chao Chen and Adrienne Kols, "Population and Birth Planning in the People's Republic of China," *Population Reports*, Series J, 25 (January–February 1982).

4. *Ibid.*, p. 590.

5. *Ibid.*, p. 589.

6. Aird, p. 287.

7. "Chinese Population Policy: A *People's Daily* Editorial," *Population and Development Review*, 8 (September 1982), 633.

8. For a good discussion of the pros and cons of this decision see Aird, and Leo F. Goodstadt, "China's One-Child Family: Policy and Public Response," *Population and Development Review*, 8 (March 1982).

9. For further discussion of this issue see my "Marriage, Family, and the State in Contemporary China."

10. See Goodstadt, p. 51.

11. Aird, p. 286.

12. "Cause of Rise in Multiple Birth Rate Examined," FBIS Daily Report, May 6, 1983.

13. Aird, pp. 285 ff.; Chen and Kols, p. 604.

14. See "Minister Views Family Planning," FBIS 118 (June 11, 1983), p. K2; and "Guangdong Official Reviews Birth Control Policy," FBIS 112 (June 9, 1983).

15. Victor Nee, "Post-Mao Changes in a South China Production Brigade," *Bulletin of Concerned Asian Scholars*, 13 (April–June 1981), 36.

CHAPTER 11

1. Judith Stacey, *Patriarchy and Socialist Revolution in China.*

2. "The Fifth National Women's Congress," *Beijing Review*, 26, no. 38 (September 19, 1983), 6.

3. *Xinhua News* (Beijing), May 1, 1983, FBIS.

4. Phyllis Andors, "'The Four Modernizations' and Chinese Policy on Women," p. 45.

5. *Ibid.*; also Marlyn Dalsimer and Laurie Nisonoff, "Implications of the New Economic Readjustment Policies for Chinese Urban Working Women," *Review of Radical Political Economies*, in press; Stacey, pp. 268–80.

6. See note 3 above.   7. See note 2 above.

8. See note 2 above.   9. Dalsimer and Nisonoff, p. 13.

10. Wang Yalin and Li Jinrong, "Urban Workers' Housework," *Social Sciences in China* 3, no. 2 (1982), 164.

11. For a clear and interesting discussion of the variety of such systems developed on one commune in Guangdong see Jack Potter, "The Implementation of Production Responsibility Systems in Guangdong, 1978–81, and Their Social and Economic Consequences," unpublished paper, no date.

12. "Study Shows Serious Boy-Girl Ratio Imbalance," *Renmin Ribao* (Beijing), April 7, 1983, FBIS.

13. Yang Fan, "Save the Baby Girl," *China Youth News* (Beijing), November 9, 1982, FBIS Daily Report (December 7, 1982).

Index

Library of Congress Cataloging in Publication Data

Wolf, Margery.
  Revolution postponed.

  Bibliography: p.
  Includes index.
    1. Women—China—Interviews.   2. Women—China—Social
conditions.   3. Women—China—Economic conditions.
4. Equality.   I. Title.
HQ1768.w65   1985   305.4'0951   83-40696
ISBN 0-8047-1243-3